SEVENTH
GENERATION

SEVENTH GENERATION

an anthology of
native american plays

edited by
Mimi Gisolfi D'Aponte

THEATRE COMMUNICATIONS GROUP

Copyright © 1999 by Theatre Communications Group

Seventh Generation: An Anthology of Native American Plays
is published by Theatre Communications Group, Inc.,
355 Lexington Ave., New York, NY 10017–0217.

Introduction is copyright © 1999 by Mimi Gisolfi D'Aponte
Epilogue is copyright © 1999 by Elizabeth Theobald

This publication is made possible in part with public funds from the New York State Council on the Arts, a State Agency.

Seventh Generation : an anthology of Native American plays /
Mimi Gisolfi D'Aponte, editor.
ISBN 1-55936-147-6 (alk. paper)
1. American drama—Indian authors.
2. Indians of North America—Drama.
I. D'Aponte, Mimi. II. Theatre Communications Group.
PS628.I53S48   1998
812'.54080897—dc21   98-4449
CIP

Book design and typography by Lisa Govan
Cover design by Cynthia Krupat
Cover artwork by Jaune Quick-to See Smith

First edition February 1999

Due to space constraints, author copyright information continues on page 389.

To Nello

Eleanor, Lucy, Olivia, John

With Love

Contents

THE WOMAN WHO WAS A RED DEER
DRESSED FOR THE DEER DANCE

THE STORY OF SUSANNA

Epilogue

Introduction

The seven plays that follow are individually exceptional works of theatre. Each was well received in an original production venue and each has traveled beyond that small initial circle to become known to a wider audience of playgoers, and now to a leading publisher of theatre books. The journeys of these plays—each different, yet each in some fashion similar to the others—become in themselves metaphors for that larger journey Indigenous Americans have undertaken from silence to voice in so many arenas of life in the United States during this century. At its close, the arena of mainstream American theatre beckons to a host of Native playwrights.

The first of its kind, this anthology opens a new chapter of play publication. As descendants of the first Americans continue to commit their extraordinary experiences to the extraordinary communal fulcrum of performed theatre and to the textualizing of that theatre, more anthologies of Native plays will follow.

The facilitating of this project must first be traced to the generosity of Paul Rathbun, creator and editor of the groundbreaking *Native Playwrights Newsletter*, begun in 1993, without whom this anthology would not have been possible. It was through *NPN*, and through subsequent communication with Dr. Rathbun, that I was able to contact most of the playwrights represented in this volume. Both his doctoral thesis ("American Indian Dramaturgy: Situating Native Presence on the American Stage," University of Wisconsin-Madison, 1996) and his editorship of the newsletter confirm his strong leadership in establishing Native American dramaturgy within the field of American theatre studies. Dr. Rathbun is on the theatre faculty of Fort Lewis College in Durango, Colorado.

I am grateful to Mr. Jim Cyrus of the American Indian Community House in New York City, who offered ongoing, generous help over a three-year period. I thank Professor Marvin Carlson of the Ph.D. Program in Theatre at CUNY Graduate Center, who welcomed my proposal to teach a "Seminar in Native American Drama," and I thank Professor Jill Dolan, whose support made that seminar a reality during spring 1997. My students proved wonderful critics and collaborators; Randall Merrifield helped Muriel Miguel in transcribing *Power Pipes* and also worked on the Suggested Bibliography. At Baruch College, many thanks to Dean Lexa Logue and her committee for reassigned time during spring 1998, to Mr. Spencer Means of the William and Anita Newman Library, and to Ana Mera-Ruiz of Baruch's Department of Fine & Performing Arts. Ongoing thanks to Steven Samuels, Terry Nemeth and Kathy Sova of TCG—wonderful partners-in-publishing, and John Istel, who years ago recommended TCG so highly. Most of all, I am deeply grateful to the many playwrights who have been kind enough to submit their plays for consideration.

The Native-Italian Connection

My interest in Native performance was kindled in the early 1970s by Professor Charles Gattnig. He noted the parallel between my Italian research concerning *tapetti di segatura*: sawdust paintings created on the marble floors of churches in Sorrento and Amalfi, in preparation for the Thursday of

Easter Holy Week; and the sand paintings created by Navajo Medicine Men in preparation for Chantways. In both rituals a meticulously drawn image is destroyed immediately upon use, and a significant sense of healing is imparted. Thus, I was initially drawn to study Native theatre, because, like much of Italian theatre, there are strong cultural underpinnings of a religious and philosophical nature that, whether or not intentionally employed by a particular playwright, have permeated and continue to permeate its development.

The performative origins of Native American theatre lie in traditional ritual, public ceremony and storytelling. Native performance, broadly defined, includes great tribal ceremonies such as the Beautyway and the Coyoteway and the Blessing ceremonies of the Navajo; the Sun Dance of the Plains people; the Hopi Kachina dances; the masked performers of the Northwest Coast; the Pueblo Matachine dances; the Southern Kwakiutl Potlatch; the Iroquois ceremonial of midwinter; the Sacred Arrow ceremonies of the Cheyenne; the Ghost Dance and the Sacred Clown ceremony of the Sioux.

Native performance, broadly defined, includes the work and guidance of spiritual leaders, shamans and medicine men and women.

Native performance, broadly defined, includes the oral tradition of storytelling by tribal elders; storytelling rich in spiritual legacy, in mythology, in transcendent values.

Native performance, broadly defined, includes the explosion of contemporary, inter-tribal powwows, held throughout the United States and Canada. At an August powwow in Queens, New York, several years ago, I spoke to Mrs. Ina McNeil, who received the "Indian of the Year" award from Louis Mofsie and his Thunderbird American Dancers and Singers, who were drumming and singing. "When we have a powwow," she said, "it's so the Indians can get together—for spiritual renewal as well as social—so not only are we having a social good time, we're having a spiritual good time, too."

In most instances Native performance offers the participant strong cultural awareness of gathering, of the circle, of the four directions, of the search for a vision, of time and space as earthly connectors to other worlds. These elements are so rich in both secular and sacred meaning that, much like the ritual of the Mass or the concept of redemption in Italian theatre, they frequently appear as specific references in contemporary Native theatre, and are sometimes sensed as present even when not referred to directly.

It is also significant that both Native and Italian theatre share ongoing appreciation and employment of popular personae, who appear prominently and continuously in various manifestations of their cultures, both literary and performative. The Pulcinella and Arlecchino characters of Italian commedia dell'arte, and the Coyote/Trickster figures of Native mythology are performance stars whose ubiquitous natures have carried them far beyond their venues of origin.

It was the privilege of Baruch College in fall 1992 to host a Folk Opera, coproduced by Louis Mofsie's Thunderbird American Indian Dancers and Singers, and Alessandra Belloni's I Giullari di Piazza (a traditional Italian folk music and theatre group, presently in residence at The Cathedral of St. John the Divine in New York City). Dedicated to "the healing of the Earth and of all Nations," and performed initially at the Lincoln Center Outdoor Festival that summer, it featured Coyote and Pulcinella meeting to sing and dance together. With the awarding of the 1997 Nobel Prize in Literature to the contemporary commedia actor/director/playwright, Dario Fo, comes further international recognition of the oral performative traditions of every culture.

Representative English-Language Plays About Native Americans

As many as seventy-five American plays were written about Native Americans during the nineteenth century. Often, favored dramatic vehicles were performed for political, as well as artistic or commercial, reasons. In 1828, the actor, Edwin Forrest, ran a playwriting contest for an "Indian" play, whose selection committee included William Cullen Bryant, then assistant editor of the *New York Evening Post*. Actor/playwright, John Augustus Stone, submitted the winning *Metamora; or The Last of the Wampanoags* (Forrest would perform the leading role across the country for the next forty years). The plot concerns Chief Metamora, the son of a chief, who has just saved the English heroine from death. Soon after, he leads his warriors against the encroaching settlers and is defeated. Pursued as he returns to his wife, Nahmeokee, only to find their baby killed by an English bullet, Metamora and Nahmeokee agree to end their lives. He stabs her, and is about to kill himself, when he too is shot to death by the victorious English. Such a story line, communicating the courage and nobility of the defeated Other, meshed well with the politics of the day. It is not insignificant that the Indian Removal Act was being debated in 1828, the year Andrew Jackson was elected president, and that it was passed in 1830 with the president's blessing.

The image of the noble savage and the icon of the gentle Pocahontas have remained favorite subjects of the American imagination. The most noted nineteenth century forbears of the present cinematic surge of Pocahontas popularity were George Washington Parke Custis's *Pocahontas; or The Settlers of Virginia* of 1830, and John Brougham's burlesque, *Po-ca-hon-tas; or The Gentle Savage* of 1855. Custis, son of George Washington's stepson, is praised by his editor for having rearranged the factual sequence of history so that the heroine's saving of Captain John Smith from her father, Chief Powhatan, would occur late in the play, thus promoting dramatic suspense. Brougham's farcical, word-play approach to his subject is foretold in these lines from the Prologue about the colonists:

Who had journeyed to enlighten
Their [the Natives'] unfortunate condition,
Through these potent triunited
Anglo-Saxon civilizers,
Rum, Gunpowder, and Religion.

(French's *American Drama*.
The Acting Edition. No. XXVIII, p. 4)

During our century, a number of non-Native authors
have written memorable plays on Native subjects; the politics exhibited in these works reflect a worldview very much
at odds with that of the previous century. In the category of
short plays, Cornelia Otis Skinner's popular monologues,
written in the 1920s and 1930s, and continuously performed
into the 1950s, include *The Vanishing Red Man*. This piece,
like Mark Medoff's one-act, *Doing a Good One for the Red
Man* (1974), lampoons the condescending attitudes and
naive ignorance about Native life exhibited by visiting
tourists from the East.

Two plays of considerable documentary value, which
exemplify the genre of historical outdoor drama as produced
in the United States, are Kermit Hunter's *Unto These Hills:
A Drama of the Cherokee* (1950) and his *Trail of Tears* (1966).
This historically accurate pair of plays was sponsored by the
Cherokee Historical Association of North Carolina and
represents collaboration by Cherokee and non-Natives
attempting to reconcile the immensely disturbing period of
history shared by their ancestors who lived in the "Great
Smokies" in the early part of the nineteenth century. These
plays continue to be produced annually in North Carolina.

Highly acclaimed in mainstream theatre circles, Peter
Schaffer's spectacular *The Royal Hunt of the Sun* (1964) and
Arthur Kopit's feisty *Indians* (1969), brought to audiences,
on both sides of the Atlantic, powerful indictments of colonial commodification of the Other: the first through dramatizing the conquests of Pizzaro in Peru; and the latter

through dramatizing the conquests of Buffalo Bill and Wild Bill Hickok, in life and onstage. Kopit's cast of characters includes the great chiefs Sitting Bull, Crazy Horse and Tecumseh. His placing of cast members among the audience has been praised by contemporary Native playwright Bruce King as a technique which breaks the "wall of magic" between players and audience: ". . . we always break that plane. The rendering of Coyote, or the rendering of tricksters, we go into the audience and bother people." (*NPN*, Paul Rathbun, ed. Summer 1993, p. 8) In 1976, Christopher Sergel adapted *John Neihardt's Black Elk Speaks*, portraying on the stage another brilliant Native leader; the play was revived again at the Mark Taper Forum in 1996.

In *The Ecstasy of Rita Joe* (1970), the Canadian playwright, George Ryga, brought to the stage the terrors a big city holds in store for a young girl fleeing the constrictions of her reservation; his compatriot James W. Nichol examined the influence of the seventeenth-century Jesuit mission on the Hurons and its disastrous results in *Sainte-Marie Among the Hurons* (1980).

Representative Plays by Published Native Americans

A remarkable Native American playwright practiced his craft quite successfully during the early part of this century, and yet his name rarely appears in theatre history books. Oklahoman, R. Lynn Riggs, son of William Grant Riggs of Appalachian stock and Rose Ella Buster Gillis of the Cherokee Nation, wrote plays during the 1930s, several of which were presented on established New York stages. Among them: *Green Grow the Lilacs*, produced by the Theatre Guild in 1931, upon which Rogers and Hammerstein's 1943 *Oklahoma!* was based. Riggs's plot, the first to be employed in the new performance genre of the musical, is to

Oklahoma! what George Bernard Shaw's *Pygmalion* is to the Lerner and Lowe musical, *My Fair Lady* (1956), and what Thornton Wilder's *The Matchmaker* is to *Hello Dolly!* (1964). It is in Riggs's *Green Grow the Lilacs* that the boisterous cowboy, Curly, first woos flirtatious Laurey; overcomes his sinister rival; and successfully defies the law for her sake. As Oscar Hammerstein stated in the September 1943 *New York Times*: "Lynn Riggs and *Green Grow the Lilacs* are the very soul of *Oklahoma!*" Another Riggs play, *Cherokee Night* (1936), addresses serious issues concerning the Cherokee people in a raw, powerful manner, by utilizing semichronological flashbacks about a group of adolescents whose difficult lives are represented during the course of seven scenes.

The contemporary era of Native American playwriting essentially begins with the groundbreaking work of Hanay Geiogamah (Kiowa/Delaware) during the 1970s; Mr. Geiogamah has kindly agreed to the reprinting of his signature piece, *Body Indian*, in this anthology. Not represented in this volume is Geiogamah's Canadian peer, Tomson Highway (Cree), author of *The Rez Sisters* (1988) and *Dry Lips Oughta Move to Kapuskasing* (1989). *The Rez Sisters* won the Dora Mavor Moore Award for best new play in Toronto's 1986–87 season; it has been performed across Canada and in various U.S. cities, and has represented Canada at the Edinburgh Festival. The *sisters* are seven women from an imaginary reservation who scramble to make money for their journey to Toronto, where they hope to win at the world's "biggest bingo game." Their laughter, their tragedies and their ability to survive even death, make this a moving, relevant play that is fast becoming a classic.

Other published, contemporary Native playwrights not represented here include the Colorado sisters, Terry Gomez, Monique Mojica and Daniel David Moses. Elvira and Hortensia Colorado (Chicimec) are well-known professional performers and storytellers whose work is often seen in New York and around the country. Their company, Coatlicue/Las

Colorado, has presented work at the American Indian Community House, where they have served on the Board of Directors; the American Museum of Natural History; La MaMa; and Theater for the New City. In addition, they have performed and toured with the Spiderwoman Theater in *Winnetou's Snake Oil Show from Wigwam City* and *Power Pipes*, which is published for the first time in this volume. Their play, *1992: Blood Speaks*, directed in production by Muriel Miguel of Spiderwoman, was published in 1996.

Terry Gomez (Commanche) presents intricately articulated, revealing dramas of familial relationships. In *Intertribal* (1996), a young girl learns about her grandmother's strength and generosity when a disturbed friend is welcomed into their home; in *Reunion* (1996), siblings gather for their father's funeral and learn that their love for one another outweighs their rivalries.

Monique Mojica (Kuna/Rappahannock) was born in New York City. She is a performer and playwright, and a founding member of Native Earth Performing Arts Company of Toronto, where she served as artistic director and portrayed the role of Marie-Adele Starblanket in Tomson Highway's *The Rez Sisters*. Her full-length play, *Princess Pocahontas and the Blue Spots* (1991), produced in Canada in 1989 and 1990, proves Mojica a word warrior doing battle with weaponry of anger and wit to redeem the unsung histories of the countless, heroic Native women, who faced the overwhelming consequences of European colonialism. She read excerpts from this play at Yale University in February 1998.

Canadian, David Daniel Moses (Delaware), is the author of two published plays, which have been recently mounted by the Native Performing Arts Company: *Coyote City* (1990) and *Almighty Voice and His Wife* (1992). The former, nominated for the General Governor's Award for Drama, successfully combines the provocative themes of sibling rivalry, the Native reservation woman as victim in a big city, and communication with the dead.

Not yet published, but produced and very much a playwright on the rise, is Bunky Echo Hawk (Pawnee/Yakama), a leading student of William S. Yellow Robe, Jr., whose work is represented in this volume. Echo Hawk's "The Essence" presents the moving portrait of a young woman who has never known her Native father until she meets him by chance while searching for clues to her own identity. The play has been given professional readings at the Native American Community House and at The Joseph Papp Public Theater/New York Shakespeare Festival in New York City, and was produced and directed by Paul Rathbun at Fort Louis College in Durango, Colorado, in spring 1998.

Playwrights Represented Here

The name of Hanay Geiogamah will soon, I hope, be included in all texts devoted to the history of American theatre. With the publishing of Geiogamah's *New Native American Drama: Three Plays* (1980), three significant and highly individual Native American plays became accessible to theatre students and practitioners everywhere (an Italian language anthology of four Geiogamah plays was published in Rome by Castelvecchi in 1994). Geiogamah's *Foghorn*, much like George C. Wolfe's *The Colored Museum*, which antedates it, utilizes stereotype as the organizing format for a comedic overview of the victimization of first Americans, with theatrically satisfying revenge events capping several of the episodes. Geiogamah's *49* is a play that brilliantly translates the essence of a tribal ceremony into a theatrical vehicle for evoking the solidarity of the Native community, particularly through its appeal to younger members by the character of the oldest Elder. *Body Indian*, published for the second time in English in this volume, is the best known and the most haunting of his works. It was developed and first performed in New York City at La MaMa Experimental Theater Club in 1972. It concerns Bobby, who has a wooden leg, and hopes to use his lease money from his reservation land allotment for alcohol rehabilitation. Drunk and passed out, he is searched by his friends for more drinking money. The body of this wounded anti-hero is often cited as an apt and telling metaphor for the horrific ramifications of Native American oppression in the United States.

The name of William S. Yellow Robe, Jr. (Assiniboine/Nakota) evokes playwright, teacher and director. Besides writing many plays which have received productions, Yellow Robe taught playwriting for many years in the Creative Writing Department of The Institute of American Indian Arts (IAIA) on the campus of the College of Santa Fe, and is presently artistic director of a new Native American company, the Wakiknabe Theater Company of Albuquerque, New Mexico. In May 1999, the Wakiknabe will perform at the Museum of the Native American Indian in New York City. Yellow Robe has mentored many young Native playwrights, among them Bunky Echo Hawk and Terry Gomez, both mentioned above. His "The Star Quilter" (1987, yet unpublished), has enjoyed a number of productions. This one-act play dramatizes the relationship of a well-positioned white woman, who purchases quilts, to use as political favors, from a poor Native woman, who becomes blind from a lifetime of weaving quilts as gifts for those she loves.

The Independence of Eddie Rose, published for the first time in this volume, is clearly Yellow Robe's signature piece, and has been the subject of dissertation studies, multiple productions and much praise. Like Geiogamah's *Body Indian*, *Eddie Rose* is a powerful play, which spares the reader/spectator neither the pain nor the dilemmas facing its protagonist. Teenager Eddie seeks to escape his dysfunctional family situation while at the same time being determined to protect his younger sister from abuse. The specificity of his experience evokes in audience members clear recollections of their own youthful vulnerability. Eddie's independence, if it is to be had, becomes ours.

LeAnne Howe (Choctaw) is a published writer of short stories and essays, who, together with Roxy Gordon (Choctaw), wrote *Indian Radio Days* (the play's original music was written by Jarryd Lowder). This "evolving bingo experience" is a stereotypical "history" of Native Americans, complete with Indian chiefs meeting Columbus, multiple wars, Tonto and the Lone Ranger, "Indian" advertisements, and Mr. President and the First Lady—most speaking their pieces against a background of contrapuntal musical selections. Farce and melodrama abound, becoming the instruments of the sharp, satiric viewpoint of the playwrights who are telling the tragic tale of their conquered peoples.

As Muriel Miguel (Kuna/Rappahannock) explained to my graduate students in spring 1997, the Hopi goddess of creation, Spiderwoman, taught the people to weave, instructing them "to make a mistake in every tapestry so that my spirit may come and go at will." The Spiderwoman Theater is a performance group to reckon with. Their work has been recognized nationally and internationally in production and in theatre scholarship. The artistic survival of this three-sister company is historical, and not unlike the survival of those seventeenth-century commedia dell'arte troupes, whose creative output continues to attract and mystify theatre students everywhere. Because Lisa, Gloria and Muriel begin their "storyweaving" with improvisation, improvisation remains the basis of both their produced pieces and their teaching. Spiderwoman contributions to both Native theatre and feminist theatre are far-reaching; their production methodology offers a paradigm of "Native-storytelling-becomes-theatre." Included in this volume is their third work to be published, *Power Pipes*, developed in collaboration with the Colorado Sisters and performance artist, Murielle Borst (Kuna/Rappahannock). Its form is episodic, moving from ritual chanting and dancing to enacted scenes to monologues to ritual chanting and dancing. The storyweaving relates to the childhood of the sisters, its horrors and its hilarity.

Drew Hayden Taylor (Ojibway) follows in Tomson Highway's footsteps as the leading young Native playwright of Canada. He was artistic director of the Native Earth Performing Company of Toronto for a number of years. He has been a successful scriptwriter for television, has had numerous plays performed and published, and has been the recipient of several prestigious drama awards. In his one-act play, *Toronto at Dreamer's Rock* (1990), three fifteen- or sixteen-year-old boys meet at Dreamer's Rock—"a real place . . . people still go there to feel its guidance." The exceptional aspect of this meeting is that the boys are from the same tribe, but from different times—four hundred years ago, the present and the future.

Taylor's successfully produced (but yet unpublished), two-act play, "The Baby Blues," is a highly entertaining comedy about a sensitive subject: a daughter and father who discover their relationship to one another during a powwow. In *Only Drunks and Children Tell the Truth*, contained in this volume, Taylor offers a tragi-comic treatment of searing questions concerning self-identity, paternity, sibling-hood and adoption. The Taylor touch is light, his search for answers profound.

Diane Glancy (Cherokee) is a published writer of novels, poems, short stories and essays, whose collection *Claiming Breath*, won an American Book Award and the American Indian Prose Award. Her anthology of nine plays, *War Cries*, was published in 1997 by Holy Cow! Press. A new one-act, "The Woman Who Loved House Trailers" (unpublished) was given a reading in New York City in February 1998. *The Woman Who Was a Red Deer Dressed for the Deer Dance* (in this volume) is composed of seventeen brief scenes, many of them monologues that suggest the narrative of a young woman and her grandmother, but also connect them to the mysterious afterworld through the deer character—the grandmother's spirit self. Glancy the poet is ever-present in the work of Glancy the playwright.

Victoria Nalani Kneubuhl, born in Honolulu of Samoan, Hawaiian and Caucasian ancestry, won the Hawaii Award for Literature in 1994. She has had ten plays produced, and three plays will soon appear in an anthology to be published by the University of Hawaii Press. The Prologue of Ms. Kneubuhl's latest play (included here), *The Story of Susanna*, opens in Babylon with Susanna of Old Testament fame being saved by Daniel, from the false testimony of the Elders whose advances she has spurned. Parts I and II follow Susanna, storyweaving, through different times and places to contemporary time and a transitional house; here, as before, she must prove her innocence and her sanity. Susanna's story is the story of every young woman in every culture whose life has been curtailed by powerful oppressors.

That brilliant scholar of Greek theatre, Moses Hadas, taught us many years ago that a hero is someone who pushes back the horizons of what human beings can do. Mikhail Bahtkin, the noted cultural anthropologist and linguistic scholar, wrote that boundaries are the locales of the most intense and productive cultural life. Joseph Roach, a leading contemporary theatre scholar, speaks of performance genealogy, a term appropriate for this body of work, which owes much to Native ritual performance.

I like to think in terms of dramatic palimpsests: much like those overworked canvases which harbor painting beneath painting beneath painting—good plays harbor multiple layers of living.

A simple listing of the subjects addressed in these seven plays is almost overwhelming—identity crises, childhood trauma, alcoholism, incest, oppression, cooptation, violent colonialization, enforced assimilation, self-hate, self-acceptance, sibling rivalry, paternity, adoption, love relationships, parent-child relationships, community relationships.

Yet when we read and see these exceptional works of theatre, we experience horizons being pushed back, intense cultural life being created, performance lineage being disseminated, layers of life being revealed. We are privileged readers/spectators—privileged witnesses.

Mimi Gisolfi D'Aponte
Brooklyn, NY
January 1999

Body
Indian

A Play in
Five Scenes

hanay

geiogamah

author's statement

Let me try to stimulate your imagination just a little. There are 512 or so Indian tribes in the United States today. If each of these tribes was to establish and sponsor its own tribally oriented theatre company, and each company produced just one new work based on that tribe's history, culture, heritage, whatever, we would have 512 new works for the theatre. Can you imagine that? Five hundred and twelve new Indian plays! And if only half of them were to do this—in, say, some nearly fantastical, dream-come-true kind of thing—then there would be 256 new Indian plays. The theatre can really help us stop the erosion of our Indian way of life. Theatre is one of the most accessible of the performing arts. We really ought to get started on this right away. There can and ought to be a whole bunch of new Indian theatres.

Body Indian was first presented by The American Indian Theater Ensemble at La MaMa Experimental Theater Club in New York City on October 25, 1972. Sets were designed by Phil Wilmon, lighting and sound by Mike Trammel, the theme song was composed by Ed Wapp, Jr., drum and rattles were by Adrian Pushetonequa and Nelvin Salcido, the male soloist was Adrian Pushetonequa and the female soloist was Zandra Apple. John Vaccaro directed the following cast:

BOBBY LEE	Bruce Miller
HOWARD	Timothy Clashin
THOMPSON	Phil Wilmon
EULAHLAH	Debbie Finley Snyder
ETHEL	Grace Logan
ALICE	Jane Lind
BETTY	Bernadett Track Shorty
MARIE	Marie Antoinette Rogers
JAMES	Keith Conway
MARTHA	Debra Key
FINA	Geraldine Keems

The original production of the play toured the United States in November/December 1972. A later production of the play toured the United States and Europe in 1973. The play was produced by Highlands University in Las Vegas, New Mexico, in March 1974, and toured nationally from March to May. Red Earth Performing Arts Company in

Seattle, Washington, produced *Body Indian* in March/April 1976, and later toured the play throughout the Pacific Northwest in 1976/1977. In 1978 the play received productions by Indian Heritage School in Seattle, Washington, and by Institute of American Indian Arts in Santa Fe, New Mexico. Native Americans in the Arts produced *Body Indian* at American Indian Community House in New York City, in February/March 1980. On October 24, 1981, the play was performed with its sequel, *Body Indian Part II*, by Native Americans in the Arts at the first Turtle Performing Arts Festival at the Native American Center for the Living Arts in Niagara Falls, New York. Tribal theatre groups, community theatre groups and American Indian studies programs continue to produce the play.

BOBBY LEE, a crippled alcoholic in his mid-thirties

HOWARD, aged sixty-five or seventy, Bobby's Indian "uncle"

THOMPSON, same age as Bobby, overweight and
obviously a heavy drinker

EULAHLAH, in her late twenties, Thompson's wife

ETHEL, Howard's girlfriend, a "visitor"

ALICE, one of Bobby's "aunts," a middle-aged heavy drinker

BETTY, same as Alice

MARIE, Bobby's cousin, Howard's downstairs neighbor

JAMES, in his late teens, Howard's grandson,
Martha and Fina's sidekick

MARTHA, in her late teens, a hip young Indian "chick"

FINA, same as Martha

setting

Howard's one-room apartment. A large old-fashioned bed
dominates downstage center. Its mattress and loose cover-
ings are dingy. Upstage right is the entrance door. Immediately right of the entrance stand kitchen props: a small two-
burner stove, a one-faucet sink and a table with oilcloth covering; they all look greasy, messy.

Stage left of the bed is a small mattress on the floor,
spread out in pallet fashion. Above the head of the mattress
and to the right of the table is a doorway to a bathroom, smaller than the entrance door.

Many empty liquor bottles are lying on the floor. Some of the labels are visible—Arriba, Lucky Tiger, Stag—all cheap wine brands. There are so many of these that the performers must stumble over and around them to make their way through the action of the play.

The railroad tracks and other special effects are provided by means of slides. Additional film effects for exterior scenes may be used at various points suggested by the text; for example, the Mint Bar where Bobby was with his aunts before arriving at Howard's, or the maiming tragedy on the railroad tracks.

author's note

The first scene should immediately establish the mood and tone for the rest of the play. It is important that an "Indian frame of mind" be established in the performances from the very start of the play. This is not something that the actors will build but something that they will sustain throughout. The following suggestions may be helpful.

1. Lines must be delivered in a clipped fashion, a kind of talk characterized by a tendency to drop the final *g* ("goin'"), to jam words together ("lotta"), to add a grammatically superfluous final *s* ("mens"), to leave a hiatus between a final and an initial vowel ("a old one"), and (in women's speech particularly) to lengthen vowels inordinately ("l—ots"). In no way whatever is anything negative or degrading intended; this is simply the way the characters in this play speak English. The actors should be warned against overplaying this "Indian" speech. It should never become garbled and unclear.

   Definitions of Indian words used in the play:

   Hites: a close friend, usually male, like a brother, but not related by blood; one who has shared many life experiences with you.

   Ka-zog-gies: a euphemism for "ass" or one's bottom. In this usage it is plural.

   Pah-be-mas: a way of addressing as friends women who are not related by blood.

   Ko-ta-kes: a misspoken euphemism for "brothers," or for "brothers who've chosen each other as brothers," or, in a special usage, "blood brothers" without being kin by birth.

Hau: translates as "yes," an affirmative reply.

Pah-bes: friends, buddies, "partners," in a special usage one's "brothers."

Al-hong-ya: money.

2. Group effort will produce both the proper restraint and gusto for the requisite Indian style of drinking. The drinking should be a controlled part of the entire performance; that is, the actors should be cautioned not to exaggerate the drinking movements, which must be performed as naturally as possible. Great swaggering and swilling of the bottles are more indicative of amateur acting than anything else. It is important that the acting not be conducive to the mistaken idea that this play is primarily a study of the problem of Indian alcoholism. At moments in the play when much drink is available, the performers may take large drinks; when the supply is dwindling, the drinks are smaller or are sipped carefully.

3. The singing and dancing should be informal and improvised extensions of the characters' thoughts and moods. Not every song will be completed; some tunes will be hummed; some songs will cut off abruptly.

4. It is not necessary to distinguish what tribes the various characters belong to, but that there is a difference in tribes, and that the characters are aware of that difference, should be made obvious.

5. A certain degree of rollicking is permissible, but care must be taken not to overdo makeup, the poor quality of the clothing, gesticulation, the "Indian" speech traits and all physical actions, most especially those used in the rollings.

6. There should be a loud, rushing sound of a train starting off on a journey to signal to the audience that the play is beginning, and Bobby's entrance can be emphasized by the distant sound of the train.

scene 1

Bobby enters from stage left and crosses the stage on crutches. He knocks on the door unevenly. Onstage are Howard, Thompson, Eulahlah and Ethel. Howard and Ethel are lying on a mattress on the floor. Thompson and Eulahlah are sleeping on the bed. Thompson rises slowly and sluggishly to answer Bobby's knock. Lights up from dim to bright as the door opens.

THOMPSON *(Opening door)*: Well, I'lll beee! B—obbye Leee! Come in, hites, come in! Long time no see. *(He reaches for Bobby's hand. They shake. Bobby lumbers into the room)*

BOBBY: Hey, guy, go down and *halp* my aunts up the stairs, will you? And pay that cab. I can't make it back down those stairs now. They're really iced. *(He hands Thompson money)* My aunts are kinda buzzin', halp them up the stairs. Don't let them fall on thir ka-zog-gies. *(He smiles broadly)* Say, tell that driver I want my sacks.

(Thompson nods in agreement, puts on a shirt and shoes, and exits. Eulahlah stirs when the door shuts. Bobby sits down in the empty chair, exhales.)

EULAHLAH (*Groggily*): Weeelll Bobbyee Leee. Heeey. (*She gets off bed and goes to hug and kiss him*) Saaay, guy, last time— (*Cough stops her speech*) . . . Hey where's Thompson?

BOBBY: He went down to pay my cab. He's coming right back up. He's halping my aunts up them stairs.

EULAHLAH (*Puzzled*): Your aunts?

BOBBY: Yeah, you know 'em. Betty and Alice.

EULAHLAH: Oooh, yeah, yeah, I know all of dem. I drank with Alice 'bout three days ago uptown. Yeah, I know dem, Bobby.

(*She continues to fondle Bobby and peers around at the others in the room, attempting to focus her eyes and gain composure as she does so.*)

BOBBY (*Nodding toward Howard and Ethel on the floor*): Heeey, what's wrong with old guy there? Is he passed?

EULAHLAH (*Giggling*): Oh, no, he's sleep. He and Ethel's been drinkin' for few days now, but he's not passed out now, just sleep. He's got cold. Doctor at clinic told him he better stay in bed for few days. He's been drinkin' l—ots since he made his lease. I guess he got sick from drinkin' too much wine. Thompson was thinkin' 'bout takin' him to hospital at Lawton.

BOBBY (*Laughing lightly at this report*): When did he make his lease?

EULAHLAH: 'Bout two weeks ago. Or maybe a week ago. Thompson hasn't made his yet.

BOBBY: I just made mine this mornin'. But my damn lease man didn't want to pay me what I wanted. I was too broke to hold out, so I just signed it.

(*Bobby fumbles for a cigarette and takes some time lighting it. He sounds exhausted when he exhales. He smokes the cigarette with deep draws.*)

I was goin' back to city today, but the roads are too bad. I saw my aunts at Mint and they told me Howard was over here. Is Marie down there?

(Bobby gestures with his lip toward the floor, but Eulahlah doesn't seem to hear him. Noise is heard from the hallway outside. After many bumping sounds, the door opens and Thompson, Betty and Alice enter. The women are frowzy. They are in a happy mood, carrying on loudly.)

EULAHLAH *(Gesturing broadly at the women)*: Hae—ye! My pa-be-mas. Heey!

(They all laugh and exchange Indian women greetings.)

THOMPSON *(With pleased smile)*: Here's your sacks, Bobby. Soun's like you got jugs in there.

BOBBY: I do.

BETTY: Welll, helll, then, open one up!

(They crack open a bottle by hitting it on the bottom and then removing the screw top, and begin to take long drinks as the wine is passed around. Drum and rattles come up as the drinking begins. Howard and Ethel are awakened by the merriment. Howard rises from the bed, sees Bobby sitting in the chair, shouts a greeting, then moves arthritically toward Bobby and embraces him. Ethel greets the other women with wan enthusiasm. The bottle continues to be passed around uninterruptedly. Ethel approaches Bobby. The light percussion continues to the end of the scene.)

ETHEL: H—ell—oo Bobby. How are you, sonny? You look preeety good. Haven't seen you in a lo—ng time, boy

BOBBY *(More settled now)*: You're E—thel, annet?

ETHEL: Yeah, yeah, Bobby, it's me, E—thel.

BOBBY: You're kin to me, annet?

ETHEL: Yeah, yeah, Bobby, we're related. On my mother's side, I think.

BOBBY (*Traces of drunken slur beginning to show in his voice*): Your dad was my dad's Indian brother. Ko-ta-kes, haw! (*He makes an appropriate gesture with his hand*)

ETHEL: Yeah, that's right, Bobby. Brothers!

HOWARD (*Interjecting*): Yeah, yeah, ya'll are kin. Ethel is related to your mother, Bobby. Your mother was my dad's sister. Ethel's dad was kin to both of them.

BOBBY: Yeah. That's the way it is . . . yeah.

HOWARD: Ethel here has a-been visitin' for few days now. Too cold to go back west. She's waitin' to make her lease.

BOBBY (*Continuing to drink from the bottle*): Is Marie down there?

HOWARD: Yeah, I think so. I heard her yellin' at them kids this mornin'. She had one of them with her when she was up here last night.

ALICE: I saw her uptown yesterday mornin'. I think she's been behavin' it.

(*The women laugh at this*)

BOBBY: I need to see her. Need to talk to her 'bout signin' up for program at Norman. She's got to sign with me.

HOWARD (*Concerned*): She'll be up here. She'll hear us through the roof. She always come up here when she hear us talkin' and makin' noise.

BOBBY: Has she been drinkin'?

HOWARD: You know how she is.

(*Betty rises and carries bottle to Bobby. The others focus on her doing this. Drum and rattles come up.*)

BETTY (*Merrily*): Here, Bobby, take a b—ig drink. We haven't seen you in lo—ng time. Drink with us, Bobby.

(Bobby grins, is pleased with Betty's attention. The others laugh and encourage him. He takes the nearly full bottle, turns it up, and downs the entire contents with a slow, steady gurgle. He gasps when he is finished. Another bottle is opened and starts the rounds. Bobby sits almost stupefied. Howard fawns over him. Bobby's teeth grit and streams of saliva run from the sides of his mouth. The others pretend they do not notice. Bobby slumps over the chair and passes out. Slowly they all surround him. There is a menacing air as they do this. The lights dim to a haze.)

HOWARD *(Gently, to avoid waking Bobby)*: Bobby. Hey, Bobby. Sonny, are you wake? You want 'nother drink? Bobby. Sit up, sonny. Ethel wants to visit with you. *(There is no sign of life in Bobby. Howard moves in closer)* Bobby. Bobby.

(They lift his body from the chair with drunken eagerness and carelessness, and carry him to the bed. One of the women adjusts his legs so that he lies stretched out on the bed.)

Bobby. Does your leg feel okay? Does it hurt you, sonny? Do you want us to take it off for you? *(He moves close to Bobby's ear)* Bobby. We goin' run out of jugs. We got to go get some more. Bobby. You got any money, sonny? We goin' run out. Bobby, heeey, Bobby, can you help us out? *(Howard touches Bobby's leg, moves back and motions to Ethel to join him. Now certain that Bobby is thoroughly passed out)* This boy always pass out pretty fast. When he got his leg cut off and start wearin' that other leg, he start drinkin' pretty heavy. *(Pause)* He was passed out on those tracks when he got hurt. *(Pause)* I know he got money on him. He always hide it in that leg.

(Howard and Ethel begin to search Bobby's pockets. They find cigarettes, folded papers, change and two or three one-dollar bills.)

ETHEL: This ain't all he has!
HOWARD: Feel in back.

(Ethel puts her hand in Bobby's back pocket with a stealthy movement.)

ETHEL: He don't have no billfold. Wait, here's some . . .

(She pulls a few bills out, looks quickly to determine their denomination and then moves quickly to cover her find.)

HOWARD *(Nervous)*: How much was it?
BETTY: Is there any more wine?

(Howard and Ethel scuffle over the money.)

ETHEL: Just little bit.
BETTY: Where?
ETHEL *(Gesturing with her lips)*: Over there . . . in those sacks.

(As Betty rises to get the wine, the distant sound of a rushing train and whistle blasts from offstage. The cast freezes. The drum and rattles grow intense. Expressions of fear slowly cross over the cast's faces as they look directly toward the audience.)

I can hear it. Sounds like it's 'bout twenty, thirty miles away.
ALICE: I can barely hear it.
BETTY: I hear it little bit.
ETHEL: Hear it?
EULAHLAH: I can hear it . . . now.
THOMPSON: Sounds like hummin'.
ALICE: The sound makes a little buzzin' feelin' on my ear.
BETTY *(To Howard)*: You hear it, Grampa?

HOWARD (*Hobbling to downstage center*): I can hear it just a lit-tle bit. Just a li—ttle bit.

(*Percussion sounds and lights intensify, then go out. When the train whistle is heard, color slide projections of railroad tracks, taken at varied sharp angles and flashing in rapid sequence, appear on the back wall.*)

scene 2

The lights come up on the company; all except Howard are sitting or lying around the room. Howard is standing in the middle of the room with a bottle of wine in his hand. He is in a jolly mood, singing and joking with the others. Bobby is sitting at the edge of the bed, his position for most of the rest of the play. Empty bottles clutter the floor. There is no indication that anything wicked has taken place, or that there is a world beyond the shabby walls.

HOWARD (*With aged gusto*): I sure like to dance. One of my boys almost won first at the fair one time. He sure was good. (*He moves around*) I taught all my kids how to sing. He can sing. (*Pointing to Bobby*) He sure can hit those high notes. (*No reaction from Bobby*) He can't drum, but he can sing.

(*The women begin to shout encouragement to Howard for his dancing.*)

I saw in Darko* paper they havin' a b—ig dance at Carnegie tomorrow night. I'd sure like to go. But evreee time this guy always get us stopped by the county laws! (*He points directly to Thompson*)

ETHEL: Are you going to war dance for us, Howard?

*Anadarko, Oklahoma.

17

HOWARD: Anytime now. (*They all laugh. The merriment increases*) Just watch me!

(*Betty and Alice shake imaginary rattles. Ethel stands and makes supportive accompanying movement. Thompson pretends to drum.*)

Fancy dance! Eee-hah! Eee-hah! Eee-hah! Eee-hah!
BETTY AND ALICE: Yo-a-hio-ya, yo-a-hio-ya.

(*Music rises offstage. The scene intensifies as Howard trips around the room with his dance.*)

HOWARD (*Loudly, breathlessly*): The drummers are gettin' ahead of me! Slow 'em down! (*There is no indication from Thompson that he hears this*) Eee-hah! Eee-hah! Eee-hah!
BETTY AND ALICE: Yo-a-hio-ya, yo-a-hio-ya.

(*Then, on cue, the dancing and singing stop abruptly with a rattle fade-out. The participants let out a whoop. While they are carrying on, Marie enters. The company focuses on her, and there seems to be an attitude of resentment toward her.*)

HOWARD (*As if surprised, speaking directly to Marie*): Marieeeee! Come in! Come in! Come over here and sit down. Look who's here. Bobby's here.

(*Howard leads her to Bobby on the bed.*)

MARIE (*Suddenly*): Welll, hiii, B—obbyee. (*She kisses him*) Where have you beeen? I haven't seen you in so lo—ng. I was startin' to get worried about you.

(*The others arrange themselves, find bottles, eye Marie; but one by one fall asleep. Meanwhile Bobby has been coming around, and now sits up on the bed.*)

BOBBY *(Adjusting)*: I came down to make my lease. I can't go back to the city today. Roads too bad. Thought I'd come here to see if you was here. They tol' me you was here.

MARIE: I thought you was up here when I heard you walkin' on the floor. I thought you'd be here for lease signin'. Did you sign yet?

BOBBY: My damn white lease man wouldn't give me what I wanted. I was gonna hold out, but I needed the money. I had to sign for what he wanted to give me. I couldn't help it.

MARIE: I'm gonna make mine Monday. He already made his. *(She lip-gestures toward Howard)* You got any money on you, Bobby?

BOBBY: I can spare you a little bit. I need all I have.

MARIE: I don't have any groceries. I tried to borrow some from Howard the other day, but he didn't even have any rations left. Thompson and his wife stay here nearly all the time now. He just barely gets by on that lease money of his. Jobs are hard to find. 'Specially for Indians 'round here. You know how it is. Money's sure scarce.

BOBBY: I was gonna tell you . . . *(Pausing to drink)* . . . I want to use my lease money to get in program at Norman. It's a AA deal for alcoholics. That preacher in the city told me they could dry me out in 'bout six weeks. I wanna go over there. I need a relative to sign my papers with me. Can you sign them for me?

MARIE: Does your caseworker at the Bureau know about this?

BOBBY *(Angrily)*: He doesn't have to know about it! I can go if I want to.

MARIE: Did they say you could go?

BOBBY *(Irritated)*: I don't have to ask them. I can go on my own, but I have to have a relative to co-sign for me to get in.

MARIE: How much does it cost?

BOBBY: You can pay if you want to. I want to pay. It costs four hundred dollars. I'll be in there for six weeks.

(When Bobby mentions four hundred dollars, some of the others stir and take notice.)

MARIE: Do you have the papers with you, Bobby?
BOBBY *(Slurring his words)*: I left them in the city.
MARIE: Do you want to lay down, Bobby?
BOBBY *(Slumping, jerking, drooling)*: Uuuhaa.

(Bobby is again stupefied from the wine. Marie rises and lays him out on the bed. This takes some effort from her. She talks to him, though she knows he is passed out. Her speech begins to sound chilling. When she has him stretched out, her actions and speech quicken.)

MARIE: Bobby. Bobby! Bobby, are you sleep? Are you sleep, sonny? Bobby. Bobby.

(While she is talking to Bobby, Thompson begins to move, as though drugged, toward the bed.)

HOWARD: He's sleep. I know he got money. Look in leg.

(Marie and Thompson begin to search Bobby's pockets. They go over his entire body, leaving his clothes disheveled, and in the process pull up the pants over Bobby's artificial leg. Frantically they begin to compete to find money stashed in the apparatus. Thompson finds money, and Marie tries to grab it from him.)

MARIE: I need some of that!
THOMPSON: No, uuuh, hey! *(With a nervous, alcoholic twitch)* I'll check. I'll check . . . for . . . for all of . . . us. *(The others freeze)* It . . . it's st . . . sti—ll there. Movin' this way. Comin' closer.

(The visuals of the tracks appear again, then go out with the lights.)

scene 3

The lights come up with the women standing center stage in a round dance formation. They begin singing and dancing to the 49 tune of "Strawberries When I'm Hungry." Marie sits uneasily in the background, obviously not welcome to take part in the women's frolicking. As the scene progresses, the women's mood gradually becomes sadder, angrier, more desperate.

ALICE: I was gonna camp at the fair this year, but Junior got throwed in 'bout a week before the fair started, and we couldn't put up our arbor. I sure like to hear that music comin' from the dance grounds.

BETTY: I haven't camped at the fair since I was a little girl. The dust bothers me, but I like the dancin'.

ETHEL: It's cheaper to camp than it is to live in town.

EULAHLAH: Daddy and 'em used to butcher before we came to the campgrounds. I really liked to fix up that meat.

ALICE *(Slowly)*: I wish I had some meat now. My kids been eatin' only commodity meat for 'bout two months now. Junior's unemployment ran out a month ago. There ain't no jobs nowhere.

BETTY: Just be glad you have your gas and lights workin'.

ALICE: They will be for just couple of days more. I got my final notice that they was gonna cut them off last week. That city truck will be pullin' up in the alley first thin' Monday mornin'.

ETHEL *(Reflecting)*: I put my nephews in government school this fall. I sure didn't want to, but at least they get taken care of there. I hate for my kids to have to go without.

EULAHLAH: I didn't mind goin' to GI school so bad. Aayyee. *(The others smile knowingly at this)* They treated me

21

pretty good where I went. Some of those schools ain't so bad, but some of them sure no good.

ETHEL: My oldest nephew plays football at Riverside. His picture was in paper two or three weeks ago. I sure felt proud when I saw it in there.

ALICE *(Almost crying)*: Everything is sure rough. I can't even get on state welfare. They say my husband is able to work. He's able, but there's no work.

BETTY *(Slowly)*: All those white people think Indians have it good because they think the government takes care of us. They don't even know. It's rougher than they know. I'd like to trade my house for a white lady's house on Mission Street. I'd like for a white lady to have my roaches. You see them at the store, and they look at you like your purse is full of government checks. I wish my purse could be full of government checks.

ALICE: I wish I had a check from anywhere.

(The bottle is moving around.)

EULAHLAH: So do I.

ETHEL: So do I. I'd get my son out of county jail if I did.

(The drumbeat comes up. Bobby has been watching the women as they lament. A pause while the bottle comes around to him, then he speaks.)

BOBBY *(Suprisingly alert)*: Every Indian needs to have a government check for twenty-five thousand. They could give you womens fifty thousand. Then you could buy all your kids shoes, clothes, bicycles, pay rent, pay fines, buy shawls and earrings, and put the money you have left in the bank to live on. That's the only way you'd ever have the money you need.

(The women turn their attention to Bobby as he makes this statement. They all laugh heartily as he finishes talking, then rise and surround him to tease him.)

ETHEL: Hey, Bobby, sonny. I bet you haven't 49'd in a long time. Come on, dance with us. You can dance with your crutches.

(The women straggle into a round dance formation, pulling Bobby up onto the floor with them. He first resists, then gives in. Bottles are in hand. They begin to sing, in high-pitched voices, the 49 song, "One-Eyed Ford," with Bobby singing along. As the dancing progresses, Bobby guzzles from a bottle and begins to falter, throwing the dancers out of kilter. One of his crutches flies across the floor as the women, with much fuss and giggling, lay him out on the bed. They stop singing and begin to glance at one another.)

ALICE *(In low voice)*: Sssssh. Sssssh. Hey, Bobby has some money, annet?
BETTY: I think so.
ETHEL: He does.
ALICE: How much?
BETTY: I think he's got lots.
ETHEL: He signed his lease today.
EULAHLAH *(Nervously)*: He said he signed it.
ALICE: Howard, does my nephew have any money?

(Howard is nearly out and does not reply.)

BETTY: I know he'd help us out if he could.
ETHEL: He's my relative. I know he'd help me out.
EULAHLAH: Me and Thompson helped him out before.
ALICE: He always comes to my house when he's here. I always take care of him.

ETHEL: He used to stay with me long time ago. He was tryin'
to get straightened up.
BETTY: He sure is a g—ood guy. Poor thing.
ALICE: You all must be good to him now, he's a poor thing.
Y'all be good to him.
BETTY: We'll be good to him.
ETHEL: Yeah, we will.
EULAHLAH: Oh, okay. We'll be good to him.

*(The lights lower as they begin to search Bobby. They find a
few dollars and stuff them into their bras. When Eulahlah
fumbles with Bobby's artificial leg, Marie startles all of them:)*

MARIE: I saw you!

*(The women quickly return to their dancing and singing,
pretending they have not rolled Bobby. Their cackling cries
are drowned out by the offstage train whistle, this time louder
than before. The railroad tracks are projected over them as
they freeze in their dance pattern. The lights go out on a slow
count as the women clutch for each other, reach their hands
out toward the audience, then freeze again.)*

scene 4

*A restlessness has settled over the group. They know that the wine
supply is quickly dwindling. Eulahlah and Thompson quarrel;
Ethel needles Howard.*

BETTY: I wish John was here. I haven't seen him . . . in 'bout
a week now.
ALICE *(In same lonely tone)*: Junior went lookin' for a job the
other day. Somebody said they saw him at Erma's. He
always shows up when he runs out of steam.

BETTY: I hope John gets his business taken care of pretty quick. His lease man is a son of a bitch. He won't even give us an advance, even when we don't have groceries.

BOBBY *(Coming suddenly to life and, slowly, in drunken movements, searching himself)*: Somebody took my money. It's almost all gone. *(Pause)* I got to use that money to go to Central State at . . . Norman. *(Pause)* What happened to it? . . . Who took it? *(Shouting)* Howard? *(Pause)* Where's . . . Marie? *(Marie makes a movement in his direction, but stops short)* Where's wine? *(Pause)* Who . . . took my . . . money? *(The group doesn't respond to any of his questions and seems not to hear them)* Why did you do . . . it . . . take my al . . . ? *(He begins to grit his teeth, and his body tenses)* I want . . . to . . . go . . . to Norman. My money . . . money . . . is . . . for Norman. Where is it? Which one of you?

(He slumps over on the bed, but doesn't pass out. He moans and grunts for the next several moments. The group sits now as though there were nothing else to do but wait for something to happen. There is a knock on the door. Howard answers it. The others watch. Enter James, Martha and Fina. The young people are greeted with blank expressions. They shake the cold off themselves, exclaim about the harshness of the weather outside and survey, with expressions of amusement and awe, the scene in the apartment.)

JAMES *(To Howard)*: How are you, Grampa?

HOWARD: Pretty good, preeetty good. What are y'all doing, sonny?

JAMES: I came up to see you, to ask you for some al-hong-ya.

(While they are talking, Martha and Fina approach Bobby on the bed. James guides Howard, now besotted, to the floor pallet.)

MARTHA (*Jostling Bobby*): Heeeey, Bobby Lee, wake up, guy. Hey, it's me, Marty, your buddy. Wake up. Where you been, dude? I ain't seen you in a long time.

(*Bobby raises his head, slowly recognizing Martha.*)

BOBBY (*Groggily*): Heeeeeey, what are you . . . ? (*Focusing on Fina*) Who's this?

MARTHA: Her name's Fina.

(*Fina and Martha giggle. They seem to have a special interest in Bobby.*)

BOBBY: Is she kin to you?

MARTHA: Yeah, she's my cousin.

(*Bobby takes a drink, offers one to Martha and Fina. He is pleased by the attention he is receiving from the two girls. Fina puts her arm enticingly around Bobby. He responds enthusiastically by dropping the bottle to the floor.*)

FINA (*Low whisper to Martha*): He's kind of good looking.

(*James is talking and laughing with Howard and Thompson, paying no direct attention to the activity on the bed. Howard occasionally glances sharply at it.*)

MARTHA (*Giggly, bouncy, high*): You want some more wine, Bobby Lee? Where is it?

BOBBY: Over there. (*He points to a sack on the floor. Martha moves to get it*)

MARTHA (*To group, sitting blankly around the room*): Golll, y'all look like y'all've been partying for 'bout three weeks. I bet y'all've been drunk a l—ot. (*Big giggle*)

26

(There is no response to her remark. Martha, James and Fina now converge on the bed, happy that they have gotten this far.)

FINA *(To James)*: Does your Grampa have any money?
JAMES: He didn't say.
MARTHA: Ask him again.
JAMES: Wait!
MARTHA *(Gesturing toward Bobby)*: I bet he's got some.
JAMES: If he did it's probably all gone by now.
FINA: Check him out.
JAMES: You check him out.
MARTHA: Heeey! I sure wish I had twenty. We could get a case and some gas. And we could go to that concert in the city tonight. Get hiii! Aye!

(The young trio all laugh at Martha's fantasy.)

FINA: If I had twenty dollars, I'd buy me a . . . a . . . a living bra! Aaaeee.
JAMES: Man, I just wish I had a twenty. And a lid. I wouldn't go to school for days. Aaaeee.
FINA *(As she fondles Bobby's torso)*: He's kinda good lookin'. Aaaeee.

(They giggle and tease each other as they get Bobby's body into place and roll it. The adults are paying no attention to any of this.)

JAMES *(Sternly)*: Check his pockets!
MARTHA *(Toward group)*: They probably took all of it already.
JAMES *(To Howard)*: Where's his money, Grampa? Grampa, hey, does he have any money? We need some bad, man.
HOWARD *(After a pause, without looking up)*: Look in shoe.

(They begin to fidget with the orthopedic shoe attached to the artificial leg, and Martha yanks out a bill.)

MARTHA *(Exclaiming at the size of the bill)*: W—ow! We can really make it with this.

FINA: How much is it?

(No reply from Martha. She giggles to herself, then signals to James and Fina that they should leave. They put on their coats and prepare to hurry out.)

HOWARD *(To James)*: Sonny, where y'all goin'?

JAMES: We're gonna drive around for a while, see who's uptown . . . There's a rock band playin' tonight.

(Martha and Fina make giggly small talk with the rest of the company as they prepare to exit. The low bleat of the train whistle sounds offstage. The youths first react as if it is a part of their high, but become gradually more concerned, agitated. The track projections flash on.)

FINA *(Giggly and ooeey)*: W—ow. It's really hummin', makin' a kinda buzzin' noise.

MARTHA: Ooooooh. It feels warm. I can feel it on my ear. Hey, this is wierd.

(The others onstage watch this silently, no movement.)

HOWARD: Sonny, can y'all come back pretty soon? I want you to help me out. Will you come check on us?

JAMES: Yeah, uh, okay, Grampa. 'Bout couple of hours.

MARTHA *(Trying to feel the track projections with her fingers)*: Psssst! Psssst! I bet these guys have been puttin' their hands on these to get a buzz. Aaaeee.

(Giggles from James and Martha; others are frozen in place.)

JAMES: We'll see ya'll pretty soon.

MARTHA: Take it easy.

FINA: Y'all be good. Be careful.

(Lights out. Sound goes off when the door closes behind them.)

scene 5

The party is nearing its end. Bobby Lee has been rolled four times so far, knows that this has happened, but has remained helpless. It is apparent on the players' faces that they have forgotten everything that has happened in the previous four scenes, that they are unaware of their abuse of Bobby. They want only to keep the party going. A soft drumbeat is heard offstage throughout the scene.

HOWARD *(Bitterly)*: I guess all the wine is gone. Is there anymore anywhere?

ALICE: Is all the wine gone? I want another one.

EULAHLAH: It's not all gone, is it?

THOMPSON: You drank 'bout four bottles of it yourself.

HOWARD *(To Thompson)*: Look over there, under that chair.

(Thompson looks, finds nothing.)

THOMPSON: I thought I saw somebody hide one under here.

HOWARD: You did. You hid it under here.

EULAHLAH: He hid it. He can drink more than all of us together.

HOWARD: I didn't hide any wine.

EULAHLAH: I know I didn't.

BETTY: Is there a bottle hidden 'round here? Is there one hidden? I thought there was more wine than this.

HOWARD: There was a lot of wine. There was 'bout ten, 'leven, maybe twelve bottles. We had a couple of bottles when Bobby came.

EULAHLAH: We had more than a couple of bottles, Grampa. Goll, there was a lot more than a couple.

ALICE *(Checking under the furniture)*: There's another bottle somewhere. It's too cold to go back uptown to get more. There's another bottle somewhere. *(Pause)* There's another bottle somewhere.

(During this discussion about the wine, Bobby silently watches from the bed, following the movements of the others as they look for bottles.)

BETTY *(Angrily)*: We bought a lot of bottles when we stopped at the liquor store on the way here in the taxi. I know we bought a lot of them. Two sacks full!

HOWARD *(To Marie)*: Hey, hey you. Do you have anything to drink downstairs?

MARIE: I don't have any wine. You drank all of it when you were down there the other day.

(Their searching becomes frantic.)

EULAHLAH: If there's no more wine in this place, then somebody go get some uptown.

(There is no response from the men. Now there is a silence. Bobby continues to observe their movement.)

HOWARD *(After all have become exasperated from searching)*: There's no more wine here. We drank it all up. If any of you want some more to drink, one of us will have to go to town to get it.

BETTY: One of you men go.

ALICE: Yeah, Thompson, you or Howard go get us some more drinks!

EULAHLAH *(Sharply)*: Goddamn you, Thompson, go get us some more drinks! *(Thompson tries to push her away, but she persists)* Get us some more drinks, you damn lazy thing. Go on! Get us some more.

HOWARD *(To Thompson)*: Yeah, sonny, you go get us some more to drink. We don't have no more. Go 'head, go get us some more. We can stay here and drink it. Go 'head.

(The others encourage Thompson to go. Thompson gives in.)

BOBBY *(Suddenly, startling them all)*: Is there anymore . . . wine? I want another drink . . . I need another drink!

HOWARD: We goin' send after some more, Bobby. Thompson here is goin' after some more uptown.

(Marie rises, goes to Bobby on the bed.)

MARIE: Bobby, do you want to go downstairs to my house with me? Howard will help you down the stairs so you won't fall.

BOBBY: I want a drink!

MARIE: Come with me, Bobby. There isn't anymore drinks here.

BOBBY *(Coming alive)*: Yes, there is, there's another drink here. *(The others turn to Bobby)*

HOWARD *(Loudly)*: Sonny, did you say there's another drink here? Did you say there's a bottle here?

(Bobby doesn't reply, reels in his wooziness.)

MARIE: Come downstairs with me, Bobby. They drank up all the wine they had here. There isn't anymore wine. Come with me, Bobby.

HOWARD *(Pushing Marie out of his way)*: Did you say there's some wine left here, Bobby? Tell me where it's at.

ALICE: Come on, Bobby Lee, be a good chief, tell us where there's another drink. We done drank up all that we had. There's no more, sonny.

EULAHLAH: Bobby Lee, hites, come on, guy, share your drink with us. Geee. We always help you out when you need it. Help us out. Share with us.

(Bobby tries to protect himself from their pummeling.)

MARIE: Bobby, I'm going downstairs now. I got to check on those kids. Howard will help you down the stairs. Come on down with him. I'll fix you a place to sleep. *(She waits for a reply; there is none)* Howard, you must bring him downstairs. He doesn't need to drink anymore. He can sleep for a while. Bobby, you come down with Howard. He'll help you down the stairs. These people are just gonna keep on drinkin'. Come on downstairs.

(Bobby remains silent. The others say nothing to Marie as she exits. They wait for Bobby to say where the wine is hidden.)

HOWARD: Bobby, do you want to go down to Marie's?
BOBBY: No! No! I'm . . . okay, here.
HOWARD: Bobby, sonny, where's that wine at?

(Bobby smiles faintly at Howard, then reaches slowly into his jacket and pulls out a full pint of wine, holds it up for all to see.)

BOBBY: Here's wine. Y'all know I always have something hidden on me . . . to drink. *(They all laugh, pretending to accept this as a joke)* If you drink, you should . . . you should always keep a small one hid on you. If you can.

(He opens the bottle and drinks it all in one long gulp. The others push and claw for the bottle, but Bobby, fending them off with his free arm, keeps it out of their reach.)

THOMPSON *(Almost crying)*: Hey, hey, Bobby Lee, hites, save me . . . save *(As the last drop drains from bottle)* CORNERRRS!*

(Bobby laughs drunkenly.)

EULAHLAH *(With pain)*: Oooooooooh, ho!

(The grip of needing a drink now tightens on all of them. Some of them show signs of "shakes.")

HOWARD: Thompson, go get us another drink.

THOMPSON *(Trembling, sweating)*: Okay, Okay! Give me money and I'll go.

HOWARD: You have money to buy it.

THOMPSON: I don't have any money. I'm broke.

EULAHLAH: Me and Thompson don't have anymore money. We spent it all a long time ago. You have money.

HOWARD: I spent all my lease money already.

EULAHLAH: No you didn't! You still have money!

ETHEL *(Joining Howard; to Eulahlah)*: We don't have any money. Howard's broke. *(Pointing to Betty and Alice)* They have money!

ALICE: I don't have any money. I've been broke for the past two weeks. I wish I had some money.

BETTY *(Sadly, to Bobby)*: I don't have . . . any . . . money.

THOMPSON: No money, no drinks!

HOWARD: Which one of you has a couple of dollars? *(No reply from any of them)* I know somebody's got some.

THOMPSON: Who's gonna give me the money?

(Now everybody searches their pockets or purses to look for money. They find nothing. Bobby moans. A loud knock on

---

* The last little shot, the final drops that usually collect in the corner of the bottle.

the door. Howard answers. The three youths enter. They are now more spaced-out than previously.)

JAMES *(Smiling, glassy-eyed)*: You said to come back, to check on you all, didn't you, Grampa?

(The two girls eye Bobby on the bed, apparently to check his vulnerability once again.)

HOWARD: Yeah, yeah, I wanted you kids to come back to check on us. Sonny, do you have any al-hong-ya on you?

JAMES *(Surprised)*: Al-hong-ya? No, I don't. Remember, I asked you for some when we came here before.

HOWARD: Yeah, yeah, but do you have any money? We need another drink.

JAMES: We're all busted.

(He giggles. The girls are waiting, talking with the others.)

HOWARD: Are y'all in your car, sonny?

JAMES: Yeah, uh, huh. We been slidin' around in it uptown.

HOWARD: What time is it, sonny?

JAMES: It's early, man.

HOWARD: Are those stores still open?

JAMES: Yeah, they're open, the ones you want. *(He giggles again)*

HOWARD *(Looking around)*: We sure need some money.

JAMES: What do you want us to do?

HOWARD: Sit down, y'all, sit down. *(Howard now takes control, his grimness exerting a force over the others)* Y'all know how Bobby Lee gets when he's been drinkin' for a long time and runs out. *(They all indicate that they know what he's talking about)* He gets real sick, haw? *(More agreement)* I was with him one time in Oklahoma City jail when he got sick, real sick. He was really havin' those dee-tees. His arms was movin' and jerkin' like cow's when you butcher it. His legs was a-shakin'. He soun' like he was chokin'. *(He strains for composure, coughs, trembles)* He tol' me he saw in his dee-tees a row of lillel chickens sittin' on those jail bars singin' Indian songs.

He said they was purple and gold and red colors. He said he felt like his head was bein' hit with a big iron 'bout ever so often. *(The two girls giggle at the bizarre images Howard is describing)* He said he felt like he was fallin' through the whole jailhouse floor into the sewer lines.

He said his hair was long as an old lady's, and his fingers were all shrunk up, like he was a-dead.

He tol' me he thought he was goin' die while he was in those dee-tees!

I don't want him to have them again! He's had them lots of times. I know what they're like. He's going have them again if he don't get a drink. He don't have any more al-hong-ya. It's all gone. He spent it all. He always spen' his money fast. He don't have anymore wine hid. I'm goin' get him some more wine before he wakes up. He's goin' need it. *(Pause)* He sure is goin' need a drink when he wakes up. Y'all know that!

(Howard moves to the bed. He signals Thompson to join him. They begin jostling Bobby's body roughly, almost brutally. The others begin, one by one, to rise and stand around the bed to watch, hiding the operation from the audience. There is complete silence. Out of the audience's view, Howard and Thompson are removing Bobby's artificial leg. James is the first to leave the encirclement, signaling his two companions that it's time for them to leave. Howard calls James back for him to assist in rearranging Bobby's body on the bed.)

(To James) Sonny, I want you to take us to white man bootleggers on Washington Street. He'll give us what

we need for this *(Indicating artificial leg)*. He'll let Bobby have it back when Bobby can get it out.

JAMES *(Disgust in his voice)*: Okay, let's hurry. It's gettin' late. We gotta' go to the concert.

(Howard and Thompson prepare to leave, placing the artificial leg upright against the bed. Complete silence until Howard and Thompson are posed at the door with the leg wrapped in a dingy blanket. Drum and rattles now begin a gradual rise to the end of the scene. The youths exit.)

HOWARD *(To those who remain behind)*: Y'all wait here. We'll be back pretty soon.

(They exit. The women begin to straighten the room, to sweep, to pick up bottles. The track visuals appear in sharp contrast over Bobby's stretched-out body. Some time passes while the women clean before the train whistle is heard. The sound grows louder and awakens Bobby. He feels around on his body and discovers that his artificial leg has been removed. He pulls himself up, speaks increasingly louder so as to be heard over the train sounds. The women do not hear him. There is a sardonic smile fixed on his face.)

BOBBY: Well, h—ell—o, Bobby Lee. How are you, hites? Lo—ng time no . . . seee.

(He reaches for his crutches, has trouble securing them. Sitting upright on the edge of the bed, he looks straight ahead at a flashing train light, an entirely different mood about him now as horror overtakes him.)

I can hear . . . a . . . train . . . that . . . train . . . my leg . . . that train's gonna . . . gonna hit . . . my . . . ley—g!

(He slumps over as loud blasts from the train echo through the theatre. The women continue tidying the room. Train sounds subside, lights begin to dim. The track visuals fade out. Silence.)

END OF PLAY

Hanay Geiogamah, a member of the Kiowa/Delaware tribes of Oklahoma, is a leading Native American director, playwright and producer. Actively involved in American Indian studies and research, he is a professor in the School of Theatre, Film and Television and the American Indian Studies Program, both at the University of California at Los Angeles. Mr. Geiogamah is a founder of the internationally acclaimed American Indian Dance Theatre, which is celebrating its tenth anniversary with a new, full-length dance-drama, *Kotuwokan!*, which he conceived and staged for the company.

He served as producer for the Turner Network Television Native American project's feature films, which include *Geronimo*, *Lakota Woman* and *Crazy Horse*. He was principal writer for the 1994 documentary series, *The Native Americans*, for the Turner Broadcasting System. Mr. Geiogamah wrote, coproduced and codirected the American Indian Dance Theatre's second Great Performances' Dance in America special, "Dances for the New Generations," which was nominated for a 1993 Primetime Emmy Award.

Mr. Geiogamah is currently producing two feature films: *Wolves*, with Frank Blythe and the Native American Public Telecommunications Drama Development Project, with script by Joseph Bruchac; and *The Indians Are Coming*, with script by Dan Jones, in association with Time Travel Productions. He is also developing an American Indian musical for Broadway, working with writer, Gregg Sarris and theatre producer, Jeffrey Seller, producer of the musical *Rent*.

The
Independence
of
Eddie Rose

william s.
yellow robe, jr.

author's statement

I am an enrolled member of the Assiniboine Tribe. My people are located on the Fort Peck Indian reservation, in northeastern Montana. I grew up in a small township called Wolf Point. I wasn't interested in making money when I entered playwriting and theatre. My goal was very simple: I wanted the name of my family, my relatives and my people to be heard. "Assiniboine." That was it. It was my way of telling this country: "See, we are still alive."

In growing up, going to white schools, we were never really taught about our Tribe—and this was a school on a reservation—we were taught everything about mainstream culture, and we heard nothing of our people. We didn't exist in textbooks, or in the lectures given by the teachers. I later discovered that it was the Assiniboine Tribe who donated the land to the school. Oh well.

In teaching playwriting, I remind myself and my students, "We are not learning to be white playwrights, we are learning to be strong Native writers. We have to be able to validate our own experience for ourselves."

Native theatre artists have been made homeless in our own homeland. I founded the Wakiknabe Theater Company as a new homeland for Native theatre artists. The world is invited to these performances, but right now my focus is on helping and developing Native theatre and Native artists.

I really don't want to sum up my work. I don't want to sound ego-driven, but I find my writing changing. Change is a wonderful thing. Some people can receive it, some fight it. There is a constant growing and changing, and I never really know what direction it will take me. I don't know who might influence it. It could be a play by August Wilson or my uncle from Frazer, Montana.

But, since I am talking about my writing, I want to give thanks. I first thank my parents, Stanley and Mina. Even though they are both no longer in this world, their teachings, inspiration, patience and love are still with me. I thank a beautiful woman who shared my life, my late wife, Diane Ruth Louise Lamar, who left this world in 1996. Her kindness and strong heart were a great source of life to me. I thank my other family members: Fish, Carol, Mary, Jackie, Josephine, Helen, Alvin, Karen and Keithy. And the new person who has decided to share my present life with me, Lori Davis. Finally, all my relations and friends who make the Fort Peck Indian reservation a place of life.

The Independence of Eddie Rose was completed in 1986, and has received numerous readings and has been the subject of several dissertations. It received its first production in June 1986, as part of the University of Montana's Montana Masquers Playwriting Festival in Missoula, Montana, under the direction of Rolland Meinholtz.

In 1987, the play was produced at Seattle Group Theater's, "Third Annual Multi-Cultural Playwrights' Festival," under the direction of Susan Finachell.

The play was presented at New York City's Ensemble Studio Theatre's "New Voices" reading series in 1989. Jack Gelber was the director.

Seattle's Group Theatre reproduced *The Independence of Eddie Rose* in June/July 1990 at the "Goodwill Arts Festival" in Seattle, Washington, under the direction of Tim Bond.

In 1998, the Theater Studies Department of Yale University in New Haven, Connecticut, produced the play, under the direction of David Krasner.

characters

EDDIE ROSE, son of Katherine,
around fifteen or sixteen years old.

KATHERINE ROSE, mother of Eddie, in her early thirties.

THEIA ROSE, sister to Eddie, ten or eleven years old,
daughter to Katherine.

THELMA ROSE, sister to Katherine, in her mid-thirties.

SAM JACOBS, a breed, in his late thirties or early forties.

MIKE HORSE, a breed, a friend of Eddie's,
fourteen or fifteen years old.

LENNY SHARB, a breed, a boyfriend to Katherine,
in his late teens or early twenties.

prologue

Early in the morning. The living room of Katherine Rose's house. Eddie Rose, Theia Rose, Katherine Rose and Lenny Sharb are in the living room. There are metal folding chairs and a table. Theia sits holding an old, gray Snoopy. Eddie is sitting on the floor and has a papersack in front of him.

EDDIE: One-it, two-it, three-it . . .

(As he gets to "three," Katherine Rose explodes and chases Lenny across the room and out of the house.)

KATHERINE: And don't you come back here, you son of a bitch! You stay the hell away from me, from my family. We don't allow thieves in this family. I'll get the cops after you. I'll kill you!

THEIA: Eddie . . . Eddie?

EDDIE: Don't cry Theia. . . . don't. Remember. Don't cry!

KATHERINE: I don't love you. I don't care what you do. I hope you die!

THEIA: Why, Eddie?

EDDIE: You'll just get her madder.

45

KATHERINE: You no-good, breed son of a bitch!

EDDIE: Come on, come with me, Theia. It'll be all right.

THEIA: No . . . No, I can't move.

EDDIE: Nothing's going to happen. Go hide. I'll help you. Hide.

KATHERINE: Stop looking at me! Stop looking at me you . . . you old breed bitch! You're not even enrolled here! At least my kids are enrolled!

EDDIE: I'll help you hide, all right?

(Eddie takes Theia to his room. Blackout.)

Act I

Same day, a half hour later. The living room. Katherine Rose stands drinking a beer. She crosses to the metal table and sits.

KATHERINE: I . . . I showed him. Even that old woman, Peterson, yes damned breed, she's . . . she's not even enrolled anyway. She . . . she was standing out on her porch watching. Her old shriveled arms holding that stink cat of hers. She looks like an old burnt-up doll anyway. Now she'll have something to tell her Mormon honeys.

EDDIE: Yeah. You did it, Mom.

KATHERINE: He won't be doing anything bad around here. My babies.

EDDIE: Yeah. Sure thing.

KATHERINE *(Cries)*: I don't want anybody doing that to my babies.

EDDIE: Real good, Mom, real good. I gotta' go. . . .

KATHERINE: Well! What's wrong with you?

(Pause.)

Huh? Are you ashamed of me.

EDDIE: Mom. I just want to go . . . go outside.

(Eddie gets up and crosses to the door, but Katherine stops him and turns him around to face her.)

KATHERINE: Don't lie. . . . Don't lie to me, my boy. Tell me what's wrong? You know I'm not the one sending you off to school. You were the one they caught drinking. You mad at me? Answer me!

EDDIE: Don't get bent out of shape, Mom.

(Breaks free for a moment.)

You . . . You'll just get mad at me.

KATHERINE *(Mocks Eddie)*: "You'll get mad at me." I suppose! Why would I do that? *(Grabs Eddie)*

EDDIE: Because . . . Because you're drinkin'.

KATHERINE: Is that all? *(Pause)* Maybe I should kick you out, too. *(Crosses back to table and sits)* What do you think? Huh? I'm not good enough to be your mother?

EDDIE: I didn't say that.

KATHERINE: Eddie? Do you love your old mother?

EDDIE: I . . . I . . . I like you. . . . I guess. See you.

KATHERINE: Come here! *(She stops Eddie)* I said come here. Come here, Eddie. *(Eddie slowly gives into her)* Good. Come here, my boy. *(Eddie crosses to her. She gets up and hugs him)* Ohhh . . . My boy . . . my beautiful boy . . . My baby . . . *(She gently caresses his cheeks)* Poor thing. I'm just mean to him. *(Kisses his cheeks and then tries to kiss him on the lips)*

EDDIE: Don't, Mom. *(He struggles and breaks free)* Please. God . . .

KATHERINE: Some man you are.

EDDIE: I'm your son. . . . God . . . I said I . . . I . . . like you. . . .

KATHERINE: Don't make me laugh. You're just a boy . . . a baby. *(She crosses to the couch and lies down)* You don't love me. You mope around, telling everyone you want to leave. Then go! I won't stop you. It'll be just me and your sister here. We don't need you. *(Pause)* I know, I know. Coming back here with silver lips and a nose from sniffing paint. Trying to act good now. You buy drinks and weed. You and your friends. Stink little shits. Don't try to fool me. You don't fool me at all. *(Her beer can drops)* Just me and my baby . . . babies here . . .

(Eddie waits a moment. Then he walks over to the couch and looks at his mother.)

EDDIE: Mom?

(He slowly crosses the floor and goes to his room where Theia is hiding. He looks into the room and returns to the couch. He gently sits on the floor. He looks at his mother one more time, then takes a book of matches from his shirt pocket and gently and quietly lights one of the matches. He holds the match in the air and looks at it. Then he eases the match toward the couch. His hands stop moving. The flame of the match burns down to his fingers. He lets the match drop. He muffles a cry with his hand, placing his burnt fingers into his mouth. He begins to cry.)

Mom . . . Mom . . .

(Blackout.)

scene two

Same day, later in the morning. Eddie is in the kitchen area off the living room. He has his papersack from the previous scene, and is placing some canned food into it. There is a knock at the door. Eddie quickly takes the sack and hides it. As he goes to the door, it slowly begins to open. He takes a frying pan and gets ready to attack. The door opens. It is Eddie's Aunty Thelma Rose. She sticks her head into the house.

THELMA: Hello. Hello.
EDDIE: Oh. Uh . . . Hello.

> *(Aunty Thelma enters. She is a large woman. She wears a scarf and an old, gray flannel coat. She carries a small papersack.)*

THELMA: Hello, my nephew.

> *(She removes her scarf. Her hair is woven into two braids. She takes off her coat and sets it on a chair. She goes to the table and clears a place for her sack, and removes some groceries and some bread.)*

How are you. *(No response from Eddie)* Eddie. *(She turns and looks at him)* Eddie? *(No response)* Do you hear me, Nephew?
EDDIE: Can't you see? You're supposed to know. Ah . . . just forget it, Auntie.
THELMA: What . . . ? Where's your sister?
EDDIE: Hiding.
THELMA: Where?
EDDIE: I don't know. We won't find her. Only if she lets us. She was in a trunk in the basement last time. She almost stopped breathing, so I punched a hole in the trunk, and she won't be blue in the face anymore. It's a good place for her. Maybe when I go off to school I'll take her with me—we can do one of those magic acts with a saw.
THELMA: Oh, dear. Hiding out in your own home, I suppose. *(Laughs)* You two kids. *(Laughs)* I came to help get you ready for school. Well, where's your mom?

EDDIE: In her room.

(Thelma heads for Katherine's room.)

Aunty Thelma. Wait up. Can I ask you something?

THELMA: Yes. What is it?

EDDIE: While I'm gone, off to school, you know. Uh ... Would you do something for me? If you can? Can you keep Theia? If you need help in taking care of her, I can send you some money, okay? I'll get a clothing order for school. It isn't much, but I can cash it, even sell it, and send you some of it. I heard about other kids who do it.

THELMA: Oh? Why?

EDDIE: You see it. She goes downtown and starts drinking, and she'll let him back in. What's the use of even having a door anyway.

THELMA: Why do you want your sister to stay with me?

EDDIE: It's not just her. I don't like the way Lenny looks at her. He does it in a funny way.

THELMA: I'll watch him. Don't worry. It'll be all right. *(Pause)* School's coming up. You should be happy you're going to school. Not a lot of young people today get a second chance to finish their schooling. Your mother and me didn't have that chance. *(Pause)* I know you'll be leaving behind a lot of your friends ... and your family, but your family will always be here.

EDDIE: That's not it. It's just as bad at that school as it is here I bet. Maybe I can hitch back home. Even in this I don't have a say.

THELMA: Not all the Indian boarding schools are that bad, Eddie. You really don't know. *(Pause)* Listen, your momma could find a job. She'll have her own money then. You kids will have money, too. She could hire someone to stay here all the time with Theia. Maybe it'll be me. I wish.

EDDIE: Me, too.

(Thelma begins to clean. She spots empty beer cans.)

THELMA: Are these from last night?
EDDIE: No. This morning.
THELMA: Ohhh . . . My. This early.

(She takes the bread and slices a piece of it. She takes a jar of jam and puts some of it on the bread and gives it to Eddie.)

She must have been very courageous then, enit?
EDDIE: I guess.

(Theia enters from Eddie's room.)

THEIA: Eddie?
THELMA: Oh! There's my girl. Come here pretty one. *(Theia goes to Thelma, who has arms out for her. She hugs Theia)* Who's the pretty one? Who's the prettiest one?
THEIA: Aunty Thelma! *(Thelma begins to make her a piece of bread with jam)* Eddie? *(No response)* Eddie?
THELMA: Your sister's talking to you.
THEIA: Is it all right to be around here? Has it stopped?
EDDIE: Yeah.

(Thelma turns Theia around and looks at her very closely.)

THELMA: Oh-quaw . . . my pretty girl. My little, pretty girl.
THEIA: We had it out this morning, Aunty Thelma. Enit, Eddie?
EDDIE: Yeah. See. She knows and she can't do anything for herself. What—
THELMA: Stop it, Eddie. I'm here now. Everything's going to be all right. He's gone now. You don't have to be afraid. Don't cry. Go and get a rag and wash your face. *(Theia does)* See. She'll be all right.

EDDIE: But it's always the same. You're not here all the time and I won't be either, but he'll be here. He shows up all the time. I'll probably run into him at that school. I'll be of no use to anybody over there in school. Not like here.

THELMA: Oh, behave now. You don't know that. *(Checks to see if Theia is near)* Listen to me, Nephew . . . my boy. You have a chance to continue your education. After they expelled you from school . . . I'm afraid you won't go anyplace. You'll be like one of these so-called basketball stars. Hanging around the streets in town, bumming people for drinks and having a wife with a big belly and kids. No ways of supporting yourself, or them. Now, my boy, you have a second chance. Don't let it go.

(Eddie stands and gets his papersack.)

EDDIE: I don't want to go to school. I've learned enough. I don't know if I want to be in this house. I wish I could leave now. Just do it without any worrying. She'll kick us out anyways.

(He exits. Thelma follows him to the door.)

THELMA: Shnu-gah. Crazy. It's just the same thing.

(Lights slowly dim on the kitchen area as Thelma begins to pick up beer cans from the floor. She finds a pair of dirty underwear and throws it on the floor in disgust.

At another part of the stage, Eddie enters a graveyard. He stops near a grave, and kicks an empty can of spray paint. He starts to clean one of the graves with his hands, and removes old, faded, plastic flowers.

Then he finds a plastic bag, with fresh paint in it and on it.)

EDDIE: Didn't even save me a sniff.

(Lights dim and come up on kitchen. Theia enters. Thelma kneels and wets her handkercheif and begins to wipe Theia's face.)

THEIA: We're the last ones again, huh, Aunty Thelma?

(Thelma holds her and then motions her to go to the bathroom. Theia does. Lights dim. They come up on the graveyard. Eddie removes a few cans of food from his sack and hides them near the headstone. He checks around for anybody who might be watching.)

EDDIE: Grandma? Watch these for me, please? I'll be back for them. Thank you for doing this for me. I hope at least you can hear me. I wish you were here. I know you can help me.

(Lights fade and come up in the kitchen. Thelma finds an ashtray filled with cigarette butts. She tries to find a place to dump it. The garbage can is full. She finally opens a papersack and places the butts into it. Theia enters with a washcloth, wiping her face.)

THEIA: How's this, Aunty?
THELMA: Oh, yes, pretty girls should always have a pretty face.
THEIA: Not greasy, like greasy fryebread, huh?
THELMA: It's good you're learning to do these things yourself. You're getting to be a big girl.
THEIA: I can learn more when I live with you.
THELMA: What? Live with me?
THEIA: He said he would ask you if we can live with you. That's what he said.

(A noise comes from Katherine's room.)

THELMA: Don't be so scared. You'll have an old, wrinkled face before you're barely a teenager. You'll look like this. *(Makes a face)*

THEIA: Not that bad, Aunty.

(Katherine enters.)

KATHERINE: What's going on out here?

THELMA: Hello, my sister. Oh. I suppose? Who else did you think it was, a ghost? Just came by to see how things are going. Came to help get my nephew ready for his trip for school. I hear you and Lenny have split the sheets.

KATHERINE: Had to. I got sick of looking at his chapped lips—old, dried-up things anyway. Who told you this? I know. Come here. *(Theia does)* Did you say anything?

THELMA: Eddie said something, but looking at this house, I could guess what happened. I was the one who asked these kids. I'm their aunty, remember? Your sister?

KATHERINE *(To Theia)*: Eee . . . Look at your hair. Go and get a brush. You look like you're from *Fraggel Rock*, bushy head. Go on.

(Theia does.)

I just don't want it going all over the place. It's nobody's business.

THELMA: As long as you didn't make a big thing of it, no one will know.

KATHERINE: That old stink thing . . . he got me really mad this time. I was saving money so Eddie could get some things on his trip to school—pop, chips, you know. And here, that son of a bitch stole it.

THELMA: Eddie?

KATHERINE: No. Lenny. He took my money. I was saving it for Eddie and he bought beer with it from the boot-legger. Even the money I made from making beaded belt buckles, he took that, too. That was early this morning.

THELMA: And you drank with him?

KATHERINE: No. It wasn't that bad. I didn't even know he did it until I went to see for myself. He came into the room with me and started to talk to me about how he loves me. "The light of my eye." I suppose, the white blood in him was talking. When I found out, I grabbed my knife I keep and put him on the run. He even tried to blame my babies.

THELMA: And he's not going to come back?

KATHERINE: I won't let him. He won't be able to get any-thing past me. I won't put up with his lies. I'm not going to get weighed down with his lies.

THELMA: Are you sure?

KATHERINE: You're making my head hurt. I just said so, didn't I? Gee, Thelma, listen to me.

THELMA: I just want to be sure this is what you really mean and you really want it.

KATHERINE: Yes! What about it!

THELMA: Nothing. I was just asking. Oh, say, did you ever hear anything from those people at that place for the job? Did they ever call you back?

KATHERINE: No. Not yet. They did say they would call me by Friday. Tomorrow. I gave them Iris's phone number. She said she would tell me when they call. By next week, I'll be making those little dentist tools. It's good money, too. I think they pay over four dollars an hour. We sure could use it. I can start to save money and get the things we need. Do things I want to do. I won't have to be stuck with these stink young guys like Lenny.

(*Theia enters with a brush.*)

THEIA: I found one, Momma. See.

KATHERINE: I suppose. I nearly forgot about her. Where did you go?

THEIA: I had to look around. I finally found one in Eddie's room.

KATHERINE: Come here, baby girl. Sit down and I'll move the herd. *(Theia does)* You have pretty hair, my girl.

THEIA: I know-a!

THELMA: No shame.

(The two women laugh.)

KATHERINE *(Mocking Theia)*: "I know-a!" . . . Oh, stink thing.

THEIA: That's what Lenny says, too. He thinks I have pretty hair.

KATHERINE: Don't you listen to him anymore. He doesn't know anything. You hear?

THEIA: Yeah but . . . okay.

KATHERINE: Now sit still.

THEIA: You're brushing it too hard.

KATHERINE: I know what I'm doing. I've brushed your hair before.

THEIA: Ow!

KATHERINE: Sit still! You don't take care of your hair. I should cut it.

(Katherine grabs Theia by her hair and shakes Theia's head.)

THEIA: Ow . . . ow-ow-weee . . .

THELMA: Don't! You're hurting her! Katherine!

KATHERINE: She's my kid! Sit still, damn you!

THEIA: I will. . . . I will, Momma. . . .

KATHERINE: Sit still!

THELMA: Katherine, she said she will.

(Katherine releases Theia and then slaps her with the brush.)

THEIA: Oww! *(She starts to cry)*

KATHERINE: Go on! Get away from me. *(Pushes Theia away)*

THEIA: Don't, Mom.

THELMA: Geee . . . you didn't have to do that, Katherine. . . . You . . .

KATHERINE: Go to your room. Don't come out until I say so.

THELMA: You don't have to treat her like this, Katherine.

KATHERINE: Don't you tell me how to raise my kids, Thelma. I've been doing it all by myself up to now. I don't need you to step in now. I said hurry up. *(She gets up and hurries Theia along by pulling her arm)*

THEIA: Momma . . . Please . . . Don't!

KATHERINE: I'll give you "don't!" You get your little brown ass to bed! *(She pushes Theia into her room and slams the door)*

THEIA *(Through the door)*: I hate you!

KATHERINE: Good. And don't talk back either.

THEIA: I'm not. Bitch.

(Katherine pulls on the doorknob.)

KATHERINE: You open this door!

THEIA: Nah-bah-nooks.

KATHERINE: You little shit! You open this door! Do you hear me! *(No response)* Now she decides to be quiet. You think you're smart, don't you?

THEIA: I am.

KATHERINE: Baby, open the door. . . .

THELMA: You won't be able to do anything. Come and sit down.

KATHERINE: These kids are growing up too fast. . . . And tough. That's good.

THELMA: I guess.

KATHERINE: I . . . I don't know if I can have them around me much longer.

THELMA: As long as you're good to them, you'll have them with you. You'll see.

KATHERINE: It doesn't look that way, Thelma. Eddie's getting to the point now where he doesn't listen to me. You know, his father didn't want him. That son of a bitch came home drunk and threw him against the wall. Then he stormed out of the house. I walked over and picked Eddie up. I . . . I couldn't hear anything. His eyes were always shiny when he was born. They were turning dull, like something inside of him was leaving. I felt his heart, and like a small drum it was still beating away. I took off my shirt and held him close. I knew he was a tough kid. They both are. *(Pause)* We only have each other. No phone, no car. We live in this box and if these other things are not supposed to be mine to have—fine. Those two kids are the only things I have in this world I can call mine.

THELMA: Oh! Not that pitiful. Stop it. We didn't get them from Kmart, under a blue-light special-a. *(Laughs)* Listen to me, my sister. I do all kinds of things, both good and bad. When they took my boy away from me, I thought I would go insane. I wanted to kill myself. I failed. Mom told me to just give him up—don't say his name. He was dead to us. But . . . but . . . I know one of these days, I'll be at a celebration and someone will walk up to me and say, "Mom." I know it'll be him. Stop thinking like you are. Besides, nearest Kmart is over a couple hundred miles from here.

(They laugh. Blackout.)

scene three

An hour later. The Tribal Detention Center. Eddie is being searched by Sam, a detention officer in his late forties. He reaches out and steers Eddie's arms into the air with a stick. The search gets detailed. Mike, Eddie's friend, is wearing a T-shirt, jeans, headband, and no shoes or socks. There are only a standing metal ashtray and two metal stools.

EDDIE: Hey!

SAM: Shut up! You got ten minutes. That's all.

EDDIE: I know, I know. You told me.

MIKE: Eddie . . .

SAM: Quiet, Mikey. Hey, see, your friend is learning the rules here. He's pretty fast in pickin' up what we do here. In a short time, a couple of days, he'll know what to do to get by. He's not a smart mouth. *(Pokes Eddie's back pocket)* Wait. What's this?

EDDIE: I don't know.

SAM: Let's see, kid. *(Removes a small candy bar from Eddie's pocket)* These guys aren't supposed to get anything. I told you that. Christ, don't you got any ears?

EDDIE: Don't get mad. I didn't know until after you just told me. I didn't even know I had it.

SAM: Yeah, right. It climbed into your pocket. Well, now you know. What do you think I should do?

EDDIE *(Softly)*: Bend over.

SAM: What did you say? *(No response)* I should give you a rap across your lips. Maybe I should turn your little ass around and toss it. Would you like it if I go and do that? Huh?

EDDIE: No . . . I don't know.

MIKE: Let him stay, please.

SAM *(Looks at Mike and mocks him)*: "Let him stay, please." Shit. Shut up, Mikey. Your girlfriend can stay. Just for ten minutes, and then you'll have to haul your ass out of here. *(Unwraps the candy bar and begins to eat it)* Hey. This is pretty good. I haven't had one of these before. I don't eat much candy. Makes my teeth hurt. Not bad, but you still can't beat a Hershey's bar.

EDDIE *(Softly)*: Have you checked your shorts lately?

SAM: You smart mouth. . . . Remember. Ten . . . *(Checks his watch)* No. Seven minutes. And no smoking, Mikey . . . or kissing.

(Sam exits.)

EDDIE: Big stink guy. When you getting out?

MIKE: I don't know. They haven't found my mom yet. As soon as the cops find her she'll come and get me and I can get the fuck out. At least until the trial. After that, I don't know, could be sixty days flat.

EDDIE: What do you suppose happened to her?

MIKE: Probably riding around somewhere, partying some-place, passed out someplace. Maybe she left town. I sure the fuck hope they do find her.

EDDIE: Damn.

MIKE: If they don't find her, I have about four days flat before my trial.

EDDIE: Don't worry then. Fuck. You'll be out in no time.

MIKE: What would you know, hey. You don't know shit about my mom.

EDDIE: Don't start talking like this. Behave.

MIKE: My mom? You want to know something about my mom, Eddie? This last summer, when we went to that celebration with your aunty Thelma? We sneaked out of her tent that night to go to the 49. I was with Denise Sky.

EDDIE: Yeah. We both wound up snagging. Better'n any fucking cowboy.

MIKE: Yeah. Then Denise went with you to get that friend of hers for you, and when you guys were gone, I went to the trees to take a piss, and all of a sudden there was this blanket that came and wrapped me up. . . . It was kind of cool at first, but it had that smell, it was stink. Then these hands were touching me. It was kind of nice at first. I heard this voice, it was saying something.

The voice said, "You can have me for all the change in your pocket." I tossed off the blanket to check this one out. And damn it . . . I fucking hate this place, Eddie. I really do. I want to get the fuck away from here. Fuck! It was my mom, Eddie. It was my own mom. *(Pause)* Talk about reaching out and touching someone.

EDDIE: Yeah. Reach out, reach out, and fuck someone up. *(Pause)* How did they catch you this time?

MIKE: Oh. After you left that night, I was with Nose and his sister, Brenda. Then we were getting stoned in his car. We really got wasted. I guess the cops came right up behind us, red and blue lights blazing away. They made us get out and searched us. Stink fuckers. They really searched Nose's sister. Poor Brenda—after they felt her up the cops let her go.

EDDIE: What did you and Nose do? *(Slams his fist into his opened hand)*

MIKE: What could we do, hey? No way, José, we weren't brave enough. Me and Nose just stood there. Those cops would've worked us over. *(Pause)* I wish we could both leave and then we could party.

EDDIE: Ah, bullshit. That's why I want to leave.

MIKE: Yeah, boarding school. Big thrill there, Eddie.

EDDIE: It might not be tomorrow for school, but it sure the hell is going to be soon.

MIKE: You're going to leave! Take me with you!

EDDIE: Behave. I'm not baby-sitting anymore, this is for real.

MIKE: You know what? I can get out. I can get out if you help me.

EDDIE: Can he hear us?

MIKE: No. Stink fucker anyway. He doesn't even watch us. We were lighting up a number just when he came to tell me you were here. You know what? Two guys got out of here.

EDDIE: Yeah?

MIKE: Shit man, they just walked out the back door, ankle to ankle. The guy here at the time didn't even care. The cops

were the ones who noticed they were gone when they
came to pick them up for court. *(Pause)* Eddie. No court
until Monday. The cops won't be around. *(Pause)* I have
a way of getting out of here. We could be gone, together.

EDDIE: You? You know how to get in, shit. How are you
going to get out?

MIKE: You'll see, you'll see. But I'll need your help once I'm
out.

EDDIE: You don't even know where I'm going. They'll pick
us both up.

MIKE: No they won't. Eddie, listen to me. Listen, hey, you
and I, we could share a room together. We'll have so
many women, we'll wear out a mattress every month.

EDDIE: Shit, wear out your wrist is more like it.

MIKE: It isn't so bad in here.

EDDIE: Yeah. Then stay.

MIKE: No . . . but, but, Eddie. If we got a place to ourselves, it
doesn't have to be around here. Nose has a car. . . . The
police took it to his house and gave the car to his parents. Since Brenda didn't get into that much trouble,
they let her hold the keys until he gets out.

EDDIE: Why?

MIKE: I don't know. I guess her mom doesn't trust their dad.
But anyway, we could get them from her and we could
really book out of here.

EDDIE: Where to?

MIKE: Off the Res. We don't have to stay in any little, rinky
town. We could go to a city. I have relatives all over the
place.

EDDIE: You got money?

MIKE: No, but I have a stash hidden at my house. We could
get it and sell some of it.

EDDIE: Why don't you just wait and see if your mother
shows up? *(Pause)* I mean, that way, I leave by myself,
and you . . . you don't have to worry about being
stopped, or picked up.

MIKE: You mean "you." *(Pause)* It's just as bad in here. I want out! Take me with you, Eddie.

EDDIE: But . . . you . . . I thought you said it wasn't so bad in here?

MIKE: Fuck. I lied, okay? This jailor here, he says he's Indin, but he's not. And . . . and he gives different ones cigarettes . . . and let's them smoke in the TV room. Let's them do a whole bunch of stuff. He leaves them alone after, but first they . . . they have to do something for him. He asks certain ones, one way or the other is what everyone says. . . . *(Pause)* Stink old fucker. *(Pause)* He . . . He's always asking me if I like to smoke.

EDDIE: Gives you a good reason to quit.

MIKE: Fuck yeah, but I'm serious as hell, hey. I want out of here. Take me with you.

EDDIE: I know you do. Look it, couldn't you tell the cops? They should be able to do something for you.

MIKE: Who do you think they'll listen to? He's been working here for a long time. They'll listen to me, duh? No way! I heard it from Nose. He's been in here more times than me.

EDDIE: Nose will let us use his car?

MIKE: Yeah . . . yeah! I can get us some money, too. We got a car. No real reason for me to stay—you're going.

EDDIE: I don't know.

MIKE: Eddie. I don't want to be here.

EDDIE: Yeah.

MIKE: I got an aunty in Seattle. It would be a long drive to Seattle, but I think I have enough money to get us there. She'll take care of us.

EDDIE: She will?

MIKE: Yeah. It would be a lot better than anything here.

EDDIE: I know

MIKE: They have concerts and better things in Seattle than we have here. Better-looking chicks. Even the white ones are supposed to be good looking.

EDDIE: What if we get caught?

MIKE: It'll be me handcuffed in the backseat of a cop car heading for reform school. You? You'll be eating a Snickers bar on a bus going to boarding school.

EDDIE: You want me to get the car and bring it here?

MIKE: Yeah. And all I need is a pair of shoes and jacket. And my stash. It's damn good weed.

EDDIE: This is a hard one, Mike.

MIKE: If you want you can get it now.

EDDIE: Your smoke?

MIKE: Sure. Just don't smoke up all my weed.

EDDIE: Okay. Sounds cool. Where do I meet you at?

MIKE: Not far from here. Near the stockyards.

EDDIE: How long?

MIKE: About a couple of hours.

EDDIE: I'll help you. You'll help me? And we book together.

MIKE: Yeah.

(Mike offers his hand to Eddie.)

EDDIE: How you gonna do that, Mike?

MIKE: You'll see. I promise you, Eddie.

EDDIE: Don't fuck around, Mike.

MIKE: I'm not. You'll see.

EDDIE: Alright. *(He shakes Mike's hand)* One-it.

MIKE: Two-it.

(Sam enters.)

SAM: Are you girls through? Time's up.

EDDIE: Let go of my hand.

MIKE: Remember. You promised. *(Mike releases Eddie's hand)*

EDDIE: Yeah, yeah.

SAM: Come on, and hurry up why don't you. You can see your little friend tomorrow. He's been a bad, little boy.

He'll be with us for some time. Don't worry. We'll watch him for you. Better'n his own mom.

(Pause.)

EDDIE: Fuck.
SAM: What?
EDDIE: Nothing.
SAM: You better get out of here. Your time's up. Come on! Let's go!
EDDIE: I'll see you, Mike.
SAM: You wait here. I'll take you to the television room.
MIKE: Eddie . . .

(Eddie stops but is pushed by Sam.)

SAM: Keep moving, kid, don't drag your ass.

(Sam and Eddie exit.)

MIKE: You have to help me, Eddie. Please help me, Eddie. Don't want to stay here. Don't want to be here. Ain't going to be here. One-it, two-it, three-it, four-it, five-it, you're it, I'm not it. Oh, fuck . . . help me please. . . . Mom . . . I don't want to be it.

(Sam enters, and Mike continues to count silently.)

SAM: You shouldn't hang around guys like him, Mikey. He's a real bad apple. Get you into a lot of trouble than you are in now. *(Crosses and sits on a stool)* You're a good boy, Mikey. I know. I know the decent ones when I see them. I had to work on it.
MIKE *(Softly)*: One-it, two-it, three-it . . .
SAM: Nah, hell, you've still got some good in you yet. And I guess it's alright if you want to smoke cigarettes. Hell.

Most young guys do that when they're your age. I know because I did. You know what, Mikey? I knowed some bad, little boys who turned out okay. Even when they did smoke. You know what I mean, Mikey? I was like you in a lot of ways. I learned to make things my own. Had to. People—Shit on them and their pity. *(Removes a pack of cigarettes from his shirt pocket)* But you're a good, little boy. I know you are. And it's alright if you want to have a smoke. You want to smoke, Mikey? You can if you want to. All you have to do is do something for me. *(Unzips his pants)* Everyone is in lock up right now, Mikey. No one will hear us. No one knows you're up here. They think I'm cleaning this place. *(Starts to rub his leg)* Come on. Don't be afraid. There's nothing to be afraid of. All most everyone here has done this before. And they don't talk about it. Come on. I'll let you smoke after you're done. It'll be good. *(Mike slowly walks to Sam. Sam readjusts himself on the stool)*

SAM: Be a good, little boy, Mike. Come on. That's it. . . . That's it. . . . Eww . . .

MIKE: Fourteen-it, fifteen-it, six-teen it . . . ain't it . . .

(Blackout.)

scene four

Later that afternoon. Katherine Rose's house. The house has been cleaned. There is a small pile of garbage near the door. Thelma combs Theia's hair very gently and sings a song to her.

THELMA: This is your grandma's song. She used to sit on a chair and slowly brush my hair and she would be singing this song. It was quiet and all I could hear was your grandma singing.

THEIA: Grandma?

THELMA: Yes. She died right after you were born. You don't remember her. Oh. I don't know. You might. She really liked you. She used to hold you and sing to you. She used to call you Pretty One. She used to baby-sit you and your brother.

THEIA: Eddie, too?

THELMA: Even Eddie. She helped raise you two kids. She watched both of you. Even fed you two. But sometimes she had problems holding you and your bottle. You were so tiny, but very big to her hands. She still could hold you though. She didn't want to let go. *(Pause)* My baby boy Paul, and Eddie and you were her only three grandchildren—but you were her favorite.

(Thelma begins to clean the hair from the brush. She takes the hair and places it into an ashtray. Then she lights a match and sets the hair on fire.)

THEIA: You're burning up, Aunty!

THELMA: No, no. You burn the hair. If you let the hair go without taking care of it, it can bring bad things to you—even ghosts. These are some of the things we did. When your grandmother died, your mom and I, we cut our hair. We women do that when someone dies. When it is someone close to you and you love them, like your grandmother, our mother.

THEIA: Really?

(Pause.)

Aunty Thelma? Is drinking something we always do? My teacher, Mrs. Johnson, she said it was because we always drink, is why we lost everything we had. It was our own fault.

THELMA: No. This is a lie, baby girl. We never used to drink at one time. Your grandma, my mother, as old as she was, never drank. She used to say it was never a part of the Indin people.

THEIA: Oh. Aunty Thelma? Eddie said I was going to be moving to your house.

THELMA: No. I think he was just saying that. I don't think your mother wants you to leave. She wouldn't want that to happen.

THEIA: Oh.

THELMA: But one day, you might. Who knows. One day you might be living with me. I didn't have a baby girl.

THEIA: All right!

(Eddie enters.)

THELMA: There you are. Where have you been?

EDDIE: Where's my mom at?

THELMA: She went out to get some groceries. I told her I would watch Theia. She should be back soon.

EDDIE: Hey, Aunty Thelma, have you thought about letting Theia stay with you?

THELMA: Yes. I told her it might happen one day, but not now. You kids still have your mother.

EDDIE: Yeah, but it would be better if you were our mother. You could take her now before she gets back.

THELMA: Oh. Not that bad.

EDDIE: Yes it is.

THELMA: Theia. Go to your room.

(Theia does).

Don't start this now, Eddie. I thought you did something crazy like running away. I was worried. Where have you been?

EDDIE: Seen a friend.

THELMA: Him? I heard he was locked up. How did you talk with him?

EDDIE: With my mouth. Christ, Mike isn't all that bad. If you've heard it from my mom—she's one to talk. Me and Mike are alike in a lot of ways.

THELMA: Like how? What makes you two the same?

EDDIE: We come back to an empty house all the time. We cook for ourselves and whoever's with us. Our mothers are the same. It's not different for him and me. Everyone says we have a mother, but we don't.

THELMA: Oh! I suppose, Eddie. Your mother is here in the house for you.

EDDIE: Yeah. Drunk and wasted, but never sober!

THELMA: Don't let me hear you say anything like that about your mother. She's my sister. You remember that. His mother . . . I feel sorry for him because both he and his mother are pitiful. Your mom and I ain't in the bars selling ourselves for a drink. His mother is always in the bars. She's a whore! Pitiful is all they are. Don't you ever compare your mother to that woman. Your father never wanted you, but she does! That should count for something.

EDDIE: Yes we are! Our own mothers have tried to "have" us.

THELMA: What?

EDDIE: You hear me, Aunty Thelma. Our mothers have tried to have us.

THELMA: What are you saying? No. Eddie. No. That couldn't have happened. You didn't know what your mother was trying to say to you. It wasn't like you think.

EDDIE: I was there. I'm always here. I try to tell you things, but you don't listen. What do I have to do to show you? You want to wait around and see it happen for your own eyes? You see how she treats me and Theia. *(Pause)* This morning, this morning, she tried to kiss me. Not like you do, but she did something in a way . . . I don't know how to . . . just don't mind, Aunty Thelma. *(Pause)*

70

When I go, I want you to take care of Theia. If you don't do it, I'll come back and do it. *(Pause)* What do I have to do? I don't know what I'm supposed to do. I can't see anything I used to. I used to be able to know. I didn't know how I did it, but it wasn't hard. I could see what I had to do and when to do it. Now I don't even know because I can't see anymore.

THELMA: Eddie. Let me see. Let me see what I can do. You are still young in a lot of ways. It'll change. Things are always changing from one day to the next. You could be wrong. You don't know what your mom was doing this morning. You could have taken it in the wrong way. You . . .

EDDIE: I know what she did, Aunty Thelma! Fuck!

THELMA: Behave Eddie. You don't know. . . .

EDDIE: Shit!

THELMA: Don't start talking like that around me.

EDDIE: Alright! Alright! I won't talk to you like that, but will you listen to what I'm saying? I have to go. I can't wait until tomorrow. Please take Theia. Take her to your home, and before I get ready to leave I'll stop by and see if you've done it.

THELMA: But Eddie, Nephew, it isn't something I can do. She's my sister. We aren't like other people. I cannot take Theia as my own. It's not our way. Just stay here and leave tomorrow. If you try to leave you might not make it, you might have some kind of trouble. You're not even ready to leave.

EDDIE: Yes I am. Just do it, please, Aunty Thelma. Please do it for me, for both us kids.

THELMA: Eddie . . . Eddie! Where are you going? Please, Eddie, stay! Don't leave. Come back here, Nephew. Please come back.

(Blackout.)

scene five

A few minutes later. The graveyard. Eddie enters. He goes to the headstone and sits. He takes out a small plastic bag with pot in it. He takes out some papers that are with the weed, rolls himself a number, takes out some matches and lights up. He kicks back and takes a big toke. He coughs a little.

EDDIE: You weren't shitting there, Mike. It is good. Thank you, Grandson. Hey, Grandma, you know what that stink guy said . . . *(He faces the headstone, and realizes something has changed. The papersack he had left is gone. The wrappers he used to cover his canned goods are on the ground. He looks around)* Oh shit. How . . . who . . . *(He puts out the joint and places it back in the bag)* Grandma. I thought you were going to watch this stuff for me. I asked you. You probably didn't hear me like everyone else. *(He hears a dog barking. He stands and picks up a rock and throws it at the dog)* Damn stink dog.

(Blackout.)

Act II

scene one

Later that night. The graveyard. Eddie is sitting near the grave, and is smoking a cigarette. Thelma quietly enters. She stops and watches Eddie.

THELMA: Nephew?

(Eddie turns quickly to see who is calling him.)

EDDIE: Damn. I . . .

THELMA: Nephew. Nephew, what are you doing here?

EDDIE: I had a stash here, and somebody already beat me to it.

THELMA: Get away from there. You shouldn't be here.

EDDIE: That's why I'm leaving.

THELMA: Come here, my boy. Come to me.

EDDIE: I thought you would be at your house or ours. I wanted to make sure I saw you and Theia before I left.

(Thelma goes to him and hugs him.)

THELMA: Please wait, Eddie. My boy. Wait. I have something for you. Please forgive me, Eddie. I'm so ew-shi-ga. I couldn't do what you wanted. Please forgive, my son.

(Eddie hugs her. He notices that her braids are gone.)

EDDIE: What? Damn! Did he do this to you? *(Eddie breaks the hug. His hand reaches for the braids that aren't there)*

THELMA: You, your mother, Lenny—none of you had anything to do with this. It was my decision.

EDDIE: Now you know, huh, Aunty Thelma? *(Pause)* You know now?

THELMA: Yes. I do.

EDDIE: I come here to talk with Grandma. Some of my friends are here. I come here to talk with them. I tell them, too, but they don't hear me. I'm all alone, Aunty Thelma. I have no one. Sometimes, certain days, I wish I was with them. I just want to be like them.

THELMA: Don't talk that way. Don't you let me hear you talk that way. I know it's hard, but don't think that way. There are a lot of people here, in this world, who will listen to you. They know you are going through this, and they know because they have gone through it. *(She steps a few feet from the grave)* I'm going to show you something. Something you can do so that you will always have someone with you. You will be able to make it through the days. It isn't hard. And when you get older, you will learn more about it. It will help you. Because from now on you will always have your people in your heart. I want you to go back to your house and get your sister. *(She touches him)* I don't want you to go into the house weak because they will get stronger from your anger and weaken you. That is how they have been living. *(Pause)* Shhh . . . now be quiet. You have to do this thing before you can go in there. That house is dead. If you go in there now, they'll win,

and you'll be dead like them. I won't let this happen.
So you must do what I ask you, for you, for your sister.
Do you understand me?

EDDIE: I guess, yeah.

THELMA: Good. Now come over here.

(Thelma takes his hand and leads him a few feet from the grave. She removes a small bowl from the pocket of her jacket and sets it down. From her other pocket she removes a small papersack, and from it takes out a small amount of sage. She places it into the bowl. Then she lifts the bowl up into the air and prays. She sets down the bowl and removes a book of matches from her coat pocket. She lights the sage with a match. The flame goes out. Thelma fans the smoke.)

Here. I want you here. *(Points to a place near the bowl)*
Now, wash yourself in the smoke.

EDDIE: What?

THELMA: Wash up.

(She rubs her arm as if she is bathing herself. Eddie dips his hands into the smoke and begins to bathe himself.)

Pray, Nephew. My boy, pray.

(Eddie does.)

Now you are ready, my . . . my son. This will help you.
Your uncles should have shown you this—you are a
man. Now I want you to go into that house of death
and bring Theia to me if you can. Don't let them get
you mad, they'll try everything to get you angry. When
you have Theia, come to my house. I'll make something for you kids to eat and a place to sleep. Go now.

*(She gathers her bowl and sage and exits. Eddie watches her.
Blackout.)*

scene two

Later that night. Katherine Rose's living room. Katherine and Lenny are on the couch. They are slowly kissing one another. Theia sits on the edge of the couch. She takes a blanket, and makes a small tent for herself. The door opens and Eddie enters. Lenny sees Eddie, then grabs Katherine by her bottom and gives her a hungry kiss.

EDDIE: Theia?

(Theia comes from underneath her tent.)

THEIA: Eddie? Eddie!

(Katherine pushes Lenny off.)

KATHERINE: Knock it off! Where the hell have you been?

(Katherine struggles and crosses to Eddie. Theia waits to make her move.)

EDDIE: Come here, Theia. Come to me.
KATHERINE: What have you been smoking? Dope?
EDDIE: Don't be afraid, Theia. I'm here to take you.
KATHERINE: Hey. I'm talking to you. Answer me!
EDDIE: Mom. Stay out of my way! I'm going to take Theia out of here.
KATHERINE: You aren't taking shit from this house.
EDDIE: I don't want to fight with you.
KATHERINE: Fight? Shit! You don't talk to me like that. You get your ass out of here.
EDDIE: Mom. You can't hold her. I'm going to walk out of here tonight with Theia.
KATHERINE: Bullshit!
EDDIE: Give her to me!

KATHERINE: No!

(Theia tries to go to Eddie but is stopped by Lenny.)

If you were a man, I would give her to you. You're nothing but a baby. I know. Now get your ass out of my house. *(Eddie is ready to move out of her way, but stops)* Go ahead! Go ahead and try it, you little baby. I'll beat the hell out of you.

EDDIE: No. Not this way. I won't hit you or that guy. I won't give you that. I'll get the goddamn cops, Mom.

(Lenny and Katherine laugh.)

LENNY: Ewww! I'm real scared, Eddie. Hey, you scare me.

KATHERINE: Shut up, Lenny. You. Good. Go ahead and do it! Get the cops. You think they'll break their ass for you? Hah!

THEIA: Eddie. Help me.

(Lenny grabs Theia and holds her tightly.)

LENNY: No. Nope. Bad, little girly. You stay with us. He's crazy.

EDDIE: Take your hands off of her, you fucker!

LENNY: Fuck you, you punk!

(Theia throws her elbow into Lenny's groin. He releases her, and she runs into Eddie's bedroom. Eddie cheers.)

Ow! Ow . . . little shit.

KATHERINE *(To Lenny)*: You dumb shit.

EDDIE: Hide, Theia! Hide!

LENNY: Fuck, Katherine, don't talk like that to me.

(Eddie laughs.)

(To Eddie) Fuck you!

EDDIE: Theia! Stay hid and I'll come back for you. Just wait and I'll be here.

KATHERINE: No you won't. *(She slaps Eddie. Eddie is ready to return the slap, but stops)* Get out! See! You can't even defend yourself. *I* would've hit back.

EDDIE: I know.

KATHERINE: Goddamn it! You smart-mouth, little shit. Get out of my house. *(Eddie turns and begins to leave. Katherine follows him to the door)* You no-good, little bastard. And don't you come back here. You can stay there with that old bag, Thelma. Your new girlfriend, huh, Eddie?

(Blackout.)

scene three

Later that night. The playground near the housing projects. Mike is hiding. Eddie comes running. Mike jumps out and nearly tackles Eddie but misses.

MIKE: Eddie! Eddie!

(Eddie stops.)

EDDIE: Oh fuck! Mike. I forgot.

MIKE: No shit you forgot. I was waiting for you. Where the fuck were you, hey?

EDDIE: I got to go to the police, Mike. I gotta' book.

MIKE: Wait. Wait, Eddie. You and I are supposed to leave. Remember? You promised me! You gotta' take me, hey!

EDDIE: No, listen, Mike. A lot of shit has happened since then.

MIKE: Where's the car?

EDDIE: Didn't get it.

MIKE: Well, we don't really need it. Where's the shoes and the coat? (*Eddie starts to take off his jacket*) Not that desperate, Eddie. (*Mike starts to laugh. Eddie starts to remove his shoes*) No. Don't do that fucker. Keep them on. When we go, we can pick up a pair for me on the way to Seattle. Havre has a Kmart. Don't sweat it.

EDDIE: I said *no*.

MIKE: What do you mean "no"? Man. You said we are going.

EDDIE: You haven't heard me. I'm going to get the cops.

MIKE: What the fuck for? Are you going to tell on me?

EDDIE: No, no, that's not it. Lenny's back and . . .

MIKE: Fuck them! When we go, we won't have to worry about that shit. Let's go now. (*Mike grabs Eddie's arm and tries to pull him. Eddie breaks away*)

EDDIE: No fucker.

MIKE: I can't stay here, Eddie. I got to go this time. No shit. If we fuck around I'll get caught by the cops. Now let's go!

EDDIE: You go to Seattle. Take my fucking shoes, my jacket. I got to go and get the cops.

MIKE: You fucker! What kind of shit is this? Man, oh man, Eddie, you stood there in that fucking place and told me, promised me, you would go to Seattle. Now let's fucking go!

EDDIE: I can't. Why don't you just stay here. If the cops pick you up, it won't be no fucking big deal. It'll mean you'll have three or four more days to stay. That's all. You knew what was going on with me. And you try to tag on to me! Fuck, Mike, you shouldn't even be out here!

MIKE: If I go back there, that old shit-faced guard will kill me! I'm in deep shit, Eddie. Please go with me. . . . Just before you left, the fucker came back and he started to tell me how he thought I wasn't a bad, little boy.

EDDIE: What . . . what happened?

MIKE: He, he wanted to know if I smoke. He offered me a whole pack of cigarettes. Zips his pants open . . .

EDDIE: Oh fuck! Mike . . . I didn't . . .

MIKE: He eased down his shorts and I seen his dick. It was just there. Small, stink, and with all this hair. He wanted me to come closer. I wanted to fucking throw up. I wanted to throw up and all I can hear is this voice. I reached out my hand and he grabbed it and put it on his dick. He used my hand to stroke his cock. . . . I touched it. . . . It felt soft. . . . He closed his eyes and put his head back like he was going to sleep. . . . And . . . I . . . I YANKED THAT FUCKER HARD! He fell off the stool and rolled on the floor groaning. I used that stick he has and bashed him in the head! Then I picked up the stool and rammed that fucker on him. I rammed him good. I started running down the hall. I took those stink metal ashtrays and used them to bash in the windows. Glass flew in front of my face. I pushed on those metal fucking doors so hard they sounded like gun shots!

EDDIE: Holy shit, Mike! I thought you were lying about that guy.

MIKE: And you want to stay here and help your mother, Eddie? You're fucking dumb, man. You want to stay here and live off people like her . . . like me and my mom? And you know what? That's good. You'll be like your mom, living off people, letting people fuck you!

EDDIE: You should have told me, Mike, because, really, I thought you were lying. I guess I should've listened. *(He goes over and touches Mike's shoulder)*

MIKE: Get away from me!

EDDIE: I don't know, Mike. I don't know what's going on. It happens every time. It doesn't change around here. For you or me.

MIKE: And you still want to stay?

EDDIE: I have something now. I couldn't run from this, and now I know I don't have to live with it. You, too, I guess.

MIKE: Oh well, I'll see you around.

EDDIE: Mike. Come here and stand with me for just a bit, huh? I want to give you something before we go our different ways.

(Mike stops.)

MIKE: All right.

(Mike goes to Eddie and stands beside him.)

EDDIE: One-it.

MIKE: Fuck you.

EDDIE: One-it . . . come on and do it. One-it.

MIKE: Two-it.

EDDIE: Three-it.

MIKE: Four-it.

EDDIE: Five-it.

MIKE: Six . . . I mean . . . *(Eddie punches Mike in the shoulder)* Ow, you fucker.

EDDIE: You flinched. Again?

MIKE: One-it.

EDDIE: Two-it.

MIKE: Three-it.

EDDIE: Four-it.

MIKE: Five-it.

EDDIE: Seven . . . oh, shit . . .

(Mike hits him. Eddie and Mike laugh. Eddie reaches over and hugs Mike.)

MIKE: Eddie?

EDDIE: Yeah?

MIKE: Did I hurt you?

EDDIE: No.

MIKE: Oh. *(Pause)* Eddie. *(Breaks the hug)* I'll see you, huh?

EDDIE: I'll pray for you, Mike.

MIKE: You gonna give me one of those medal guys? Saint something.

EDDIE: No. I'll pray for you like Indins do. It's different. Okay?

MIKE: I don't know how to do that. We'll get lost for sure.

EDDIE: I'll find you. It'll be different. We'll always be brothers.

MIKE: Yeah.

(Mike begins to exit.)

EDDIE: Mike. *(Mike stops. Eddie removes his shoes and gives them to Mike)* Take 'em. You'll go longer.

MIKE: Yeah. Beats the fuck out of having blisters.

(Blackout.)

scene four

Early the next morning, around three A.M. Katherine Rose's living room. Katherine is wearing only a shirt. Lenny is only in pants. Katherine is looking for Theia.

KATHERINE: She's around here somewhere. Lenny. Go and check Eddie's room again.

LENNY: Shit. I don't wanna be doing this hide-and-go-seek shit all night long.

KATHERINE: You should've kept an eye on her. Where the hell is she?

LENNY: Just when it's getting good. Shit. Let's just leave her and let her crash wherever the hell she's at. You and me can get back to what we were doing.

(Katherine goes behind the couch. She finds a pile of clothes and starts to sort through it.)

KATHERINE: No. I want to make sure she's . . . Oh.

LENNY: You remember how good it is, huh?

KATHERINE: Dream on. Look. *(Points to Theia, who is under the clothes. She removes some clothes to get to Theia)* Baby girl . . . Little, baby girl . . . get up, my baby girl. *(No response)* Come on, baby girl, you have to go to bed now.

(Lenny crosses to behind the couch.)

LENNY: Damn. If we're not going to do anything until you've done your good-mother shit, I might as well do it and get it done. *(He picks up Theia's arm)* Get up, girly. Time to get your ass to bed. *(He begins to lift Theia; she awakens)*

THEIA: Momma? Mom . . . let me go!

LENNY: Whoa . . . settle down! Christ! Bad girl!

KATHERINE: Just put her down. Put her down, Lenny!

LENNY: I can carry her if she would stop fighting me. Ow!

KATHERINE: Hey! Put her down! Christ!

(He does, and nearly drops Theia. Theia races to her mother and grabs Katherine's leg. Katherine falls.)

There, there, baby girl, don't. . . . Shit.

THEIA: He touched me!

LENNY: Oh! Big fucking lie! I didn't either.

KATHERINE: I know, baby. I know, baby.

LENNY: I didn't fucking touch her. All I did was pick her up. You seen it.

KATHERINE: All right! I heard you. Christ. Come on, baby girl. I'll put you to bed. Follow Momma.

(Katherine gets up and leads Theia to her bedroom. Theia watches Lenny. Lenny slowly follows them.)

LENNY: Hurry it up, huh?

KATHERINE: Yeah, yeah.

(They go to the bedroom. Lenny stands at the door and watches.)

THEIA: If you keep drinking tonight, Momma, will I have to go to school tomorrow?

KATHERINE: Yes. Now get your brown ass to bed. Take your clothes off. I don't want you to sleep with your clothes on anymore. Where are those pajamas you have?

(Theia is undressing.)

Hurry. I want to get ready for bed, too.

(Lenny touches himself.)

You won't leave your mother because you love her. Don't you, baby girl?

THEIA: I guess so. *(Pause)* Momma?

KATHERINE: What?

THEIA: Why is he watching me?

(Lenny walks away from the door.)

KATHERINE: Who?

THEIA: Him. Lenny.

KATHERINE: Where?

(Katherine turns to see. Lenny is by the table lighting a cigarette.)

THEIA: He was right there watching me.

LENNY: No, I wasn't. *(Crosses to the door)* You better get used to the idea of having me around. I'm not going to hide every time you're around. Daddy says so.

THEIA: Is that true, Mom?

KATHERINE: We'll see. Now get in bed.

(Katherine enters the living room. Lenny crosses to the couch and sits.)

LENNY: Well?

KATHERINE: What the hell were you doing? That's my little girl. You remember that. Nothing better not happen to her, or I'll cut your shit-eating eyes out.

LENNY: What? I'm going to be her daddy. You're just upset with all those fucking lies they've told you about me. I love you Kathy baby. I wouldn't do anything. Trust me.

(Katherine takes a drink from one of the wine bottles.)

KATHERINE: You damn right you haven't done anything. Nothing is going to happen. Especially to my baby girl. You're supposed to be so fucking tough. You won't know what tough is until I cut your boney ass.

LENNY: Behave, Kathy. *(Tries to force a laugh)* Fuck. Give me a break, huh?

KATHERINE: Don't try to fool me. You sure in the hell can't fool me. I know you.

LENNY: Okay, okay, you know. I could've helped you with her if you wanted me to. All you had to do was ask.

KATHERINE: I can do it myself. I don't see why I would ask you for your help now.

LENNY: Can I have a drink? *(She tosses him the bottle. He drinks)* Here. *(Offers her the bottle. She doesn't take it)* You're not going to drink anymore?

KATHERINE: No. Why?

LENNY: I thought now would be a good time to visit on the chair . . . or the couch. She's in bed. I think now's a good time to do it. You know?

KATHERINE: You shit!

LENNY: That's why I came back. I wouldn't have come back here. I'm not used to being treated like this. You were the one who told me to come back here. After you threatened to slice the shit out of my ass. . . . And . . . I can come and go whenever I damned well please.

KATHERINE: Well, then go! *(She walks away from the couch)* I didn't force you to come back. I have my ways, too. You're not the last one for me. I'll have others. Some of them will be better than you.

LENNY: Uh-huh.

KATHERINE: I mean it. *(She walks toward the couch and sits)* You shouldn't worry. You're free.

LENNY: I know I am. *(He sits closer to her. She moves away)* I don't have anything tying me down.

KATHERINE: Men never do anyway.

LENNY: I can stay if I want to.

KATHERINE: So . . . you are going to stay, huh?

LENNY: Yeah . . . I mean . . . there's nothing here for me. I don't have any family here . . . no relations . . . can't find work. But I might stay here, for the sake of staying.

KATHERINE: I might go. Yeah. I might be able to get work off the Res. I'll take my little girl with me. Soon. You'll see.

LENNY: When in the hell is this supposed to happen?

KATHERINE: When Eddie leaves. I won't have to worry about him riding my ass all the time. I can think better.

LENNY: Oh shit! I thought you had a job waiting for you. *(Laughs)* You'll have a big surprise for you when you do leave.

KATHERINE: Well I am. Don't laugh at me. *(Slaps Lenny a couple of times on the head)* Stop-Making-Fun-Of-Me!

LENNY: Ow, ow, but why wait? You should do it now, big shot.

KATHERINE: I will. It'll make it easier for me with Theia in school and Eddie gone.

LENNY: For what? Partying?

KATHERINE: Piss on you!

LENNY: Hey . . . don't get mad, hey, Kathy baby, but it's the truth.

KATHERINE: I know I can do it. I just haven't found the right man. Maybe if I can find one who's strong enough . . .

LENNY: Oh, Christ! *(He pulls away from her)*

KATHERINE: One who's strong and smart enough, I won't be in the place I'm at. Their fathers weren't much of anything. Couldn't depend on them to do anything right. I had to raise them and their fathers. Big kids without diapers, is what their fathers were like. I don't have time to be doing that. There are things I want to be doing, too.

(Lenny chuckles.)

LENNY: Like what?

KATHERINE: I want to do things without having to worry about anybody else but me. I want to go places and see things. Meet different people and things.

LENNY: Then join the fucking army! *(He laughs)* Or the marines.

(She moves closer to make eye contact with him. He doesn't look at her. She slaps him.)

Ow! Fuck! *(She moves further down the couch from him)* Why the fuck did you do that for? Huh? *(Tries to grab her and misses)* Damn. I was just teasing you. You didn't have to hit me.

KATHERINE: You're making fun of me. You aren't listening to me.

LENNY: Yes I am. I heard you. Goddamn you're crazy. But I didn't hear you that good is all.

KATHERINE: Oh, Christ, at least Eddie can listen to me. The only thing you want to do is grab my tits and try to get me to go to bed with you. You don't know me.

LENNY: Sure I do.

KATHERINE: Ahh! Get me a drink. *(No response)* Please.

(Lenny gets up and gives the bottle to her.)

LENNY: I've been listening to you. You want a life of your own. See. I know what you're talking about. I've been through the same thing.

KATHERINE: What? What have you been into? You had kids? You just like making them and leaving.

LENNY: No. When I was in this rehab center in Seattle. *(He sits)* I couldn't wait to party.

KATHERINE: What? What were you doing in there?

LENNY: I was being treated . . . for drugs.

KATHERINE: Oh. Big change, huh?

LENNY: Yeah. They had an AA program at the rehab center I was in. Learned a lot from Bill W. *(Pause)* There were a bunch of us in there. Most of them were these black guys and some Mexicans . . . a few Orientals. Poor man's UN—that's what we used to say. The rest were white, and just a few of us Skins. My brothers.

KATHERINE: What?

LENNY: There was this AIM guy who said we should unite while we were in there. That way we could have a voice.

KATHERINE: He told you that? Christ. You're barely Indin.

LENNY: I know. Fuck. *(Pause)* Anyway, they had these little cots . . . well, beds, and we had these gray, wool blankets. It was pretty warm. It didn't snow much in Seattle, but it was still cold. They had a place for us to wash our clothes. Had a TV—color and everything. They even had showers and baths, whirlpools—big metal fuckers, with hot water all the time. It was a pretty decent place.

KATHERINE: That's what you should do now. You could use a wash. *(Tries to get to her feet)* Holy-lee.

(Lenny tries to stop her, but she gets away from him.)

LENNY: Come here.

KATHERINE: No. Err . . .

LENNY: I have something sweet for you. *(Touches himself)*

KATHERINE: When did all this happen anyway?

LENNY: What?

KATHERINE: Your bath . . . no . . . when you went to this halfway house?

LENNY: Just last year. *(Gets up and crosses to her)* What do you feel like doing?

KATHERINE: Finish drinking this.

LENNY: Then what? Get our clothes off? Hey, Kathy baby, baby Kathy girl, well . . . you know, the kid's asleep.

KATHERINE: Christ. If this is all you think about. You must've went crazy in that place in Seattle. Or, hey, did they have women in there, too?

LENNY: No.

KATHERINE: No? Then what did you do? Play with yourself?

LENNY: Nothing. I don't have to do that. I can still get it when I want it.

KATHERINE: Don't lie. Huh, Lenny? What did you do? Play with yourself?

LENNY: I didn't do any of that shit. Nothing didn't . . . *(Pause)* I was only in there for a few weeks, and then I got out. It wasn't like I was in jail or anything like that. We took care of each other so nothing like that would happen. We watched and made sure something like that didn't happen.

KATHERINE: Like what, Lenny?

LENNY: You know . . . so . . . so no one would fuck us. Rape us. *(She laughs)* It's not funny! Fuck! *(She watches him)* It didn't happen . . . but, but there was this young kid. He was a pain in the ass to everyone. He just wouldn't shut his fucking mouth and one night, one night, they decided to throw him a blanket party. *(Pause)* Everything echoes in the halls, but, but no one heard him that night. He was always talking, and then one night . . . no one heard him. There was this guard. He had to hear. . . . But he didn't even bother to check. *(Pause)* It never happened. *(Katherine goes to him and touches his shoulder)* No one heard it. . . . No one listened to me when I tried. . . . No one.

KATHERINE: Lenny . . . Lenny . . . Lenny? I'm sorry what happened to you. You can stay here if you want, but I have to go to bed. And please, don't get mad, because, I don't want you with me. I just don't want you. . . . Don't ask me to come with you. All right, Lenny? You can sleep as late as you want.

LENNY: Where are you going?

KATHERINE: To my room. I want to sleep.

(Katherine steps back and starts to ease herself toward her room. Lenny reaches for her.)

LENNY: Just like in AA—after I shared that . . . you're not going to go to bed with me?

KATHERINE: I don't want to.

LENNY: Fuck!

(Katherine moves toward the knife under the couch. Lenny slowly follows her.)

Kathy.

(He goes to the other end of couch and removes the knife.)

KATHERINE: No . . . no . . . Len . . .

LENNY: This is mine now. Just like you are. *(She goes for the door. He races after her and gets her in a stranglehold)* No . . . no . . . Can't let you do that.

KATHERINE: Please . . . Ow! Don't Lenny!

LENNY: Fuck you then!

(He hits her in the back and knocks her down.)

KATHERINE: Please don't hurt me, Lenny. . . . Help!

(He hits her again.)

LENNY: Shut up, you damn old cow!

(He kicks her.)

KATHERINE: Help! Help me! Eddie!
LENNY: You fuckin' bitch. I'll show you. You think I was a smelly breed who's not good enough! I'll get what I want.

(He stands for a moment and then goes into Theia's bedroom.)

KATHERINE: No! No! Stay away from her, Lenny, please! Leave her alone! She didn't do anything to you.

(Katherine gets up and stumbles after him, but when she gets to the bedroom door, it is locked. We hear some things being tossed around inside.)

My baby! My baby!
THEIA: Mommy? Eddie? Is that . . . No!

(Theia screams. We hear a police siren. Police lights. Blackout.)

scene five

Early morning, the next day. Eddie stands near the front door. Thelma enters the living room carrying a suitcase. She walks over to Eddie.

THELMA: Let me do it, my son. It would be better if I do it.

EDDIE: No. I have to do it.

THELMA: You must not forget, she is still your mother. She's kept you alive . . . till now. *(Eddie nods yes)*

(Katherine enters from her bedroom and sits on the couch. She stares straight out and doesn't say a word. Her face and arms are bruised. She looks for an ashtray, sees one on the other side of the couch and reaches for it. Thelma sees Katherine struggling to reach the ashtray and goes to her, but stops midway and places her hands over her mouth. Thelma then goes to the table and looks for her braids. She finds them and gives them to Eddie. He looks down. Thelma holds him and he looks at her. She releases him and hands him three papers she's taken from her coat pocket. She picks up the suitcase and exits.

Eddie walks to the door of his bedroom, stands for a moment, and sneaks a look at his mother. Then he goes into the bedroom. Katherine looks over her shoulder and blows a cloud of smoke in his direction. The bedroom door reopens and quickly Katherine turns away. Eddie appears carrying a papersack. He shuts the bedroom door. He goes to the front door and sets the sack down. Then he goes to the couch and stands behind it.)

EDDIE: Mom? *(Softly)* Mom? *(He takes out the papers given to him by Thelma)* I'm going to see Theia at the hospital. They told Aunty Thelma she'll be in there for a few days. The doctors want to watch her. I have something for you. The cops told me and Aunty Thelma that you're going to have to sign these. They told me you said no. *(Holds out the papers)* Here they are. *(No response)* They told me and Aunty Thelma what they are. You have to sign them right away. I'll give them to Aunty Thelma and she'll take them to the agency. *(No response)* Ma?

KATHERINE: What . . . what are these? *(She slowly reaches up and takes the papers)*

EDDIE: That first one there . . . That's a complaint against Lenny. They have him and will hold him, but you have to sign so they can get him to court. You have to sign there, on the—

KATHERINE: Papers. Those dumb son of a bitches. They think these mean something. This is going to change anything. Oh God. *(She looks up at Eddie)* Why . . . why the hell did they give me all these damn papers? *(She waves them like a fan)* See. Eddie. See. You see. This is what I go through when I try to get help for us. They give me all these damn papers. What good are they?

EDDIE: Just . . . just sign them.

KATHERINE: What is it I'm signing again? I forgot. Come here and help me, my boy. Read these papers for your mother.

EDDIE: It's a complaint, Mom. The cops say you have to sign it and they'll get Lenny to court and put him in jail.

KATHERINE: That's a big damn joke. *(Crumples the papers)* He's going to be out in a few months anyway.

EDDIE: We have to do something.

KATHERINE: No.

EDDIE: At least do that. Sign the damn papers.

KATHERINE: It wasn't my fault what happened. I couldn't do anything. I was here by myself. I had no one to help me. You're supposed to protect me and your baby sister from things like this.

EDDIE: I was kicked out.

KATHERINE: You left me!

EDDIE: You kicked me out! Putting on a big show for him.

KATHERINE: You're trying to be smart. That's all you're trying to do. *(Picks up the papers)* You better shut up, or I'm not going to sign these.

EDDIE: Yes you will. *(Crosses to Katherine)* Don't say that—If you don't, Aunty Thelma will.

KATHERINE: She will, huh?

EDDIE: Why are you fighting for Lenny? When it's time for you to take up for us.

(She crosses to him and slaps him.)

KATHERINE: Don't say that! Damn you! *(Hits Eddie again)* You little, no-good . . .

(Eddie runs from her.)

EDDIE: Yes. That's what we want!

(Katherine crosses to the couch. He follows.)

KATHERINE: If Thelma wants you, she's going to have to fight me first. I'm not going to give up my baby girl to that old bitch.

EDDIE: Mom. Do it!

KATHERINE: I'm not going to give up my kids for a bunch of papers. It happened to Thelma, but it's not going to happen to me. I won't let it. They don't think I can take care of my baby. That's all it will mean. Just like Thelma. Everyone was talking about how she couldn't take care of her little boy. It's not going to happen to me.

EDDIE: Don't do this, Mom.

KATHERINE: Have your Aunty Thelma sign. *(Picks up the papers and tosses them to Eddie)* She'll get what she always wanted.

EDDIE: Momma, please.

KATHERINE: Please my ass.

EDDIE: I've never said no to you.

KATHERINE: You shouldn't. I'm your mother. You, you don't know what you're talking about. And here, you, you were going to try and lead this family. And see, you can't do it.

EDDIE: That's not it, Mom.

KATHERINE: Yes it is! Don't lie, Eddie.

EDDIE: All the times you asked if you were doing the right things. What I should have said was, "No." It was the truth. And I said, "Yes." I don't know why, but I just did. And now, I'm sorry as hell I ever did.

KATHERINE: And all this time you were telling me you loved me, you were lying to me? *(Stands up)* You always hated me?

EDDIE: I always hid it. And now I don't even try.

KATHERINE: Don't say that, Eddie. *(Pause)* After all I've been through with you? It doesn't mean anything to you. When your dad threw you out of his life, it was me—me—Eddie. I picked you up, wiped your bloody nose, wrapped your busted arm. I healed you and gave you life. I loved you. *(Looks at Eddie)* You don't care anymore?

EDDIE: I don't know what to do. Every fucking time! At first I said, "Yes," just so I could get away from you. And now, after what happened—it happened to me, too, Mom. *(Pause)* My mother is Aunty Thelma. She helped me stay here with you. I thought you would change. And you didn't. You may never change . . . may never change. *(Looks at her but she turns away. He waits, and then she looks at him)* I feel sorry for Lenny, and for everybody who was in this house, but I don't feel it. So I think it. That's what I do. And I would sit here and look, and then nothing changed. Nothing moved. Just us. And soon we were moving around and around, always on the same path, never really going anywhere. *(Pause)* I cry, but I cry because I can't tell you. I hide my tears because they don't mean anything to you. The tears don't mean anything to me. I can't cry at our own funeral, Mom. My tears are nothing but water— laughing or crying, they taste the same. *(Pause)* It'll probably start up all over again, but I don't want to be a part of it. I don't know if you'll have Lenny with you, or who'll take his place, but it isn't going to be me. *(He begins to gather up the scattered papers)* I want out. *(He hands her the papers. She sits motionless)*

KATHERINE: No, Eddie. It isn't true. You know it isn't. . . . *(She hugs him and doesn't let go)* You're just mad is all. You know I can take care of you kids. You know I can. Say yes. . . .

(Eddie slowly takes his mother's hands off. He eases her back down on the couch.)

EDDIE: No, Mom. No. You can't. Give me back my life. I want to leave here, alive. *(Gives her the papers)* Here. *(Reaches into his pants' pockets and gets a pen)* Here. Use this. *(Katherine takes the papers and looks at them)* The first one is the complaint. *(Katherine signs it)* And the next two are the custody papers. *(Katherine looks at Eddie. She signs the papers. She slowly hands them to him)* Thank you. *(Pause)* Thank you, Mom. You gave me life again.

(Eddie takes the papers and places them in his sack. He takes out the two braids and holds them up. He crosses over to Katherine. He gets an ashtray.)

Mom. Mom. Here. *(Holds the braids out)* These were Aunty Thelma's. *(He takes a book of matches)* I'm going to burn mine. I want you to have the other and please burn it, Mom. *(Eddie hands her a braid)* And later . . . I'm going to pray for you . . . and Theia. Aunty Thelma says she knows some people who can help Theia. They'll help you, too, if you want them to. I don't want anymore bad things happening to you, her or me. *(Pause)* At least try and heal one of our cuts.

(He lights a match and touches it to one of the braids. Katherine stops him.)

KATHERINE: My boy, women do this. Just go.

(Eddie gives her the braid and the matches. She lights a match and holds it near a braid. The flame burns to the end and touches her hand) Ow . . .

(She lights another match. Her hand is trembling as she holds it in the air. Eddie reaches out and helps steady her hand. Blackout.)

END OF PLAY

William S. Yellow Robe, Jr. is an enrolled member of the Assiniboine/Nakota nation. He was born and raised on the Fort Peck Indian reservation in northeastern Montana. He attended Northern Montana College and the University of Montana. Mr. Yellow Robe is an actor, director, playwright, consultant, poet and lecturer. He is Founder and Artistic Director of Wakiknabe Theater Company (an Inter-Tribal Native theatre) in Albuquerque, New Mexico.

Mr. Yellow Robe taught theatre and playwriting at the Institute of American Indian Arts in Santa Fe, New Mexico, from 1993 to 1996. During this time, he had the honor of presenting two of his students' works at The Joseph Papp Public Theater/New York Shakespeare Festival's "New Works" series. In his last year at the Institute, Mr. Yellow Robe and his students published a collection of student plays in an anthology entitled, *Gathering Our Own*.

William S. Yellow Robe, Jr. has written over twenty-seven plays, which have received readings and productions in theatres across the country, including the Mark Taper Forum in Los Angeles, the American Conservatory Theater in San Francisco, The Joseph Papp Public Theater/New York Shakespeare Festival in New York, Seattle Children's Theatre in Seattle, the Honolulu Theatre for Youth in Honolulu and the Ensemble Studio Theatre in New York. His still-to-be-published, one-act play, "The Star Quilter," was presented by the British Broadcasting Corporation in the BBC's "Radio Drama" series.

Mr. Yellow Robe is the first playwright to receive the Princess Grace Award for playwriting. He is a recipient of a National Endowment for the Arts Award for Playwriting, a Jerome Fellowship from the Minneapolis Playwrights' Center, and an Honorable Mention for the James Arthur Baldwin Playwriting Award from the University of Massachusetts/ New World Theater. He is a member of The Dramatist's Guild, Hellgate Writers, and the Wordcraft Circle of Native Storytellers and Writers. His poem, "The Last Round Dance," will be published in Wordcraft Circle's newsletter. He is a former member of the Northwest Playwrights' Guild. Mr. Yellow Robe serves on the board of advisors for Red Eagle Soaring Theatre Company of Seattle, Washington.

William Yellow Robe, Jr. currently devotes his energies to the Wakiknabe Theater Company (Wakiknabe means "we return home" in the Assiniboine language), and a student organization on the University of New Mexico campus, Wakiknabe II. Wakiknabe and Wakiknabe II produced three plays in 1998.

Indian
Radio Days

An Evolving
Bingo Experience

leanne howe
and roxy gordon

With contributions by the WagonBurner Theater Troop:
Jodi Byrd, Claire Cardwell, Joe Coulter, Justin Data,
Maria Hernandez, Debbie Hicks, Brenda Lynch, Ken McCullough,
Steve Thunder McGuire, Judy Morrison and Scott Morrison;
and original music by Jarryd Lowder.

Roxy Gordon (left) and LeAnne Howe

author's statement

LEANNE HOWE

Roxy Gordon and I wrote *Indian Radio Days* on the front porch of his Dallas home in the summer of 1988. I would drive over after working all day for a Wall Street brokerage firm whose regional office was in Dallas, Texas. We would write the scenes from the play and talk with friends who came by to listen to the script progress.

The year before (1987) our play *Big PowWow* was produced by Sojourner Theater Company in Fort Worth, Texas. *Big PowWow* was the first collaboration between an all-black theatre company, an all-Indian cast and Indian playwrights. From that experience we decided to write a radio play.

Out of the experience of Indian artists and activists coming together to work on *Indian Radio Days*, WagonBurner Theater Troop (WTT) was born. WTT is a community of

Indian artists and Indian activists who enjoy working together, who mentor younger Indians and who merge art and activism as a teaching tool for Indians and non-Indians. In 1993, WTT really created *Indian Radio Days* for the stage. WTT members grew into those characters in the script, created new music and sometimes developed new characters for each performance. As an American Indian this is how I believe our stories are supposed to be created. From the collective.

American Indian playwrights and writers tend to create stories from the experiences of our people. In turn, our work belongs to our ancestors, and the next seven generations of American Indians. I call this Indian process "Tribalography."

In other words, our stories, our plays, our art, will one day become part of the intellectual assets of our tribe's culture.

My great-grandmother was named *Anolitubby*, which in Choctaw means *Tells and Kills*. I believe this play incorporates aspects of Native storytelling. Future performances should strive to perform this "never-ending story."

There are many people to thank concerning *Indian Radio Days*. They are Jodi Byrd, Claire Cardwell, Joe Coulter, Justin Data, Eric Goekel, Judy Gordon, Maria Hernandez, Debbie Hicks, Jon Kerstetter, Jarryd Lowder, Brenda Lynch, Corey Beth Madden, Oliver Mayer III, Ken McCullough, Steve Thunder McGuire, Judy Morrison, Scott Morrison and Paul Rathbun. Finally our families and tribes. Without them *Indian Radio Days* would not exist.

Indian Radio Days (*IRD*) was first performed on October 7, 1993, at CSPS Theater in Cedar Rapids, Iowa, with a grant from the Iowa Arts Council. The play was coproduced by LeAnne Howe, Jarryd Lowder and CSPS Theater. Original music was composed by Jon Kerstetter, Eric Goekel and Jarryd Lowder. Sets were designed by Steve Thunder McGuire. LeAnne Howe was the director. The members of the company were Dan Coffey, Joe Coulter, Justin Data, Maria Hernandez, Debbie Hicks, LeAnne Howe, Steve Thunder McGuire, Frank Mitchell, Judy Morrison and Scott Morrison.

On Columbus Day, 1993, *IRD* was broadcast by WSUI/AM 910 (NPR affiliate). It had been prerecorded before a live audience at CSPS and edited for broadcast via satellite to other public radio affiliates in the Midwest and Alaska Native radio stations.

In 1994, *IRD* was performed by the WagonBurner Theater Troop (WTT) at Iowa State University, and at the University of Iowa. The play was produced by Jarryd Lowder. Original music was composed by Jon Kerstetter, Eric Goekel and Jarryd Lowder. Sets were designed by Steve Thunder McGuire. LeAnne Howe was the director. The members of the company were Jodi Byrd, Claire Cardwell, Joe Coulter, Justin Data, Maria Hernandez, Debbie Hicks, Brenda Lynch, Ken McCullough, Steve Thunder McGuire, Frank Mitchell and Judy Morrison.

On February 22, 1995, Mark Taper Forum, Los Angeles, California, produced *IRD* as part of their new playwrights reading series. Original music was composed by Jarryd Lowder. The director was Owen Le Beau. The members of the companay were Stuart Bird, Jack Burning, James Apaumut Fall, Jade Herrera, Jane Lind, Valentina Lopez-Firewalks, Adan Sanchez and Larry Swalley.

On February 26, 1995, WTT performed *IRD* at the University of Northern Iowa in Cedar Falls, and in April 1994 and 1995 WTT performed *IRD* at Lake Forest College, Lake Forest, Illinois. The play was coproduced by LeAnne Howe and Jarryd Lowder. Original music was composed by Jon Kerstetter, Eric Goekel and Jarryd Lowder. Sets were designed by Steve Thunder McGuire. LeAnne Howe was the director. The members of the company were Jodi Byrd, Claire Cardwell, Justin Data, Debbie Hicks, LeAnne Howe, Brenda Lynch, Ken McCullough, Steve Thunder McGuire and Judy Morrison.

On August 19–20, 1995, WTT performed *IRD*, at the National Museum of the American Indian in New York City. Original music was composed by Jon Kerstetter, Eric Goekel and Jarryd Lowder. Sets were designed by Steve Thunder McGuire. LeAnne Howe was the director. The members of the company were Jodi Byrd, Claire Cardwell, Justin Data, Debbie Hicks, LeAnne Howe, Jarryd Lowder, Brenda Lynch, Ken McCullough, Steve Thunder McGuire and Judy Morrison.

characters

FEMALE ANNOUNCER

NARRATOR

INDIAN BINGO WOMAN

FIRST CHARACTER

INDIAN BINGO LADY

INDIAN WOMAN

INDIAN CHIEF WHO MET
THE MAYFLOWER

FRENCHMAN

CHOCTAW INDIAN

EUGENIA CHRISTI

COMANCHE INDIAN

JOHN MUESEBACH

CHIEF LEFLORE

RED WING

COMMERCIAL ANNOUNCER
#1, #2, #3, #4

BONES

SIMON ANOLITUBBY

OJIBWA INDIAN

FRED SEEDBOX

MARTHA BULL COMING

BARTENDER

LONE RANGER

JIM MONTGOMERY

LOWAKE HARRIS

FLAMING ATTIRE

PRINCESS WANNA BUCK

KEVIN COSTNER

JANE FONDA

CLAUDENE LEVI-
ECHOFEMME

CHIEF JUANITA JACKSON

HARVEY
LITTLE GREEN MAN

SOUND/MUSIC
TECHNICIAN

Staging

The stage is created to look like an actual radio production room. There are three microphones placed stage left, stage right and center stage. Stage lights come up as the theme music begins the opening scene. Lights stay up throughout the performance.

Stage left should resemble an old-time radio show production booth. The Female Announcer stands stage left throughout the performance. The Female Announcer performs many of the commercials with the help of other members of the cast. From time to time, the Female Announcer hands news items to the Narrator, center stage.

At center stage is a microphone where the Narrator stands throughout the performance. Cast members remain offstage until their scene. The stage right microphone is for the sound/music technician and the Extra.

Typically, *Indian Radio Days* is performed with at least ten cast members. The Extra's job is to hold up the audience cue cards that appear throughout the script as "Theatre Audience Directions." This role is much like a cheerleader. The Extra also helps the sound/music technician.

There are no breaks in the performance.

Bingo cards are inserted into the theatre programs and the audience plays bingo throughout the play. The Indian Bingo Lady comes on stage periodically and ad-lib's about life on the Reservation where her brother is Chief. She also gossips about life and the goings-on in the bingo hall, a business also managed by her brother. The director should decide how many of these segues are enough.

After each performance, cast members can give the bingo prizes to the audience. In former performances of *Indian Radio Days* these prizes have been "Church Lady fashions" or secondhand clothes wrapped in brown paper bags.

Sound/Music Technician

The sound/music technician is an extremely important member of the cast. There are audio cues throughout the play. These are designated as fade-up, fade-out or cross-fade. It is recommended that the director and sound technician collect the music and the "sounds" to be used in advance of rehearsals. The sounds of burps, gulps, a champagne bottle pop, etc., are meant to fade into narration and add to the scenes.

In the original productions, theme music was written and prerecorded. However, any music can be used to standardize these themes. Sounds were also prerecorded: bingo hall sounds (Bingo); ocean tides (Ocean Solo); the sounds of rattling bones (Black Hawk 1, Black Hawk 2, Black Hawk 3, Black Hawk 4, each one successively louder and fuller); various kinds of gunfire (WW2, Gunfight); Galloping Horse; Radio Noise. Theme music from films, such as *Dances with Wolves*; French music clips (Frenchie); and songs, such as "Stranded in Iowa," "People," "You're So Vain," "Half-Breed" and "Danke Schoën," were used in the play and aired for five to thirty seconds, depending on the scene and director's pacing.

Fade-up "Radio Noise" and "Indian Radio Days Theme."

FEMALE ANNOUNCER *(Soft, droning, FM voice; she strikes bell)*:
You are listening to AIR/American Indian Radio's production of *Indian Radio Days*. The time is now twenty-
nine minutes past the hour.

*(Narrator walks to microphone. He changes accents and
mood for each change in scene.)*

NARRATOR: I am talking with the first American Indian. He
is naked and dirty. He is burned dark brown by the sun.
He carries a flint-tipped spear. He is the first American
Indian.

(Fade-out "Radio Noise" and "Indian Radio Days Theme.")

FIRST CHARACTER *(Matter-of-factly)*: I'm not an American
Indian. I am not Mongolian. I'm from inner space. I
am the First Character.

(Audience is directed to applaud the First Character.)

NARRATOR: Please, for the listening audience, tell us, if you will, what you mean by that?

FIRST CHARACTER: I'm the FORE American. Indians came later.

NARRATOR: That's very interesting. Where are you from?

FIRST CHARACTER: According to my somewhat crude, but accurate, rock and sun calendar, this is the Pleistocene epoch, man.

NARRATOR: And you state, you are not an American Indian?

FIRST CHARACTER: Nope. White people made American Indians.

NARRATOR: What did you say?

FIRST CHARACTER *(Exasperated)*: Listen, man. *(Drops the accent)* We were all just people. And, in fact, people before people that you define.

(Fade-up and then out "People.")

NARRATOR: If you aren't an Indian, who are you? Can you tell us the name of your tribe?

FIRST CHARACTER: PEOPLE!

(Fade-up "West Africa.")

First, we were all together on the central plains of Africa. One of your ancestors was over there, too. *(Exasperated)* Then, before we knew what happened, there was continental drift. *(Shocked)* I mean, there was an ocean in between us. So, we grew up over here, and you grew up over there. We couldn't even talk to each other anymore. So, we took a trip. My ol' lady didn't think I ought to go to France, but I had this gallery opening in a cave over there. *(Excited)* And, then, I run into these ol' boys that had heavy eyebrows. So, I taught 'em how to paint. Didn't make any money, though. But I taught 'em medicine, too.

NARRATOR: Let me interrupt, here. Ah *(Short pause)* could you clarify some of those statements for us, please?

FIRST CHARACTER: No.

FEMALE ANNOUNCER *(Strikes bell)*: You are listening to AIR/American Indian Radio's production of Indian Radio Days. The time is now twenty-nine minutes past the hour.

(A cast member demonstrates the effectiveness with roll of toilet paper for audience as the Female Announcer reads the commercial.)

This portion of AIR is brought to you by White Cloud Indian Toilet Paper. Squeezeably soft to the touch. Biodegradable. It won't rub you the wrong way!

(Fade-out "West Africa.")

INDIAN BINGO LADY: AD-LIB BINGO ROUTINE *(Fade-up and then out "Bingo")*

(Audience is directed to applaud after bingo routine. Fade-up "Indian Ocean.")

NARRATOR: We've had a change of ethnicity. Our last guest said he wasn't an American Indian. You say you are?

INDIAN WOMAN *(She has a very matter-of-fact persona)*: I'm the Indian.

NARRATOR: Can you elaborate on that?

INDIAN WOMAN: I'm THE Indian.

NARRATOR: Well, who was he then?

INDIAN WOMAN *(Emphatic)*: He never existed. We've been here from the beginning of time. This is Turtle Island, after all!

NARRATOR: Clarify that for me, if you will, and tell our listening audience, if you can, who are "*we*"?

INDIAN WOMAN: Mister, what's wrong with you? We are The People. We have always been here. That white man was some kind of Impostor. He was WHITE after all.

NARRATOR: How did Indians get here if, as you say, you are The Indian?

INDIAN WOMAN: Well, obviously, we've always been here.

NARRATOR: You don't think you came from Africa?

INDIAN WOMAN *(Exasperated)*: Africa? Are you kidding? I guess you believe that Bering Strait Theory, too!

(Audience is directed to boo and hiss.)

FEMALE ANNOUNCER *(Hits bell)*: You're listening to AIR's production of *Indian Radio Days*. The time is now twenty-nine minutes past the hour. Coming up next hour is the invasion of the English, French and the Germans.

(Fade-out "Indian Ocean.")

NARRATOR: I'm now standing on a rock. I dare say, *the* Plymouth Rock, from all appearances. Who are you, sir?

INDIAN CHIEF WHO MET THE MAYFLOWER *(Cups hands together as if he is hollering at a boat way in the distance)*: No! No! NO! NO! We've got to send you back! It would only encourage others like yourself to attempt this dangerous and foolhardy trip across the ocean in those flimsy boats. Besides, we don't have the room. And who knows what will happen next? You may try and take our jobs and drive the price of corn to an all-time low. No, No, No, NO! You must go back!

NARRATOR: Who are you people?

INDIAN CHIEF WHO MET THE MAYFLOWER: I'm one of the Indians who met the *Mayflower*.

(Audience is directed to boo and hiss.)

NARRATOR: So it's untrue that you welcomed these poor English prisoners and debtors with open arms to the New World for an American Thanksgiving dinner?

INDIAN CHIEF WHO MET THE MAYFLOWER: What do you think, fellow?

NARRATOR: Well, this is not what we're taught in the history books, so I didn't know.

INDIAN CHIEF WHO MET THE MAYFLOWER: Fellow, do you mean history books or dime novels? *(Turns to the audience and hollers)* No. No. No. NO! Go back. That's right. I'm afraid you cannot stay. I'm sure captains Pete Wilson, Rush Limbaugh and Newt Gingrich will understand.

(Fade-up "Radio Noise" and "Indian Radio Days Theme.")

FEMALE ANNOUNCER *(Strikes bell)*: You're listening to American Indian Radio's production of *Indian Radio Days*. The time is now twenty-nine minutes past the hour.

(Fade-out "Indian Radio Days Theme.")

NARRATOR: I'm on location on the Gulf Coast at the mouth of the mighty Mississippi River with two early adversaries in January 1704—a Choctaw Indian and a Frenchman. The Choctaw is dirty. He is forty years old. He is mostly naked. Bird feathers stick out of his hair. He is carrying some skins. Written on his chest in big block letters is: "LIFE'S A BEACH." Tell me, gentlemen, can you explain to our listening audience what you think of each other?

(Fade-up "Frenchie." Frenchman, very scared, staccato voiced, curses in French, a long string of nonsuperlatives.)

In English, please.

FRENCHMAN *(French accent)*: Monsieur. I don't know what will happen to me. I am zhousands of miles from my home. And, I am standing in zee breast of zee savage. What do you zhink I zhould be feeling?

CHOCTAW INDIAN *(Laid back. Makes the sound of smoking. Lights a match, inhales, pauses and exhales into microphone. Mocks the French accent)*: I've got these skins, man. Ver-ry nice. Ver-ry thick. Good for hats.

FRENCHMAN: Monsieur Savage. Hum. Let us discuss zee bezinezz.

(The two walk away from the microphone arm in arm. Narrator shrugs his shoulders. Fade-out "Radio Noise" and "Frenchie.")

INDIAN BINGO LADY: AD-LIB BINGO ROUTINE *(Fade-up and then out "Bingo")*

(Audience is directed to whoop and holler. Fade-up "Hashi Mi Mali.")

FEMALE ANNOUNCER *(Strikes bell)*: You're listening to *Indian Radio Days*. This is AIR/American Indian Radio. The time is now twenty-nine minutes past the hour.

(Cross-fade "Hashi Mi Mali" and "Gunfight.")

NARRATOR: It's October 12, 1892. A posse of thirty U.S. marshals have so far failed to remove Ned Christi, dead or alive, from his Ozark Mountain home outside of Tallequah, Oklahoma. A full twelve hours of battle, some thirty-eight rounds from a cannon, two thousand rounds of rifle ammo, have brought these marshals no closer to capturing Mr. Christi. And with me here is Ned's beautiful daughter, Eugenia, to tell us what is going on. Say something to the audience, Eugenia!

EUGENIA: Hey, everyone!

NARRATOR: Eugenia—I can call you that, can't I, darlin'?

EUGENIA: Yes. But don't call me darlin'.

NARRATOR: Eugenia, this battle seems to be taking on ominous proportions, what with the talk that your father is the last Cherokee warrior and all. And, of course that bundle of dynamite those marshals are wrapping might finally finish your father off. Would you say now, after all this, that war is in your father's veins?

EUGENIA: Well, I guess you could say that.

NARRATOR: Can you elaborate on that?

(Fade-out "Gunfight.")

EUGENIA: Well, after breakfast yesterdee, my dad said, "Girl, we've been unearthed, underrepresented, considered uncivilized, and still they are unconvinced that I have a reason to be fed up. We've been distilled, dissuaded, disbanded, dug up, and now, because I won't surrender, I've been lied to, lied about, worked over, robbed, and damn near ruined. The only reason I'm sticking around is to complete the war they began." So there, darlin'!

(Eugenia slugs Narrator in the belly and stomps away from the microphone. Audience is directed to whoop and holler. Fade-up "Indian Radio Days Theme.")

FEMALE ANNOUNCER *(Strikes bell)*: You're listening to AIR/American Indian Radio's production of *Indian Radio Days*. The time is now twenty-nine minutes past the hour.

(Fade-out "Indian Radio Days Theme.")

NARRATOR: I am on the San Saba river bank in central Texas on March 2, 1847. I am about to witness a historic event. The wild Comanche Indians have just agreed to sign a no-fault treaty with John Muesebach of the German Colonial Society of Frankfurt. We will see firsthand how that peace treaty came about. Here, coming towards me is a Comanche Indian. He looks very much the same as the Choctaw Indian, dirty. Sir, any comments on this unfolding situation?

COMANCHE INDIAN (*Loudly, with terror*): I eat white people for breakfast! I am KO-MAN-CHE!

NARRATOR (*After a pause*): Hmmm. Well, ah, ah, ah-h-h. Okay, let's move on. John Muesebach is dressed in a black German-style coat. He wears horn-rimmed glasses and is smoking a white clay pipe. I believe he is shy. He seems very confused.

(*Fade-up and then out "Roll Out the Barrel."*)

JOHN M. (*Loudly, with passion*): Sieg Heil! (*Salutes like a Nazi soldier*) Sieg Heil! I am very pleasing to meet you, Mr. Indian.

COMANCHE INDIAN (*Imitates the salute*): Friedrich Nietzsche—God, what an idiot!

JOHN M.: I have come from de Fadderland to make allies with me Comanche brodders.

COMANCHE INDIAN (*Growling*): What for?

JOHN M.: So we can settle our families here. Grow cabbage. Make sour Krauts. Make beer.

COMANCHE INDIAN: I don't know about you sour Krauts. But a beer sounds pretty good to me. Maybe this free trade can be all it's cracked up to be. Will you stop around the tribe's bingo hall, say around midnight, and we can discuss this proposition?

(*Fade-up and then out "Radio Noise" and "Hashi Mi Mali."*)

FEMALE ANNOUNCER *(Strikes bell)*: You're listening to *Indian Radio Days*. This is AIR/American Indian Radio. This portion of AIR is sponsored by Red Woman Chewing Tobacco. The tobacco of the New World! Just a pinch of Red Woman Chewing Tobacco between the cheek and gum gives you all the flavor of a full-blooded, red woman. AIR is also sponsored by Cheap Cherokee. Nothing runs farther and faster on the road, *and* it won't die on the trail. . . . If you're interested in test-driving a Cheap Cherokee, contact your local dealer. The time is now twenty-nine minutes past the hour.

(Fade-up "The Bone Picker.")

NARRATOR: I am here in Jackson, Mississippi, with Chief Greenwood LeFlore in 1850. He is fat and wearing a dusty, black waistcoat. Under his waistcoat he wears a T-shirt that plainly says: "WHERE'S THE BEACH?" He wears a bow tie. He is a man without a country. He is staggering. Excuse me, sir. I'm told you are an Indian.

CHIEF LEFLORE: I'm an Indian.

(Fade-out "The Bone Picker.")

NARRATOR: You don't look like an Indian.

CHIEF LEFLORE: I don't know what an Indian is supposed to look like.

NARRATOR: We tend to think of Indians looking like Sitting Bull or Chief Joseph. You look like a United States senator, or maybe a Presbyterian minister.

CHIEF LEFLORE: I quit trying.

NARRATOR: Quit trying what?

CHIEF LEFLORE: Quit trying to look Choctaw.

NARRATOR: Was it hard to look Choctaw?

(Fade-up "Ocean Solo.")

CHIEF LEFLORE: It became increasingly so for me. Especially after Andy Jackson betrayed me and my family. *(Small bitter laugh)* You know, I fought for him in the War of 1812. I made speeches to my people about how good this one white man was. But I was wrong. I thought Andy had seen enough dyin' to last him a lifetime, but I was wrong. I think on the walk to Oklahoma, the Trail of Tears, the Choctaws lost four thousand, maybe more.... *(Voice trails off)* I watched 'em fall down from exhaustion day after day in the rain, snow. I listened to the babies cry. Have you ever tried to carry a little baby for ninety days straight? Their little bodies become bruised from being handled, day in and day out, and it was all my fault. Some of us got cholera. Do you know what cholera did to Nahotina? *(Coughs and stops)*

NARRATOR: Mr. LeFlore, what are you talking about?

CHIEF LEFLORE: I'm talkin' about life, boy. I'm talking about being, at one time, anyway, the Southern District Chief of the Choctaw Nation. I'm talkin' about the forced relocation on the Trail of Tears of people out of Florida, Tennessee, Mississippi, North and South Carolina, Alabama, Louisiana and even Maine, and to hell and back. Everywhere. I'm talking about the Indian ethnic cleansing. Boy!

NARRATOR: Then, for Christ's Christmas, sir, why don't you want to look like a Choctaw?

(Fade-out "Ocean Solo.")

CHIEF LEFLORE: Because being Indian is a very complicated matter, and I have not always been accepted. You see, my father was a French Canadian. My mother was Choctaw: *n'est-ce pas.* I once believed what the father said. Now I am a full-blooded Choctaw: *Tchatas sia hoke!* Okay. That is final. Even if you can't recognize me here in this great city.

(Fade-up "The Bone Picker.")

NARRATOR: Mr. LeFlore just pulled a bottle of liquor out of his pocket and drank it all down to the last drop. He has just fallen over. *(Walks up to the body, pulls out handkerchief, and touches it to him to see if he's dead)* He appears to be dead.

FEMALE ANNOUNCER *(Strikes bell)*: You are listening to AIR/American Indian Radio's production of *Indian Radio Days*. The time is now twenty-nine minutes past the hour.

(Fade-out "The Bone Picker" and fade-up "Red Wing.")

NARRATOR *(With force)*: The Civil War has just ended. We are here with Pretty Red Wing on the western plains of Nebraska in 1864. She is awaiting the return of her husband. He has been out in Colorado hunting antelope with Black Kettle's band of Cheyenne. It has been reported that a Colorado militia officer named Chivington has attacked Black Kettle's band and has left many casualties. Red Wing is anxiously awaiting word of her husband. Red Wing, can you come to the microphone? Before we get into details, how is it to work with Black Kettle?

RED WING *(Breathy, like Marilyn Monroe)*: Well, he was wearing a very modest pant-coat. I think it was gray. No, no, it was buckskin, and he had a designer vest and silver earrings to complete the outfit. He looked divine.

NARRATOR: Aside from his attire, can you tell us how it was to work with Black Kettle?

RED WING: Well, you see, Black Kettle is a good American. He flies the American flag on his . . . lodgepole.

(The Extra holds a flag in front of his pelvic area as a sight gag.)

NARRATOR: Why would an American Indian fly the American flag?

RED WING (*Breathy, like Marilyn Monroe*): I don't know, I don't know.

(*Fade-up and then out "Galloping Horse." The Extra runs to microphone and gives Narrator a message.*)

NARRATOR: This news from Indian Country just in via Pony Express. The Colorado Militia under the direction of Pastor Chivington has just attacked Black Kettle's company. War! Good God, y'all! Pretty, little Red Wing, aren't you worried about the death of your lover?

RED WING: I think, if it is true, it has interrupted the antelope hunting.

NARRATOR: Don't you have any feelings for Black Kettle?

(*Fade-up and then out "Radio Noise" and "War."*)

RED WING: I'm worried about the hunt. We worry about the people's survival. That's the Indian way.

(*Audience is directed to applaud. Fade-out "Red Wing."*)

FEMALE ANNOUNCER (*Strikes bell*): This concludes Part One of *Indian Radio Days*. You are listening to AIR/American Indian Radio. The time is now twenty-nine minutes past the hour. Coming up next is Black Hawk's Skeleton and Martha Bull Coming. But first a word from our sponsors.

COMMERCIAL ANNOUNCER #1: Coming up this Saturday on RSN/Racist Sports Network is a classic rivalry that's guaranteed to give you testosterone fits! The 'Skins will try to fend off the Immigrants, live from RFK Stadium, featuring Senator Ben Nighthorse Campbell on the play-by-play. BE THERE!

COMMERCIAL ANNOUNCER #2 *(Sexy female voice)*: Receive the goodness of what nature has to offer. Land of Flakes Butter. Mmm . . . Pure. Simple. Sweet and true. Land of Flakes butter in the dairy aisle of a supermarket near you.

COMMERCIAL ANNOUNCER #3 *(Pitiful Indian child's voice)*: Do you live in fear of the unknown, but feel powerless to make changes? Call the live, one-on-one Indian Psychic Association. Get your personal information on success, love and lucky bingo numbers. Call now and receive an authentic Native American drum from Taiwan. Call 1-800-INDIANS.

COMMERCIAL ANNOUNCER #4 *(Concerned Sally Struthers voice)*: Every child needs food, clothing, shelter and the almighty, everlasting, loving hand of God. You can sponsor a needy child through the Indians for Christ Program. Only fifty cents a day will provide a child with the physical and spiritual nourishment that he or she needs so desperately. Or several thousand dollars a day can provide us with a multimillion-dollar combination cathedral and luxurious vacation complex. Please give generously to the Indians for Christ Program. Call 1-800-4-CHRIST.

(Fade-up "Stranded in Iowa." Audience is directed to whoop and holler.)

FEMALE ANNOUNCER *(Strikes bell)*: You are listening to Part Two of *Indian Radio Days* on AIR/American Indian Radio. The time is now twenty-nine minutes past the hour.

(Fade-out "Stranded in Iowa.")

NARRATOR: We're in the newly created territory of Iowa, in the Office of the First Governor, Robert Lucas. Chief Black Hawk's skeleton is here in the room. Let's have a word with Black Hawk if we can. Chief, sir, how is it that you ended up here?

(Fade-up and then out "Black Hawk 1.")

How do you like hanging with the governor here in Iowa territory?

(Fade-up and then out "Black Hawk 2.")

Is it true that your bones were stolen from your burial scaffold by a greedy doctor and later confiscated by Governor Lucas?

(Fade-up and then out "Black Hawk 3.")

Well, Chief Black Hawk does not seem at liberty to answer any questions at this time. Perhaps he needs to confer with his lawyer. Thank you Chief Black Hawk.

(Cross-fade-up and then out "Black Hawk 4" with "WW2.")

INDIAN BINGO LADY: AD-LIB BINGO ROUTINE *(Fade-up and then out "Bingo")*

NARRATOR: I am in the final battle of the Mousse-Argonne French Campaign, 1918, during World War I. I am talking with Simon Anolitubby, another Choctaw from Oklahoma. He is a soldier in the United States Army. How did you get here, soldier?

ANOLITUBBY: I enlisted, SIR.

NARRATOR: What's an Indian doing here?

ANOLITUBBY: I am a good American. I fly the American flag. I am a code talker, SIR.

NARRATOR: A code talker? What is a code talker?

ANOLITUBBY: One day, a Captain John Smith, our commander happened to overhear us conversing in our language. He said, "Corporal, how many of you Choctaw do we have in this battalion?" I said, "We have eight who can speak Choctaw fluently, SIR." So he said, "Round 'em up on the double. We're gonna get these Krauts off our backs."

NARRATOR: What happened?

ANOLITUBBY: We translated messages and handled telephone calls from the field. The German code experts were flippin' their wigs tryin' to break the new American code. Within twenty-four hours after our language was pressed into service, the tide of battle had turned. The Allies were on full attack. We were praised by our company commanders and told we'd all get medals.

NARRATOR: When did you boys receive them?

(Fade-out "WW2.")

ANOLITUBBY: We never did. Turns out the government didn't think we were U.S. citizens 'cause we are Indians. The Navajo or the Hopi boys didn't receive any medals for code talking either.

(Simon Anolitubby salutes the audience after his soliloquy. Fade-up and then out "Winnebago.")

NARRATOR: I'm am standing in the remains of Cloquet, Minnesota. It is the day after Columbus Day, October 1918. The town and approximately one million acres of the surrounding area have been burned to ash. Sitting on a stump in front of me is an Ojibwa man smoking a cigarette. Sir, can you tell us what has happened here?

OJIBWA INDIAN: We had a BIG cookout to celebrate Columbus Day.

NARRATOR *(Shocked)*: You call this a cookout?

OJIBWA INDIAN: Just kidding. *(Takes a drag, exhales)* Naw, what really happened is a spark from the paper-mill logging train started it. You see, before trees turned a profit, us Indians used to burn the undergrowth every year. In some places it made it easier to hunt. Other places it got rid of the bad brush. . . . Let the tall stuff grow better. But seeing as how we got pushed off the land, and no one's been taking care of it . . . and kaboom!

(Audience is directed to whoop and holler. Fade-up "Radio Noise" and "Indian Radio Days Theme.")

FEMALE ANNOUNCER *(Strikes bell)*: You are listening to AIR/American Indian Radio. The time is now twenty-nine minutes past the hour.

NARRATOR: I'm still somewhere in the U.S.A. The year is 1924. Indians have just become citizens. The federal government has declared that Indians are Americans, too. I am standing here in Watsonville, California, with Fred Seedbox. He is a Hupa Indian and a hand on an artichoke ranch. Mr. Seedbox, can you describe how this law affects you?

(Fade-out "Radio Noise" and "Indian Radio Days Theme.")

FRED S.: I don't know. Can it make me any money?

NARRATOR: Mr. Seedbox, being an American citizen doesn't mean you're going to make more money, it means you can be a participant in the American political process.

(Audience is directed to boo and hiss.)

FRED S. *(Dryly)*: Oh.

NARRATOR: How will that affect you?

FRED S.: Mister, I don't have the slightest idea what you're talking about. All I know is that I harvest the food for lovers. That's all.

NARRATOR: "The food for lovers!?" *(Sings "Indian Love Call" a cappella)*

FEMALE ANNOUNCER *(Strikes bell)*: You are listening to AIR's *Indian Radio Days*. The time is now twenty-nine minutes past the hour.

INDIAN BINGO LADY: AD-LIB BINGO ROUTINE *(Fade-up and then out "Bingo")*

NARRATOR: I am here in New York City with Martha Bull Coming, an Abenaki Indian also of New York. We're at the famous Wall Street bar, Harry's at Hanover. It's 1935. Martha, can you tell us why you've called this press conference?

(Fade-up "Champagne Bottle Pop.")

MARTHA B.C.: 'Cause Indians can't drink, damn it!

NARRATOR: Are you referring to the issue that Indians cannot handle alcohol?

MARTHA B.C.: Sure we can handle it. See, I just picked up this glass. I'm handling it okay.

NARRATOR: No, no, no, no. Alcoholism among the Indian population is the highest of all the ethnic groups in this country due to the fact that Indians are allergic to liquor. Now, true Caucasians, Asians, Africans, well, people all over the world are alcoholics, but scientists say they might be on the verge of a breakthrough, establishing that Indians are the most vulnerable to alcohol in this country.

MARTHA B.C.: I'm drinking a Shirley Temple. So there. What are you going to do about it?

NARRATOR: Is that why you called us here? To drink a Shirley Temple?

MARTHA B.C.: I'm testing the law.

NARRATOR: The law that prohibits Indians from consuming alcoholic beverages, I presume?

MARTHA B.C.: That's the one. Look at me! I'm downing the whole drink in one swallow.

(Fade-up and then out "Gulp Sounds.")

NARRATOR: Martha, that was a Shirley Temple.

MARTHA B.C.: OK, arrest me! I know my rights.

(Audience is directed to applaud.)

I said: Arrest me! Get your handcuffs and nightsticks! I know what I'm doin'!

(Audience is directed to applaud.)

BARTENDER *(New York accent)*: One more Shirley Temple, madame?

MARTHA B.C.: Hell, yes! Drinks for the house and fresh horses for my men. *(Fade-up and then out "Burp")* Excuse me. Here, give it here. I'm downing this one, too. *(Fade-up and then out "Gulp Sounds." Pause. Slurs words)* Damn, I'm getting fucked, or drunk, or something.

BARTENDER: Lady, there ain't no alcohol in a Shirley Temple.

MARTHA B.C. *(Soberly)*: Oh.

(Fade-up "Indian Radio Days Theme.")

FEMALE ANNOUNCER *(Strikes bell)*: You are listening to AIR's *Indian Radio Days.* The time is now twenty-nine minutes past the hour.

(Fade-out "Indian Radio Days Theme.")

INDIAN BINGO LADY: AD-LIB BINGO ROUTINE *(Fade-up "Bingo")*

(Audience is directed to applaud. Fade-up and then out "Kazoo Playing Lone Ranger *Theme with Galloping Sounds.")*

NARRATOR: We've had a change of ethnicity again. This afternoon I'm meeting with the Masked Man himself. Do you have any words of wisdom after working with Tonto all these years on radio and films?

LONE RANGER: Never trust a damn Indian.

NARRATOR: Why is that?

LONE RANGER: Because I just found out what *Kemosabe* really means! . . . Horse's ass!

(Fade-up "Israeli Music.")

NARRATOR: I'm here at the formation of the State of Israel. It's 1949, and I'm in the capital of the newly formed state of Israel. Jim Montgomery, a Lakota Indian from America, is here with us today. Can you tell us how you came to be here?

JIM M.: Well, man, I came home from the war, and the Rez was pretty damn boring. I mean, man, I'd been sleeping with those French chicks, and them squaws weren't cuttin' it. In fact, they were cuttin' me, so I split.

NARRATOR: But why Israel?

JIM M.: I heard Golda say we Indians was Jews.

NARRATOR: What? You're kidding.

JIM M.: No, man. We're the ten lost tribes. Just ask the Mormons. You could have knocked me over with a feather when I heard that.

NARRATOR: So then, Jim, you came to Israel to establish communication between the ancient tribes of Israel and the Lakota Tribe?

JIM M.: Yeah! That ain't bad! And the woman promised she'd lay some farmland on us. Except I'm not a farmer, I'm a WARRIOR LOVER.

(Fade-out "Israeli Music.")

NARRATOR: Do you mean that Mrs. Meir said she'd give land to American Indians?

JIM M.: No, man, she said she'd give it to Jews.

NARRATOR: Mr. Montgomery, do you mean you consider yourself to be Jewish?

JIM M.: Not anymore. I came because of this ten-lost-tribes thing, and they made me a Palestinian. It was my nose that did it. I guess the joke's on me. *(Big laugh)*

(Audience is directed to trill. Fade-up "Radio Noise" and "The Bone Picker.")

FEMALE ANNOUNCER *(Strikes bell)*: You are listening to *Indian Radio Days* on AIR/American Indian Radio. The time is now twenty-nine minutes past the hour.

NARRATOR: I'm in Minneapolis, Minnesota. It's 1952, and I'm speaking with Lowake Harris, who is a member of the Menominee Nation. The U.S. government has recently announced the termination of her tribe, saying they are no longer Indians under current government law. Lowake Harris, can you tell me what this means to you?

(Fade-out "Radio Noise" and "The Bone Picker.")

LOWAKE H.: It don't mean a goddamn flippin' fuck to me.

NARRATOR: But isn't it wonderful to no longer have the federal government telling you what to do?

(Audience is directed to trill.)

LOWAKE H.: Nobody on this planet, on two legs, EVER told me what to do.

NARRATOR: But what about the Bureau of Indian Affairs? The BIA?

(Audience is directed to boo and hiss.)

LOWAKE H.: Those goddamn wimps? They never told me squat.

(Audience is directed to laugh.)

NARRATOR: Do you mean your life hasn't been administered by the BIA? Where did you get your education? Didn't you go to BIA schools?

LOWAKE H.: I went to Haskell. But I got my education in the dorms doing deals and sneakin' out the window.

NARRATOR: I'm sure that didn't benefit you?

LOWAKE H.: It benefited the hell out of me.

NARRATOR: Then in your opinion does the American government no longer owe you anything?

LOWAKE H.: Screw you and the white boys! They ain't paid their debts, and from now on you can call me MS. HARRIS, Indian attorney-at-law.

(Audience is directed to applaud. Fade-up "Hashi Mi Mali.")

FEMALE ANNOUNCER *(Strikes bell)*: This ends Part Two of *Indian Radio Days.* You've been listening to AIR. Coming up next is Princess Wanna Buck, Joseph Flaming Attire and Wayne Newton. But first a word from our sponsors.

(Audience is directed to applaud. Fade-out "Hashi Mi Mali.")

COMMERCIAL ANNOUNCER #1 *(Confident male voice)*: Try new Straight Arrow Brand Condoms for the utmost in prophylactic protection. Straight Arrow Brand Condoms are made from the intestines of buffalo and are naturally lubricated. They come in three sizes: Big Chief . . . Bad Warrior . . . and Little Brave. You're always prepared to defend yourself and your partner with Straight Arrow Brand Condoms.

COMMERCIAL ANNOUNCER #2 *(Child's voice)*: Mom, do you ever get that not-so-fresh feeling?

COMMERCIAL ANNOUNCER #3 *(Confident Indian woman voice)*: Why, yes, daughter, and when I do, I reach for new Moontime Organic Tampons. They're made from the cattails that grow by rivers and ponds and were used by Native American women when they were also feeling not so fresh. Here, try Moontime Organic Tampons.

COMMERCIAL ANNOUNCER #2 *(Child's voice)*: Thanks, Mom.

(Fade-up "Indian Radio Days Theme.")

FEMALE ANNOUNCER *(Strikes bell)*: You are listening to Part Three of *Indian Radio Days* on AIR/American Indian Radio. The time is now twenty-nine minutes past the hour.

NARRATOR: Pine Ridge, yes or no?

(Audience is directed to shout "YES!" Cross-fade "Indian Radio Days Theme" and "Gunfight.")

We are now here in Pine Ridge, South Dakota. The year is 1973. There is a constant exchange of gunfire between the militant members of the American Indian Movement (AIM) and the FBI. Nighttime is upon us, ladies and gentleman. However, a member of the American Indian Movement has stepped into my line of vision.

(Fade-out "Gunfight.")

He appears to be a security guard. He is wearing an American army field jacket. He holds at his ear a radio. I suppose he is in contact with the insurgents. *(Whisper)* I am going to try and overhear what he is listening to . . .

(Cast member walks close to Narrator. They carry a small radio at his ear.)

I believe it's music. He's coming toward me. I'll aim the microphone at his radio . . .

(Fade-up "You're So Vain.")

FEMALE ANNOUNCER *(Strikes bell)*: You are listening to AIR/American Indian Radio. The time is now twenty-nine minutes past the hour.

(Cross-fade-out "Radio Noise" and "You're So Vain.")

INDIAN BINGO LADY: AD-LIB BINGO ROUTINE *(Fade-up and then out "Bingo")*

(Fade-up "Don't Rain on My Parade." Audience is directed to whoop and holler.)

NARRATOR: It is July 16, 1992, and we are here on the Cattaraugus Indian Reservation in western New York State. A conflict between the Seneca and the state of New York has become very tense as Indian protesters drop burning tires off a highway overpass and clash with state police. I have with me here one of the Seneca protesters, Mr. Joseph Flaming Attire, not his real name. Mr. Flaming Attire, what is this protest all about?

FLAMING ATTIRE *(Effeminate voice)*: I bet you thought no Indians lived in New York, did you?

NARRATOR: Mr. Flaming Attire, that's not the point. Two hundred New York State troopers have been sent to the reservation. A thirty-mile strip of the New York Thruway is shut down. That, sir, is the point.

FLAMING ATTIRE: We're doing this because first of all our lands were condemned. Our sacred land was dug up, dug over, dug away, and we don't dig it!!!

(Fade-out "Don't Rain on My Parade.")

It was desecrated while we were caged up like farm animals. Then the state of New York felt it had the authority to build an interstate through what little land we had left. So we showed them what sovereignty is all about and fought them like mad in court and got the title to the land they built the damn interstate on. And seeing as how this is our land, we're shutting this sucker down.

NARRATOR: Doesn't this protest seem a bit extreme?

FLAMING ATTIRE: Well, we were reading this little book about a Boston Tea Party . . .

(Fade-up "Indian Ocean.")

INDIAN BINGO LADY: AD-LIB BINGO ROUTINE *(Fade-up and then out "Bingo")*

FEMALE ANNOUNCER *(Strikes bell)*: You are listening to AIR/American Indian Radio. The time is now twenty-nine minutes past the hour.

NARRATOR: We're now at the Newest Age Flora, Fauna and Native American Shop in College City, Iowa, where I've just surprised the fabulously popular Princess Wanna Buck serenely shopping the crystal discount aisle. She's well known by new pagans, old hippies and self-aware non-Indian advocates. She's returned to the

Midwest to offer her intensive workshop: "Know Your Indian Inner Child." Pardon me, Princess Wanna Buck.

(Fade-out "Indian Ocean.")

PRINCESS WANNA BUCK: I'm sorry, I only give autographs at my book signings or for my workshop participants.

NARRATOR: Could you share a few thoughts with our radio audience, please?

PRINCESS WANNA BUCK: A media moment . . . My spirit guides anticipated this opportunity . . . to bring more yearning souls of the warm embrace of the "FORE REAL" PEOPLE TRIBE.

NARRATOR: There are questions as to your legitimacy as an Indian teacher, prophet and tribal leader.

PRINCESS WANNA BUCK: Well, there was an unfortunate confusion between myself and that greedy fraud, Chief Wendy Wanna-Be. She can't even open an American Indian Express account after that ghastly lawsuit.

NARRATOR: How do we distinguish a fake from a legitimate Indian teacher—

PRINCESS WANNA BUCK: —some say prophet.

NARRATOR: —with authentic—

PRINCESS WANNA BUCK: —spiritual—

NARRATOR: —authentic, spiritual wisdom to sell?

PRINCESS WANNA BUCK: O-o-oh, the desperation and insight in that question! Inquiring minds recognize that tribal identity is more than bloodlines, earth tones and stuff like that. *Indian* is not an identity that can be purchased cheaply with mere money. The *Fore Real* People Tribe is from the depths of primeval time. We were Native Americans in a prehistoric life, reunited in this astral plane. Your native prebirth self can be found and embraced on a guided, intense weekend for only seven hundred and eighty dollars plastic—or discount for cash and family groups. But you must excuse me now, I have to restock my crystals.

(Fade-up and then out "Indian Radio Days Theme.")

FEMALE ANNOUNCER *(Strikes bell)*: You are listening to AIR/American Indian Radio. The time is now twenty-nine minutes past the hour. Coming up next is Ronald Reagan and *Indians in Space*, but first this.

NARRATOR: It's 1995, and we're at the premiere of *Son of Dances with Wolves*. In this sequel film, Kevin Costner's character is saved from a military execution by his eldest son and a bunch of wacky Sioux warriors. Maybe we'll get a chance to talk with him. Oh, here he is now. Kevin, excuse me. How are you?

KEVIN: Fine, thanks.

(Women in the audience are directed to applaud and tear clothes off.)

NARRATOR: What statement do you wish to make with the *Son of Dances with Wolves* film?

KEVIN: Well, let's see. I guess first of all, I'd like to thank the producers, the entire cast and my family.

(Women in the audience are directed to applaud and tear clothes off.)

Oh yes, and you all, too. Brad Pitt, eat your heart out!

NARRATOR: Perhaps, you misunderstood me. But, you seem confident that you'll do better with the sequel at the Academy Awards than you did with *Dances with Wolves*.

KEVIN: Yeah, man. I thought the first one was an important film. I pushed real hard for having Indian actors speaking their own language, you know. But it's hard to

score with any sequel nowadays, but I hope this one
will get the recognition it deserves.

NARRATOR: Please tell us if you can, how did you arrive at the
title: *Son of Dances with Wolves*?

KEVIN: Well, that's easy. I went out to Sedona. I took off my
clothes. I rubbed my left cheek and then my right
cheek. Built up a little friction. All of a sudden it went
into my head. Shu manni tu tanka-o-wa-she-chew. Shu
manni tu tanka-o-wa-she-chew. Shu manni tu tanka-o-
wa-she-chew.

(Fade-up "Dances with Wolves Movie Theme.")

NARRATOR: What does it mean?

KEVIN: Ah, well . . . Dances Bad White Boy.

(Fade-out "Dances with Wolves Movie Theme.")

NARRATOR: We're here in South Dakota again at the Indian
massacre site of Wounded Knee, where the filming of a
made-for-television movie, *Lakota Woman*, has just been
completed. Actress and producer, Jane Fonda, just
walked by. Jane, oh my God, what luck. Jane, could you
tell us why you have gone to such efforts to bring this
historical event to the American viewing audiences?

JANE: Well, you know my dad always taught me to work for
the rights of those who are oppressed. You know that I
helped raise money for the Vietnamese people during
the sixties. It wasn't a popular stand, but it was right.

NARRATOR: And now here you are making an Indian movie
in South Dakota. I understand you have many Indians
working on the movie.

JANE: Yes, it was important to me to have the Indian people
telling their own story. My husband, Ted Turner, and
I feel so strongly about doing the right thing with
Indian people. You know, we work so hard to . . .

Go Braves!!!! Scalp those suckers! I mean . . . we worked hard to see that Indian issues came to the public's attention . . . *Get those tomahawks chopping! We need a home run, boys!* Excuse me, I mean, you know, Indian people have been so misunderstood!!!! *Go Braves! Go Braves! Go Braves! Go Braves!*

NARRATOR: Jane, are you all right?

JANE: Oh, yes! *Go, Ted, my brave warrior!* I mean . . . the Indian people have been so mistreated . . . and yet no one seems to listen. *Go Braves, another RBI for everyone!* I mean . . . *(She is dragged offstage kicking and screaming by a man wearing a white doctor's coat)*

JANE FONDA COMMERCIAL: Fat, fat go away, go and land on Doris Day. Just kidding folks. All you Fonda fans out there . . .

(Fade-up "Indian Radio Days Theme.")

Get off your butts and work off white guilt as well as build muscles with Jane Fonda's Indian workout special. That's right, for $39.95 you will be able to lose inches and stop overeating on the Rez. Also a small portion of your money will go towards funding a Native Weight Loss Program. With that initial payment of $39.95, you'll receive a workout tape featuring traditional dances and you'll *FEEL BETTER FAST*. Raising your self-esteem is ninety percent of the program and, just think, you'll know you've helped send a plane full of fat-free food to one of a dozen or more reservations in America, easing Natives' overeating blues, too. Act now, and you'll also receive Robert Redford's "Sun Dance Workout" tape. Get rid of that unwanted flesh, the Indian way. Call 1-800-INDIANS.

(Fade-out "Indian Radio Days Theme.")

COMMERCIAL ANNOUNCER #1 *(Southern preacher's voice)*: All you Midwest farmers, this is your lucky day! We know farmland isn't the cash cow it used to be. So if you'd like to turn your tired, your poor, your huddled barns into something worthwhile . . . Indian Bingo Make-Over Barn Kit could be the answer to your prayers. Here's how to apply. Just pick up the phone and dial 1-800-INDIANS, and we'll work out all the details. Also, each of you will receive a free bow and arrow for just trying out our thirty-day Indian Bingo Make-Over Barn Kit! Just sign on the dotted line, and an Indian representative will be on his or her way to help you get relocated—I mean, rebuilt—soon!

(Fade-up "Brandenburg Concertos.")

NARRATOR: Tonight, we have with us as our guest on *Firing Blanks*, the renowned ethnocentric—

CLAUDENE LEVI-ECHOFEMME: —ethnocritic, ethnocritic . . .

(Fade-out "Brandenburg Concertos.")

NARRATOR: —ethnocritic, Claudene Levi-Echofemme. Dr. Echofemme has ventured into Euro-tribal reservations *sine qua non* and made a most startling and axiomatic discovery. She will reveal to us an aspect of this culture that has so fascinated Indians all over this continent. Dr. Levi-Echofemme, share with us, if you will, *ad hominem*, some of this groundbreaking analysis of European and Euro-American culture.

CLAUDENE LEVI-ECHOFEMME: In my newest book, I build on the theory I introduced in *Consumer Culture*. I'm sure all you OTHERS out there are familiar with the cannibalistic tendencies of Judeo-Christian traditions.

NARRATOR: I gather, then, that you can tell us, *ex cathedra*, why Europeans prefer meat characterized by a lack of pigmentation.

CLAUDENE LEVI-ECHOFEMME: My newest book, *Professional Cannibalism*, examines this cultural phenomenon and makes connections between the pagan tradition of transubstantiation and the Europeans' phallogocentric fascination with white meat, dark meat, etc. In addition, I looked at the European anal tradition, which we all know is inferior to our own oral traditions, and found many instances of these cannibalistic ideological productions.

NARRATOR: Yes, doctor, all orality aside, can you explain this moon of the misbegotten interpretation of Eurocentric tribalism to our *pluperfect* mother-loving studio audience.

CLAUDENE LEVI-ECHOFEMME: From Jonathan Swift to Hitler to Jeffrey Dahmer, it can be assumed that whites are cannibals. Moreover, the history of colonization on this continent is already littered with examples of European cannibalism that constructed the body of the native OTHER as edible.

NARRATOR: Claudene, we all know, of course, that Hitler was a vegetarian, and I suspect, *in absentia*, that you intend to implicate the Donner party here? And by extension, *pro patria mori*, you go so far as to say, on page 232 of your new book, that Eurocentric tribal productions center on this cannibal figure culminating in its most recent incarnation—Hannibal the Cannibal Lecter.

CLAUDENE LEVI-ECHOFEMME: Indeed, Bill, unlike the Trickster in our own cultures, the European culture has constructed its own trope of the flesh eater, whatever. This anal history, as I fondly call it, began with Chris "Cannibal" Columbus, who ventured into Indian Country with his famous shopping carts: the *Pinta*, the *Nina*, the *Santa Maria*. In other words, the semiotic tracing of their postgastric condition delineates Columbus's desire for the OTHER as food source.

NARRATOR: And speaking of entrees, Ms. Doctor, you isolate, *in utero, in vitro, in victus*, the three main culinary treats that Europeans found most alluring, which they thought were *worth dying for.*

CLAUDENE LEVI-ECHOFEMME: Bill, according to Anglopologists, Indians ate corn, beans and squash. Thus, while we were cultivating a civilized form of food production, Europeans were dining weekly on consecrated flesh.

NARRATOR: Excuse me, Claudene, but haven't you ever considered your research reductive and just plain preposterous? We all know that Europeans were the ones who noticed Indian cannibalism, and they were the ones who brought, among other things—

(Audience is directed to shout "Smallpox, gonorrhea, syphilis.")

Ah . . . civilization to the wilds of this continent. Whites taught the savages the error of their ways, and even gave the Indian the wheel, *nolo contendere,* and, as Adams points out, *a propos* of this subject, puree of Park Avenue matrons was served at Gloria Steinem's fiftieth birthday party, and French feminazi Hélène Cixious lectured in a coat made from the skins of Algerian street boys. This is the literal distortion *ad nauseam* of the vegetarian body.

(Audience is directed to boo and hiss.)

CLAUDENE LEVI-ECHOFEMME: Bill, dear, be honest, lots of whites are quick to challenge my reading of this culture and its habits, and you're no different; apparently what you really don't like about my research is that I'm an outsider, an Indian with an attitude. And Bill, I'd like to point out that I recently discovered that one of my ancestors was an eighteenth-century English princess who was on a boat to America at the time of her death, so you see, the argument that I am an outsider is misinformed. Bill, really, whites are just too damn close to their own practices, literature and histories to teach, study or write about them. Their problem is that they refuse to bend and accept that Indians might have something to teach them. Only those with a history should study the history of others.

(Audience is directed to applaud. Fade-up "Brandenburg Concertos.")

FEMALE ANNOUNCER *(Strikes bell)*: Whoa, are you listening to HOT AIR or what? Yes, you are! And the time is now twenty-nine minutes past the hour. Coming up next is *Indians in Space.* But first this:

INDIAN BINGO LADY: AD-LIB BINGO ROUTINE *(Fade-up and then out "Bingo")*

(Fade-up and then out "Radio Noise" and "Hashi Mi Mali.")

NARRATOR: I'm standing outside the Hollywood Bowl. The year is 2000. I have been tipped that a famous Indian will announce, today, his decision to run for the presidency of these United States. He's approaching me now. He's wearing a cowboy hat, boots and white, Western suit. I'm going to try and speak with him. Can you tell me your name, sir—excuse me, madame?

CHIEF JUANITA JACKSON: I am Chief Juanita Jackson. I decided to announce my candidacy for the president of the United States. I thought, if Wayne Newton could come out of the closet, I could, too. He made me proud. And Wayne's just the tip of the iceberg.

(Fade-up "Danke Schoën." Men in the audience are directed to applaud and tear their clothes off.)

NARRATOR: What are you talking about? What do you mean Wayne Newton's coming out of the closet? What iceberg?

CHIEF JUANITA JACKSON: It's time for Indians to unite, rise up, put on their beads and take control.

(Fade-out "Danke Schoën." Cross-fade up "Winnebago." Men in the audience are directed to applaud and tear their clothes off again.)

NARRATOR: But what has Wayne Newton got to do with this?

CHIEF JUANITA JACKSON: Well, he's a good-looking guy. He's rich, and he's got a cute little . . . *(Pause)* mustache. He likes horses, and he's an Indian probably . . . *(Pause)* the most successful Indian in North America. Now, finally, it comes out in the newspapers, he's an Indian. So, I thought, if he could do anything, after "Danke Schoën," I could run for president!

NARRATOR: I didn't know he was an Indian!

CHIEF JUANITA JACKSON: Hell, yes! He's a Cherokee. It's been twenty years since I met a human being who wasn't a Cherokee. Now I find out that Cher says she's a halfbreed, too.

(Fade-out "Winnebago." Fade-up and then out "Half-Breed.")

NARRATOR: So what's the point to all this rhetoric? Being a Las Vegas nightclub singer hardly makes you capable of running this country. What makes you think that an unknown woman, much less an Indian woman, could run for president? And win?

CHIEF JUANITA JACKSON: What about Ronald Reagan? He was a woman—I mean a movie-star president.

NARRATOR: Yeah, well, look what happened. I mean now we've got Ronald Reagan and *Death Valley Days* running nightly on TV. Don't tell us that is good for the country.

CHIEF JUANITA JACKSON: I didn't say I could win. Indians don't necessarily show up and do what they *could* do. You see, it's just that there are Indians everywhere. You just don't know it.

(Audience is directed to applaud. Fade-up "Indian Ocean.")

COMMERCIAL ANNOUNCER #1 *(Star Trek imitation)*: From the people who brought you *Star Track: The Trail of Tears* and *Star Track II: The Wrath of Andrew Jackson*, we proudly present the new, syndicated TV series *Star Track: Caravan*. Although Graham Greene was unavailable, we have found a cast of actors who look Indian with enough makeup on to fool even the Sioux. Join Captain Pick Hard, a descendant of French fur traders; Elijah, the animated wooden Indian who longs to be human; and First Officer Number 11143, the only DIB-ed Indian onboard. Watch them travel through space and time to fight the Indian Confederacy's enemies and seek out new lands, new reservations and bravely go where no Indians have gone before.

NARRATOR: Ah, I'm standing here on Mars, the so-called Red Planet, with Harvey Little Green Man. Harvey is a biotechnician for the *Indians in Space* Project. Tell me, Harvey, how could you Indians, who were once the poorest people in the United States, finance this off-world operation?

HARVEY: BINGO.

NARRATOR: What did you say?

HARVEY: Gaming facilities, man. Lots and lots of VERY successful gaming facilities.

NARRATOR: I guess you know that there is a ship filled with pioneers from Earth on its way here as we speak. How will you and the other native peoples deal with that?

HARVEY: Damn! We came up here to establish new home-lands. We kept telling the OTHERS to stop their pol-luting ways or Mother Earth would be uninhabitable. Now, looks like we're just gonna have to build another chain of high-stakes bingo palaces and casinos so we can get away from those folks again.

(Fade-out "Indian Ocean.")

INDIAN BINGO LADY: AD-LIB FINAL BINGO ROUTINE
(Fade-up and then out "Final Bingo")

(Fade-up and then out "End of Indian Radio Days Theme.")

NARRATOR: There you have it. You've been listening to AIR/American Indian Radio's production of *Indian Radio Days*. The clock is now running. According to the 1990 Commerce Department's Census Bureau, there are thirty-eight-percent more people who chose to be recognized as American Indians today, as com-pared with the 1980 census. Oh yes, I'd like to add that my great-grandmother was an Indian, too.

END OF PLAY

A Choctaw enrolled in the Choctaw Nation of Oklahoma, LeAnne Howe has written short stories, essays, plays, film scripts, and has given literary readings throughout the United States, Japan, Jordan and, most recently, in Romania. Her work has appeared in the literary periodicals: *Story*, *Callaloo*, *Fiction International* and *Cimarron Review*, as well as in ten anthologies, such as *Spider Woman's Granddaughters* (Boston: Beacon Press, 1989), *Reinventing the Enemy's Language* (New York: W.W. Norton, 1996) and *Native American Literature* (New York: Harper Collins, 1995). Her other works for the theatre include: *The Shaman of Ok* and *Big PowWow*. Her awards include fellowships from The MacDowell Colony, The Ragdale Foundation and The Atlantic Center for the Arts. She is the mother of two sons: Joseph Craig and Randall Craig, and the grandmother of Chelsey Craig and Alyssa Craig. She currently teaches Native American literature at Grinnell College in Grinnell, Iowa, and lives with her husband.

Roxy Gordon. Born in Ballinger, Texas, 1945. Attended the University of Texas (UT) in Austin, where he edited the official student literary magazine, *Riata*. Stayed at UT way too many years, then went to the Fort Belknap Reservation in northern Montana. Born Choctaw, not knowing much about the rest of Indian America, but he wanted to find out. Finding out started then. He met the Assiniboine and Gros Ventre. He and his wife Judy Gordon lived in a one-room log cabin in Lodgepole, Montana. Together they published and produced the weekly reservation newsletter, *Ft. Belknap Notes*. Gordon went to San Diego, attended a college by the ocean where he and Judy met Richard Brautigan, Robert Creely, Jim Morrison, Ed Dorn, Clayton Eshelman and Michael McClure. At Brautigan's urging they hung out with him and literary folks in North Beach. Back to Texas. Gordon's first book, *Some Things I Did*, was published by Encino Press in Austin. Later he and Judy edited and published a music magazine called *Picking Up the Tempo*. Gordon later went to Dallas to work for the Mysterious Rhinestone Cowboy, David Allan Coe. Performed with various bands and published books as Wowapi Press with Judy. He has had work published here and there and other places. Made recordings released in England, the latest, *Smaller Circles*, was released on CD in 1997. He and Judy have two sons: J. C. Gordon and Quanah Gordon. Gordon's Assiniboine name is Too Gah Juke Juke Hoke Sheena: "First Coyote Boy."

"I've never quite left Montana. Long ago adopted into the Assiniboine John Allen family. John was tribal councilman and chairman for many years. His wife, Minerva, is a well-known poet. I've had long-time involvement with the American Indian Movement. Been to visit Peltier twice in Levenworth."

Power Pipes

spiderwoman
theater

Spiderwoman Theater. Top (left to right): Elvira Colorado, Murielle Borst, Hortensia Colorado. Bottom: Lisa Mayo, Gloria Miguel, Muriel Miguel.

author's statement

MURIEL MIGUEL

DIRECTOR, SPIDERWOMAN THEATER

This is what I remember.

We had just come from an event at the American Indian Community House. We were eight Native women and a non-Native stage manager sitting at a round table in a restaurant. We were laughing and teasing and happy to be with each other.

Sitting there looking at my sisters and my friends faces,
I thought: How beautiful!
I thought: How strong!
I thought: How noisy!
I thought: Wow, what talent!

The teasing and laughter continued. During the conversation someone said, "At this table we have actors, singers, dancers and a stage manager. Wouldn't it be great to do a project together?"

I thought: "Yes, Yes!"

Then out of nowhere came this image:

I saw rows and rows of women dancing and playing pipes. They were emerging from an arched doorway. Their dresses were glowing and shimmering. Flowers, birds and feathers were woven in their hair. They were beautiful, extraordinary creatures that had never been seen before.

They were goddesses.

And, that's how it all began.

And, that's how I remember.

In 1993 *Power Pipes* was produced by the Randolph Street Gallery in Chicago. In 1994 it was produced by Mexico Fine Art Museum Gallery of Theatre; the Walker Art Center in Minneapolis; and at the Cleveland Professional Arts Center. In 1995 *Power Pipes* received a production at the Brooklyn Academy of Music in New York; and at American Indian Community House (AICH) in New York City. The play's cast of actors/improvisors has featured:

Gloria Miguel	MESI TULI OMAI
Muriel Miguel	NAOMI FAST TRACKS
Elvira Colorado	OBSIDIAN WOMAN
Hortensia Colorado	SHE WHO OPENS HEARTS
Murielle Borst	WIND HORSE SPIRIT WARRIOR
Lisa Mayo	OWL MESSENGER

characters

MESI TULI OMAI

NAOMI FAST TRACKS

OBSIDIAN WOMAN

SHE WHO OPENS HEARTS

WIND HORSE SPIRIT WARRIOR

OWL MESSENGER

scene 1

PIPES

We hear panpipes from far off. The sound gets louder. Enter six women playing pipes. They dance to the four directions. Then they form a circle center stage. They disperse to their respective places on stage. Lights go down. Mesi Tuli Omai is on the platform upstage right. She wears a moon headdress. She turns slowly as moonlight comes up. All make sounds in the dark. Primordial wailing, crying.

scene 2

COSMOS

a) invocation

Naomi Fast Tracks runs to center stage. She looks out into the cosmos. She pulls Obsidian Woman to her and they look out together. Obsidian Woman then pulls She Who Opens Hearts to her, and Naomi Fast Tracks then pulls Wind Horse Spirit Warrior to her. Mesi Tuli Omai pulls Owl Messenger to her.

b) drone

They all look out together. They begin a drone. They receive the drone from the cosmos. The drone is pulled into their bodies. Out of their mouths come words:

WIND HORSE SPIRIT WARRIOR AND SHE WHO OPENS HEARTS *(Together)*: We, we, we, we, we, we . . . *(They move around the stage, jumping, whirling, turning, pulling the energy from the cosmos into their space. They continue their words:)*

NAOMI FAST TRACKS AND OWL MESSENGER *(Together)*: We look, we scavenge, we find, we gather. . . . Look, scavenge, find, gather . . .

MESI TULI OMAI AND OBSIDIAN WOMAN *(Together)*: We put the earth back together, we make the truth about ourselves.

(Mesi Tuli Omai, Owl Messenger and Naomi Fast Tracks go to perches. Obsidian Woman crosses upstage right behind ramp. She Who Opens Hearts and Wind Horse Spirit Warrior exit. Owl Messenger sets an arrow in the center of the circle.)

scene 3

INTRODUCTIONS

Each actor tells who she is, what her medicine is. She does so with sound and gestures. The gestures are repeated by everyone outside the circle. All these introductions overlap. Obsidian Woman slowly crawls and scratches to center stage. Her skirt is over her head. She is wearing large gloves, their backs painted red, with stiff brushes in the palms. All are scratching. Mesi Tuli Omai is growling. Obsidian Woman enters the circle. Drum in short spurts, then it stops.

OBSIDIAN WOMAN: I dig.

(Drum, rattle.)

MESI TULI OMAI: Now!

(Drum, rattle.)

Now!

OBSIDIAN WOMAN: I dig. I dig. I search, and I reveal.

(She takes her skirt away from her head. Scratching stops.)

MESI TULI OMAI: Now!

(Drum, rattle.)

OBSIDIAN WOMAN: I carry the energy of my ancestors
And draw the energy around me.
I dig. I dig. I search, and I reveal.
I dig. I dig. I search, and I reveal.

MESI TULI OMAI:
Nae
E mis penne
nae.

(She is descending the platforms upstage right. At each level there is a drum rattle. As she rolls into the circle, rainforest sounds begin. Voice begins as Mesi Tuli Omai stands. She shows blood.)

Enough!
(Blows dart upstage) Unite with Kuna Yalla!
(Blows dart stage left) Children destroying themselves.
(Rain-forest sounds) Nourish, protect the seven generations.

(Blows dart downstage) Listen, balance.
(Blows dart down right) Answer the ancient voices.
Angua.
My name is Mesi Tuli Omai *(She starts to dance. Drum
 begins)*
Spirit of the rain forest.
My medicine is love.
Love is my power.
I heal with love.
I blow darts of love into the minds,
Hearts and souls of the people.
(Keening begins) Gather together.
Honor the spirits.
Sing to the spirits.
Dance to the spirits.
Pray to the spirits.

*(She dances to perch. Wind Horse Spirit Warrior dances in.
She carries a dream catcher.)*

WIND HORSE SPIRIT WARRIOR: I am Wind Horse Spirit Warrior.
 I live in between the worlds.
 I go in and out of the spirit world. *(Dances in and out of
  the circle)*
 I am the past, the present, and the future.
 I am the guardian of the spirit world.
 My medicine is my dreams.
 My breath can devastate,
 Destroy and heal.
 I run. I listen. I seek the truth. *(War whoops. All make war
  whoops)*
 I am Wind Horse Spirit Warrior. *(She dances upstage
  center)*

*(She Who Opens Hearts enters, slithering onto the stage,
into the circle. She eats everything. She pulls a heart apart.*

She blows into the heart in four directions. All make the same gesture. Whistling and blowing sounds.)

SHE WHO OPENS HEARTS: I gather all the eyes, hearts, mouths, embryos, bones, wombs, hearts. I am nourished. I am fed with the strength of creation. I am She Who Opens Hearts. This is my medicine. I am She Who Opens Hearts. This is my medicine.

(Owl Messenger stands stage left.)

OWL MESSENGER: When the darkness hits my eyelids, I awake.
I am Owl Messenger
Standing behind the rainbow.
Behind the colors of the rainbow, I see the layers.
I am here. I see the layers.
I'm here to bring the messages from layer to layer.
I go to the place where everyone speaks the same
    language.
I blow the messages to all.
Then I take my needle attached to a long sinew, and
    I begin
To connect the layers, breathing the messages into the
    cosmos.

(She sews as if she is using a huge needle. All sew with sounds of needles going through skin. These are connecting sounds.)

I am Owl Messenger. I am male and female.
I bring the messages from those passed on
To the living, to the future, to all creatures.
I connect up, down, diagonally.
My needle, going between the layers, connecting,
    blowing the messages.
Then I pull, causing the layers to converge
Until they are all in one concentrated spot.

Blow and pull,
Blow and pull,
Bringing the messages together.
This is my medicine.

(Naomi Fast Tracks dances a woman's traditional dance, holding a stool. She dances into the circle.)

NAOMI FAST TRACKS: It's the rubbing.
It's the rubbing.
I hear without words.
I hear with my hands without words.
It's the rubbing.
I reach out.
I rub the heart.
It's the rubbing.

(They all rub together.)

It's the rubbing.
Naomi
Naomi Fast Tracks, that's me.
My medicine is to hear with my hands.
My large hands reach out and rub the heart.
I hear.
It's the rubbing.

scene 4

PAN DULCE

OBSIDIAN WOMAN: Me. *(She brings a stool downstage center and stands in back of it)* Me. Me. Me. *(She sits)*
SHE WHO OPENS HEARTS: Meeeeeeeeee. We were going to have tea. I was sitting in the living room.
OBSIDIAN WOMAN: I was in the bedroom.

SHE WHO OPENS HEARTS: We were going to have tea with pan dulce.

OBSIDIAN WOMAN: She came in and asked me if I was going to have tea.

SHE WHO OPENS HEARTS: "Do you want to have tea?" She said, "I will be right there."

OBSIDIAN WOMAN: I said, "I'll be right there," but I really didn't want to be right there. I was upset because she came in and bothered me.

SHE WHO OPENS HEARTS: I arranged the pan dulce on a plate and put it on the table. I called her again. I called her three times.

OBSIDIAN WOMAN: I guess I wanted coffee, but I figured since she hadn't made coffee, I would take the tea.

SHE WHO OPENS HEARTS: Well, I am not going to call her again. (She moves into the circle with a stool and sits) She knows the tea is out here. She'll come when she feels like it. That is what always happens, you tell her and tell her, and she comes when she feels like it.

OBSIDIAN WOMAN: Probably going to come in and call me again. I wish she'd stop calling me. I'll come when I'm ready.

SHE WHO OPENS HEARTS: I sat down and started to drink my tea. The pan dulce was there on the table.

OBSIDIAN WOMAN: I didn't want any pan dulce anyway.

SHE WHO OPENS HEARTS: She came out. She said, "Where's my tea?"

OBSIDIAN WOMAN: Where's my tea? (She goes to She Who Opens Hearts)

SHE WHO OPENS HEARTS: It's over there!

OBSIDIAN WOMAN: You don't have to snap.

SHE WHO OPENS HEARTS: What do you mean?

OBSIDIAN WOMAN: It's over there. . . . It's over there. . . . It's over there.

(She chases She Who Opens Hearts from her stool.)

SHE WHO OPENS HEARTS: You don't have to snap. . . . You don't have to snap.

OBSIDIAN WOMAN: I don't have to snap.

SHE WHO OPENS HEARTS: You snap all the time. Snap, snap, snap.

(She chases Obsidian Woman from her stool. She sits.)

OBSIDIAN WOMAN: I snap. I'm not going to drink my tea here.

(She goes to her stool)

SHE WHO OPENS HEARTS: She steps on me. She just doesn't realize it.

OBSIDIAN WOMAN: I will just lie down, read my book and have my own thoughts. She is probably sitting out there sulking.

SHE WHO OPENS HEARTS: I took the pan dulce into the kitchen, slammed it down on the counter. Fuck it! She is always doing this.

(All scream.)

OBSIDIAN WOMAN: I was very angry, very, very angry. I had all this rage inside of me.

(All make anger sounds, stamp feet.)

SHE WHO OPENS HEARTS: I was angry. I was really very angry.

OBSIDIAN WOMAN: I am not going to let it bother me. I am going to read my book.

SHE WHO OPENS HEARTS: I stuffed all the pan dulce back into the bag.

OBSIDIAN WOMAN: She can put all her pan dulce back into the bag. She always does this to me. Now she is not going to talk to me.

SHE WHO OPENS HEARTS: I wouldn't eat the pan dulce. I stuffed myself with cookies instead. *(She goes to Obsidian Woman)* I hate it. Why can't I say, "Come out here?"
OBSIDIAN WOMAN: Leave me alone.

(She Who Opens Hearts puts Obsidian Woman on her lap.)

SHE WHO OPENS HEARTS: What is your problem? I'm always afraid there is going to be a split.

(Obsidian Woman falls to the floor.)

OBSIDIAN WOMAN: There is silence between us.
SHE WHO OPENS HEARTS: There is silence between us.
OBSIDIAN WOMAN: Can you hear the silence? Can you hear the silence? Can you hear the silence?
OBSIDIAN WOMAN AND SHE WHO OPENS HEARTS *(Together)*: Can you hear it?
ALL *(Outside the circle, watching)*: Make the offering.

(Obsidian Woman and She Who Opens Hearts take orange flowers from their hair and place them in the circle. Wind Horse Spirit Warrior shakes the rattle. Obsidian Woman and She Who Opens Hearts return to their perches.)

scene 5

GOTCHA

WIND HORSE SPIRIT WARRIOR: I've got you.
ALL: Gotcha!
WIND HORSE SPIRIT WARRIOR: Remember. It's time.
Remember the stone.
You sweat, you climb.
You sweat, the stone sweats against your fingertips.
Touch the stone. Remember the color.
The turquoise color? I've got you.

ALL: Gotcha!

WIND HORSE SPIRIT WARRIOR: You sweat, you climb, you
　　sweat, you climb.
　　Womblike travel to the heart of the stone
　　Eye to eye
　　Eye to eye.
　　Centuries a sentinel, alive
　　Eye to eye,
　　Eye to eye—I've got you!

ALL: Gotcha!

WIND HORSE SPIRIT WARRIOR: Make the offering.

ALL: Make the offering

WIND HORSE SPIRIT WARRIOR: Remember.
　　Homage extended.
　　Homage received.
　　There is a growling in your soul, now that we've met
　　Eye to glowing eyes.
　　Got you!

ALL: Gotcha!

scene 6

PICNIC WITH 49ERS

*In the circle there are only the two flowers, but the women see all
sorts of food offerings. They are very excited about being fed. They
have a picnic.*

WIND HORSE SPIRIT WARRIOR: Fry bread.

　　*(All come down from their perches. They bring their stools
　　and bags. They put out a blanket.)*

SHE WHO OPENS HEARTS: Napoles, Gorditas. I've got Gorditas.

OWL MESSENGER: Food, food, food.

MESI TULI OMAI: A picnic.

OBSIDIAN WOMAN: Jalapenos.

MESI TULI OMAI: Strawberries.

SHE WHO OPENS HEARTS: Gorditas.

NAOMI FAST TRACKS: Cauliflowers—artichokes.

OWL MESSENGER: Really good.

NAOMI FAST TRACKS: Roses.

WIND HORSE SPIRIT WARRIOR: Bananas.

MESI TULI OMAI: Look what I have in this box!

NAOMI FAST TRACKS: Stuffed roasted chicken.

SHE WHO OPENS HEARTS: Gorditas. Napoles.

WIND HORSE SPIRIT WARRIOR: Bananas.

MESI TULI OMAI: Delicious red strawberries, dipped in chocolate.

OBSIDIAN WOMAN: They remembered.

ALL: Strawberries.

NAOMI FAST TRACKS: I didn't get strawberries. Nobody gave me a strawberry. *(She passes out strawberries)* I haven't had a strawberry
In centuries.
Strawberries
Strawberries
Hey.
It's party time.
It's party time.
Get down tonight.
It's party time.

(All get out the drum. 49er songs are Native fun songs. There are English verses, which follow.)

LEAD: Eh - ya - eh - yo
　　　Yo - eh - hi - ya.
ALL: Eh - ya - eh - yo
　　　Yo - eh - hi - ya
　　　Eh - ya- eh - yo
　　　Yo - eh - hi - ya
　　　Eh - ya - eh - yo

Yo - eh - hi - ya
Eh - ya - eh - yo
Yo - oh
Way - ya - ha,
Way - ya - ha - yo.

Riding the subway,
Our eyes met.
You played the fiddle,
And I flipped.
Now here I am, a
Prisoner of Love.
Hi - ya
Way - ya - ha, Way - ya - ha - yo.

You said you'd have my ring, dear
Not even a zircon.
You say I'm bossy.
So are you.
My Chiefy Wifey,
Hi - ya
Way - ya - ha, Way - ya - ha - yo.

Hey, old man, where are you?
I'll wait for you
Till I'm very old.
In the meantime,
I'll love a younger one.
Oooooooooooooo . . .
LEAD: Just kidding
Hi - ya
Way - ya - ha Way - ya - ha.
Forgive me, don't leave me.
It was a mistake, I'm sorry.
I'd rather bleed than hurt you,
Sweetheart.

ALL: Send kisses.

LEAD: Kiss, kiss, kiss, kiss.
Hi - ya
Way - ya - ha, Way - ya - ha.
I saw a rainbow, and stars fell.
You said you loved me.
Why'd you lie?
You passed me with a white woman.
My heart I gave,
But what the hell.
Hi - ya
Way - ya - ha, Way - ya - ha - yo.

(Owl Messenger dances.)

Eh - ya eh - yo
Yo - eh - hi - ya
Eh - ya - eh - yo
Yo - eh - hi - ya
Eh - ya - eh - yo
Yo - oh
Way - ya - ha, Way - ya - ha - yo.
I used to be a raving beauty.
You can see
I'm growing older.
I surely miss not snagging
The cute ones any more.
Hi - ya
Way - ya - ha, Way - ya - ha - yo.

(Owl Messenger dances across stage to upstage left.)

scene 7

POSSUM STORY

OWL MESSENGER: I propose a toast.

ALL: A toast, a toast.

OWL MESSENGER: A toast to the offerers.

WIND HORSE SPIRIT WARRIOR: A toast to the rememberers.

SHE WHO OPENS HEARTS: To the forgotten ones.

MESI TULI OMAI: To the givers.

NAOMI FAST TRACKS: A toast to the cooks.

ALL: Yeah.

(All toast with whatever is in their hands. Owl Messenger drinks and transforms into Possum.)

OWL MESSENGER *(Flirtatiously)*: I'm beautiful. Look at how my tail glistens in the sunlight. *(She lies on stage right stairs)* Starry, starry night.

ALL: Hairy, hairy man.

OWL MESSENGER: Starry, starry night.

ALL: Hairy, hairy man.

OWL MESSENGER: Hey, hairy, hairy man. What are you doing here? I haven't seen you for millennia. Not since you stole my bushy tail and gave it to your wife. And she never even wore it. *(Singing)* Starry, starry night. When is a possum not a possum?

MESI TULI OMAI: Don't know myself.

OWL MESSENGER: I must transform to my higher self. *(She goes to center stage)* When the wed, wed wobin goes bob, bob, bobbin' along.

ALL: That's her higher self?

OWL MESSENGER: A possum is not a possum when she is not enrolled. When she is disenfranchised.

MESI TULI OMAI: Does she have a federal number?

WIND HORSE SPIRIT WARRIOR: But is she a possum over the border?

OWL MESSENGER: It was tough when I was a little possum. The other little possums said things like, "Your mother is not enrolled, and your father is a Central American possum."

WIND HORSE SPIRIT WARRIOR: She's a Spanish-speaking possum.

OBSIDIAN WOMAN: Alien, alien, alien.

SHE WHO OPENS HEARTS: Under that fur . . .

NAOMI FAST TRACKS: Her back is wet.

SHE WHO OPENS HEARTS: She must be a wetback.

OBSIDIAN WOMAN: Alien, alien, alien.

OWL MESSENGER: So you're not a real possum. But my heart is possum. I was brought up possum.

SHE WHO OPENS HEARTS: Her mother is a Chihuahua.

OBSIDIAN WOMAN: Alien, alien, alien.

WIND HORSE SPIRIT WARRIOR: She's a dog-ass possum.

OWL MESSENGER (*She sings and dances the Muskrat Ramble*): I'm part muskrat.

(All start to leave the picnic.)

WIND HORSE SPIRIT WARRIOR: That's not a traditional possum dance.

MESI TULI OMAI: Is that a Rappahannock dance?

NAOMI FAST TRACKS: It's not traditional.

(Possum transforms back into Owl Messenger.)

OWL MESSENGER: Is the picnic over?

ALL: Yup! Picnic's over.

OWL MESSENGER: Where's everybody going?

ALL: We're leaving.
Home.

(Blanket and drum are removed.)

NAOMI FAST TRACKS (*Looking at everyone*): You can stay. You can stay, too. (*Comes to center stage*)

scene 8

MADDU

NAOMI FAST TRACKS: Maddu was a little girl.
Maddu was a pretty little girl.
She had a chunky little body.
She had long legs and long arms.
Maddu had straight brown hair.
She wore it just below her ears with bangs.
Maddu was a little brown girl.
Maddu had great big cheeks.
And brown round eyes.
Maddu wore high, white shoes.
Dirty
Maddu wore cast-off clothing.
She was a quiet girl
Never talked.
All of Maddu's thoughts were in herself.
All the borders of her life stopped at her front door.
Maddu had a friend
A real friend.
Maddu and her friend always knew each other
Always knew each other.
They even had the same haircut.
They played, they sang.
When her friend came within her borders
Maddu's borders stretched out beyond that house.
Maddu, her friend
Maddu, her friend
One day her friend went away.
That little friend was moving beyond her borders.
Her little friend came to the house
Into her house.
They sat on a white kitchen chair
Maddu and her little friend
Talking about going away

Out of Maddu's boundaries
Outside her front door.
They said, "Say good-bye."
Maddu knew, but she didn't know.
Oh, Maddu, Maddu.
Next morning it was the same
Every morning the same.
She got up
Every morning, no different.
Her little friend came in the front door.
Maddu's little friend
Put into her hand
A little blue, wool purse
Two little gold balls that made the clasp.
She opened it, and inside
There was something that belonged to him.
He said, "Take it."
"Take it and hide it."
"Maddu, take it and hide it."
This morning was not like every morning.
"When they find what is in the purse,
You will have to come and see me.
You will have to come and see me."
"Promise, Maddu."
"Maddu, promise."

WIND HORSE SPIRIT WARRIOR: Promise.

NAOMI FAST TRACKS: I promise.

WIND HORSE SPIRIT WARRIOR: Promise.
      Promise forever.

scene 9

PROMISE I

WIND HORSE SPIRIT WARRIOR: I see a little boy and a little girl.
      They had many exciting adventures. The boy taught the
      girl how to play and that it was OK to be a kid.

They had a special bond.

One day, the boy's mother had to go far away. She went to the outer realms and wasn't coming back. The little boy stood at the edge and watched his mother go. He said, "'Bye, Mommy, 'bye." He was so confused, he didn't understand the little girl understood. She knew. She stood next to him on the edge and took his hand.

NAOMI FAST TRACKS: I promise.

WIND HORSE SPIRIT WARRIOR: Now I don't have anybody.

NAOMI FAST TRACKS: Maddu, little boy, little girl, promise. *(This is said all through Wind Horse Spirit Warrior's monologue)*

WIND HORSE SPIRIT WARRIOR: Don't worry, I'll always love you.

I'll never leave you. Promise.

Promise forever.

The two friends grew up, and no matter what happened they always had a special bond. Sometimes she goes on a special adventure without him. He watches her go. He waves and says, "'Bye-'bye," as she walks away. They stop and remember that they will always belong to each other.

They are one heart, one soul.

They promise.

(Mesi Tuli Omai leaves the upstage arch.)

ALL: Hey, where are you going?

WIND HORSE SPIRIT WARRIOR: I thought this was pretty heavy but . . .

OBSIDIAN WOMAN: She doesn't know where she is going.

WIND HORSE SPIRIT WARRIOR: That's nothing new.

(Mesi Tuli Omai enters again.)

SHE WHO OPENS HEARTS: Here she comes.

OBSIDIAN WOMAN: Don't look at her.

(Mesi Tuli Omai crosses to Naomi Fast Tracks, who is on a blanket.)

MESI TULI OMAI: Shoo, shoo, shoo.

(She grabs Naomi Fast Track's blanket. They fight over it. Mesi Tuli Omai finally gives it up.)

I don't need your old blanket. My stool that's all I need. *(She travels around the circle as if it is many different terrains)*

scene 10

CUNA STORY

Mesi Tuli Omai scurries across the upstage left archway three times.

MESI TULI OMAI: Tough road.
    I'll never make it. All alone. Crashed. Smashed.
    All alone. *(She crosses to center stage with her stool and sits. Music recording of panpipes)*
    I found a way to escape. Just stay in one place. Just sit down in one place, close your eyes and go off.
    It was hot in the city the summer I got my first moon. On my eleventh birthday.
    That same week my only friend was struck and killed by a car.
    I was so sad. . . .
    I sat by my window, closed my eyes and went off on a faraway trip. *(Droning sound)* I traveled many miles, all the way to Naragana, on the San Blas Islands, where my father came from, where the Cuna people would have a special celebration for me. A traditional healing ceremony for me. There I found myself naked, sitting in a clay tub of water. Men and women were dancing around me. A special woman cut my hair, another woman poured water over me.

(All enter carrying stools. Three sit facing the circle; three with their backs to it.)

The men went into the rain forest to bless the polly-walla tree and to take the fruit that would make the blue dye. My face and body were covered in blue dye. My father took me around the island, he blew a large conch shell. Ami Oma Sisquat. *(She makes the sound of the conch)*

(Wind Horse Spirit Warrior and Owl Messenger play pipes.)

"Today my daughter is a woman. Ami Oma Sisquat. Today she is ready to be a wife." Then everybody came to my saipu to dance and drink Chi-chi, a ceremonial drink.

(All make traveling sounds.)

Home again, sitting by the window, I thought, "My life will be different now."

(All wail. This scene turns into the subway scene. During the last speech, everyone has moved into the center and is now in position for the next scene, the subway sequence.)

scene 11

SUBWAY

Naomi Fast Tracks begins the sound of the motor of the subway train. Wind Horse Spirit Warrior runs to stage left of everyone, straphanging. Everyone sways together as the subway jolts to a stop. She Who Opens Hearts makes the sound of the train screeching around a corner. Owl Messenger makes the sound of the doors

opening, while Obsidian Woman makes the station announce-
ment. Mesi Tuli Omai crosses downstage, then crosses back up to
her stool. While she is downstage, Wind Horse Spirit Warrior
crosses to her stool stage right. This sequence is repeated three
times. Everybody leaves the subway except She Who Opens
Hearts. Mesi Tuli Omai starts to exit, realizes that it is the wrong
stop, returns, sits, becomes a stranger.

scene 12

RAPE STORY

part one

SHE WHO OPENS HEARTS: That guy's been staring at me since
I got on. Maybe it's just my imagination.

MESI TULI OMAI: Humph. *(She changes seat on subway with*
back to She Who Opens Hearts)

SHE WHO OPENS HEARTS: He's still staring at me. There's no
one else in this car except him, that woman and me.

(Warning sounds, drumsticks.)

I should have got off at the last stop.
Where did those three other guys come from?

(More warning sounds.)

Thank God there are three more people on this end.

(Warning sounds.)

They are walking toward me. They are sitting down next
to me. I gotta get off. No, don't! Lady, help! Help me!

(She Who Opens Hearts tries to fight off the men who sud-
denly swarm around her as Mesi Tuli Omai leaves car. She

Who Opens Hearts struggles, but is pushed to the floor of the subway car. Rattles and drums mark the accelerating pace of She Who Opens Hearts's terror as pantomime gang rape begins.)

scene 12

RAPE STORY

part two

Scene freezes. She Who Opens Hearts gets up. Mesi Tuli Omai enters. They sit in original subway positions. They clap to signify repeat of scene up to the attack. This time Mesi Tuli Omai (as the passenger) does not exit, but instead comes to the aid of She Who Opens Hearts. Together they pantomime fighting off the gang.

MESI TULI OMAI: Stop! Help! Police!
ALL: RAAAAPE!!!!!!

(She Who Opens Hearts and Mesi Tuli Omai exit and freeze. Two beats. Both clap.)

scene 12

RAPE STORY

part three

Scene begins for the third time, but now four deities enter scene, joining Mesi Tuli Omai and She Who Opens Hearts. All look directly into audience.

SHE WHO OPENS HEARTS: They are sitting down next to me.
   I gotta get off!!!!
WIND HORSE SPIRIT WARRIOR: Do you believe the warning?
OBSIDIAN WOMAN: Listen to your warning.
NAOMI FAST TRACKS: Who are your protectors?

OWL MESSENGER: Did you ignore the messages?

MESI TULI OMAI: Answer the voices.

(Repeat five deities' warnings.)

SHE WHO OPENS HEARTS: If I could just make it to that pole.
Oh no, no, no—they are trying to pry my fingers loose!
(As deities offer support with hands and voices) Oh, no you
don't, you motherfuckers! I'll crush your fucking balls!
I'll kill you!!

OWL MESSENGER: Ding, ding! *(End of sequence)*

*(Repeat of first subway sequence, i.e., sound of motor, of
train, of screeching, of doors opening and of conductor
announcement. This last is the cue for Wind Horse Spirit
Warrior to rise and exit the subway car. She freezes at Mesi
Tuli Omai's voice, staring out at the audience.)*

scene 13

SONG AND DANCE

MESI TULI OMAI: You wander around on your own little cloud.
When you don't see the why or the wherefore
You walk on me when we both disagree
'Cause to reason is not what you care for.

ALL: Shut up! *(All turn sharply to Mesi Tuli Omai)* I've heard
it all a million times before. Take off your coat, lie
down and close the door. Shut up!!!

*(They all move their stools to the perches. The sound of the
chorus of "Don't Sleep in the Subway" comes on. They all
dance in place for one chorus, then they move into a Rockette
chorus line, Busby Berkeley style. They then break up and
begin a variation of women's traditional dancing for one
chorus. They then get their stools and return to their center*

177

stage subway positions. They begin the subway sound sequence again, leaving Wind Horse Spirit Warrior for their perch positions. Wind Horse Spirit Warrior moves to center.)

scene 14

QUEEN STORY

WIND HORSE SPIRIT WARRIOR: All hail, great master! Grave sir, hail!
I am Ariel. I come to answer, to fly,
To swim, to dive into the fire,
To ride on the curled clouds.

(All begin to tease her out loud.)

ALL: Hey, this ain't fair!

(All continue to tease. Wind Horse Spirit Warrior complains about her treatment to Owl Messenger.)

OWL MESSENGER: Oh, let her talk!
WIND HORSE SPIRIT WARRIOR: I'm a tempest without a teacup,
I'm a tragedienne without a tragedy,
An empress without an empire,
A jewel without a crown,
A rule without a ruler,
NAOMI FAST TRACKS *(Laughing)*: A rule without a ruler?
WIND HORSE SPIRIT WARRIOR: I was once a ruler of a vast queendom.
I was tall, I had legs that came to here. *(Indicates chin)*
My lips were ruby red,
I had midnight black hair that ended in curls.
I was a knockout, if I do say so myself.
ALL *(Overlapping)*: If she does say so herself. . . . She'd better say it, 'cause no one else will. . . . Get real. . . .

WIND HORSE SPIRIT WARRIOR: I had men who would die for me. Men had multiple orgasms just looking at me.

(Side comments are teasing and sneering.)

My skin was like silk on steel.
And, when I would walk, rose petals were thrown at my feet.
I took baths in milk,
And when I woke up in the morning my breath didn't even smell.
My palace was like . . . Did you ever see the 1970 movie *Camelot?*
Like that, but better!
(She breaks into song) "If ever I would leave you . . ."

(All burst into song, mockingly.)

Shut up!!
When I traveled, I was carried on a long, silk, red divan.
With red pillows and red fringe.
Did you ever see Cecil B. DeMille's version of *Cleopatra?*
It looked like that, but better!
Legions of men sang to me. *(She sings a snatch of an* Aida *aria)*

SOMEONE: That's an opera.

WIND HORSE SPIRIT WARRIOR: *AIDA!*

> *(She hops up on a platform)* See, now I'm far away! *(She sings another stanza and then moves halfway down the ramp)*
> Now it's getting closer! *(Sings another snatch, and then runs down to center stage and sings in full voice, hopping triumphantly around the stage)*
> Then, unfortunately, I fell in love with a man who was already taken by another, and we vowed to love each other for eternity. Unfortunately he died, dead, dead, dead, DAMN! I was so heartbroken that I

bought a secret, painless, potent potion. I put on my best dress, threw a party, laid in my bed, and before I drank the poison I yelled, "Love, give me strength!" Did you ever see the 1968 Franco Zeffirelli film, *Romeo and Juliet?* Like that, but better!

I had one hell of a funeral!

I flew up to meet the Creator!!! *(She runs upstage onto center platform)*

The Creator said, "You have two choices—everything else is taken. You can be a legendary rock star who eventually dies fat in his own excrement, or you can be a cute, attractive, good-looking, poor, little girl from the Native persuasion—because to say Indian isn't politically correct."

So I jumped into this body, and I looked around.

OWL MESSENGER: So what's the point?

WIND HORSE SPIRIT WARRIOR: I hate being a kid! And I can't wait till I get the fuck out of here!

(All laugh uproariously at her. They all laugh together. Then a transformation begins. All suddenly stop laughing except for She Who Opens Hearts. She has been caught laughing last. She has been picked. She is wrong.)

scene 15

SHAME STORIES

Now She Who Opens Hearts leaves platform, moves to center, faces upstage, then downstage, then faces upstage again.

SHE WHO OPENS HEARTS: OH, NO! Oh, no! Oh, shame, shame! *(Moving upstage right)* Shame, oh, shame, oh, shame! *(Moves, circling backward across the stage. She comes to rest upstage left, and stands erect but seems to be vibrating jerkily as if being shaken. She circles around, and jerks back into first erect position)* Eh, eh, eh. I've been used. I've been taken. *(She covers her breasts and genitals with her hands. She stands erect again, vibrates jerkily again)* Shame. Shame! I've been used. I've been taken.

(As she speaks these words, Mesi Tuli Omai enters in darkness, sets her stool outside of the circle and sits facing upstage, watching She Who Opens Hearts.)

MESI TULI OMAI: If I sit like this, you only see my back. Nobody will know what color I am. *(She shows her left hand over the top of her head, then shows her right hand over her shoulder)* Now you know I'm not white. I'll show my face, but I won't look at them. *(She turns clockwise on the stool, eyes unfocused, then back)*

SHE WHO OPENS HEARTS: Shame. Shame. Shame. *(She crawls up on ramp)* Eh, eh, eh.
India mecca mecca
India mecca mecca
No that's not me, that's not me.
Yo no soy India mecca, mecca.
(Crawls into circle) Shame, shame, oh, shame! *(Covers herself, trying to hide)*
Can't breathe
Can't breathe
Pieces, pieces, pedacitos, pedacitos.
You've broken me up in pieces, in pieces.
Can't breathe, can't breathe. *(She hides herself)*

MESI TULI OMAI: Squawk

SHE WHO OPENS HEARTS: India mecca mecca.

(Mesi Tuli Omai crosses up to behind She Who Opens Hearts.)

MESI TULI OMAI: I hear them. Squawk. Squawk. *(Slapping herself)* She's dark.
She's dumb.

(Other body slaps come from outside circle.)

Don't let her in.
Don't look at her.
Throw her out.
She's black.
She has no talent.
Don't work with her.
She doesn't exist.

(Mesi Tuli Omai freezes, hanging from her waist. She Who Opens Hearts freezes, hiding head. Owl Messenger crosses to downstage center.)

OWL MESSENGER: I would like you to meet some people that are very important to me. *(Pointing to a spot downstage center)* This person is a psychic and a visionary who sends her visions into the future and beyond. *(She looks to stage left door and then crosses to upstage center ramp)* This person is an artist, cook, storyteller. She is sweet, kind, gentle, loving and very sad.

(All run across and become the other person.)

It has been said of this person that he brings a large light into the room. He is charismatic, handsome, and he has a beautiful smile. And he is a full-blooded Indian. I'm very proud of these people.

(The three deities begin to sing "Beezebug.")

OBSIDIAN WOMAN: Shame! *(She stops their singing)*

(Mesi Tuli Omai makes a hissing panther growl and a panther clawing motion at the same time.)

SHE WHO OPENS HEARTS: Sal Rafaela
Sal, salgrande chiquita.

MESI TULI OMAI: She doesn't need love.

    Hate her.

    What is she?

    She must be an Indian. *(She laughs)*

OWL MESSENGER: Shame, shame!

OWL MESSENGER, MESI TULI OMAI AND SHE WHO OPENS HEARTS: Shame!

(All together. All slump.)

MESI TULI OMAI: Love me.

    Love me.

    Love me. *(Takes terrified gulp of air after each exclamation)*

    Hate her, hate, hate, hate.

    She's no good.

ALL: Shame!!!

SHE WHO OPENS HEARTS: Habla Rafaela. Speak. Con esa Voz. Dilo todo estuvistes. Tell it all.

OWL MESSENGER: Beezebug, beezebug.

OWL MESSENGER, MESI TULI OMAI AND SHE WHO OPENS HEARTS: Beezebug, beezebug!

(All cross to stage right, chanting—they continue to chant during Owl Messenger's speech below.)

OWL MESSENGER: You're my little keeter. *(Crosses to stage right)* You're light, you're pretty, you're smart. Beezebug, Beezebug. I gave you a wonderful grandmother. She's an Indian. You can go anywhere. You can be better than me. You don't have to go into service like me. Black man, I no longer deny you. I love you. *(She crosses stage left)*

(The next three speeches are spoken almost simultaneously.)

SHE WHO OPENS HEARTS: Yo soy, I am without shame
India mecca mecca
See my shame.
See my Indianness.
See it come out of here
Out of here.
This is Indian.
And this
India mecca mecca
India mecca mecca.

MESI TULI OMAI: Don't, don't.
Put the pieces back together.
I love myself, I'll heal myself.
I don't need your love.
I love myself.
I'll heal myself.
I don't need your love.
I'll heal myself.
I love you.
I love you.
I'll put the pieces back together.
I'll heal myself.
I love you.

OWL MESSENGER: I would like you to meet my grandfather, John Wesley Spencer, born 1848 during slavery. A kind, honest, hardworking man who provided for his family. His family was his life. His family was his life.

(The three deities clap; others bow. All position themselves as in a square dance. Obsidian Woman, Wind Horse Spirit Warrior and Naomi Fast Tracks come forward, exchange places with others; all face audience.)

scene 16

COLUMBUS

OWL MESSENGER: The *Nina*!

(*Naomi Fast Tracks holds up a paper boat, the kind children make for hats.*)

MESI TULI OMAI: The *Pinta*!

(*Owl Messenger holds up a second paper boat.*)

SHE WHO OPENS HEARTS: The *Santa Maria*!

(*Wind Horse Spirit Warrior holds up a third paper boat.*)

OWL MESSENGER: Five hundred years. The Old Boy got lost.
SHE WHO OPENS HEARTS: Genocide!

(*They crumple the paper boats and throw them on the floor. Wind Horse Spirit Warrior spits on them. Everyone disperses.*)

scene 17

DRUM PREPARATION

Obsidian Woman puts blanket down center stage. Everybody assembles at center with stools. Naomi Fast Tracks carries drum and puts it on the blanket. All sit around the drum doing various things in preparation for singing. They settle. They sing a Kiowa war dance.

scene 18

DRUM

KIOWA WAR DANCE

(MADALINE HENRY)

WAY - YA - YA - HEH - YA - HEH - YO
WAY - YA - YA - HO - WAY - YO - HEH - YEAH +
3 - YO.

WAY - YA - YA - HEH - YA - HEH - YO
WAY - YA - YA - HO - WAY - YO - HEH - YEAH +3
- YO.

WAY - YA - YA - HEH - YO
WAY - YA - YA - HEH - YO
WAY - YA - YA - HO - WAY - YO - HEH - YEAH +3
- YO.

YO - WAY - HA
WAY - YA - EH - HEH - YA
HO - WAY - YO - HEH - YEAH +3 - YO.

*(Repeat last two stanzas. When that is complete, they return
to their perches, where we find Mesi Tuli Omai sitting
upstage center, singing along with her Walkman—Paul
Ortega's "Trail Song." Naomi Fast Tracks is seated on perch
stage right of her.)*

scene 19

JUMPING ARROW

Mesi Tuli Omai walks around in the circle.

MESI TULI OMAI: I'm still traveling, searching, searching.
Do you know what's important to me? *(She goes stage
left and sits on perch)*

Love and companionship.
Now this search takes me on a long and bumpy road.
I'm telling you.
The men I've found on that road . . . those men.
I'm still looking for that perfect man.
As time goes by, the type of guy changes.
Now I'm looking for that perfect old Indian.
(She sings snatches of Paul Ortega's "Trail Song") That's
    my perfect old Indian-looking song.
Once I thought I found him.
I was in an airport in Western Canada,
One of my real-life trips.
I felt eyes on me, I looked around.
I saw him.
Tall, skinny,
Long, gray piggies
Big cowboy hat, boots. *(She sings for a bit)*
On the jet, we sat together.
He looked at me and grabbed my hand.
We talked and we talked and we talked.
He was a rancher, a cowboy.
We were the same age.
He was married, but I was hooked up to someone else, too.
And he said, "I want to wrap you in my buffalo robe."
And he kissed me. Imagine that!

ALL: Imagine that!

MESI TULI OMAI: His name was Angus Jumping Arrow.
He sure jumped me.
When we landed, he went his way and I went mine.
    (She sings a bit more of the same song)
I'm still traveling on that road of love.
It's a tough one, let me tell you.
And I need all the help I can get.

*(She continues singing. Naomi Fast Tracks sidles up to her
and sits directly stage right of her.)*

scene 20

FISH STORY

NAOMI FAST TRACKS: I've got a romantic traveling story, too.
I was in Amsterdam,
And I finally decided I was going to do this thing
I was really scared about.
I was going to MAKE LOVE TO A WOMAN, EEEEEEEE!
So I met this woman
Long legs, big breasts, short hair, tall, good looking.
I was staying in a really nice apartment.
I was girlfriend sitting because
This girlfriend, she had thirteen personalities.
Her name was Sue.
And Sue had a friend, Mai Lee.
She had six personalities,
All of them violent.
Altogether, they had nineteen personalities.
So I was staying in this really nice apartment.
One morning, I got up and went into the kitchen.
In the sink were these putrid, really slimy and smelly fish heads and fish bodies.

MESI TULI OMAI: *Fish bodies? (She moves to sit next to Naomi Fast Tracks)*

NAOMI FAST TRACKS: I said, "What are those fish heads and things doing in the sink?" Sue said, "Oh, Mai Lee is going to make us a Chinese dinner." "No, you cannot do that, you will die." "Mai Lee is going to make us a Chinese dinner!" The very tall, good-looking woman was there, too. I was trying to act cool, so I said, *(Yelling)* "Get those fish heads out of the sink!" Of course, they all thought I was the heavy, so they took the fish and buried it in the garden.

Here's another romantic part. Before I left, I kissed

the tall, good-looking woman. She kissed me on the lips. She said she would meet me in the women's bar. I went there and went up to the balcony. Finally they came, and I came running down the stairs, and I kissed her, and she was drunk. And Sue was drunk, too. Sue didn't have any shoes on. She had black pants on and a huge leather jacket with nothing underneath. And every once in a while she'd open it and say, "Ahhhhhhhh!" So they kicked her out of the bar. Did I tell you it was raining out? It was raining out. She went screaming into the street, and every once in a while she'd run up to a car and open her jacket and go, "Ahhhhh!" And finally she squatted between two cars and peed in the gutter.

(Mesi Tuli Omai leaves, continuing her journey around the circle. Naomi Fast Tracks follows her and continues her story.)

I thought I would never make it with a woman. Here's another romantic part. The tall, good-looking woman? Kissed me in the rain. And then we got to the house, and we made coffee and everything. And then she took me by the wrist and said, "Come to bed with me." This is it, I'm going to make it with a woman!!

(Mesi Tuli Omai turns and leaves, going upstage to perch.)

I'm going to make it with a woman! *(Follows Mesi Tuli Omai up to the perch)* I opened the door to my bedroom, Mai Lee was in my bed. Mai Lee was naked. She had twigs stuck all over her body. I told you it was raining out? It was thundering and lightning. Mai Lee was screaming to the thunder, "I hear you, Father."

(Mesi Tuli Omai leaves perch to continue around circle, with Naomi Fast Tracks following her.)

I was really disturbed because she had tiger balm smeared all over her body, and on the tiger balm she had oregano. I threw her out of the room. I took off all my clothes and went to bed with the tall, good-looking woman. I was so preoccupied, I couldn't do anything but kiss.

(Mesi Tuli Omai stops moving.)

Well, we were in bed for a while there, and I started to smell this really bad smell. I got up and opened the door and into my face billowed clouds of dark, putrid, greasy-smelling smoke. Mai Lee had fried the fish heads.

I rushed out of my room into the kitchen, and I slipped on the guts and scales on the floor. I said, "This can't be happening to me!"

Here's the romantic part. The tall, good-looking woman took me to her mother's house.
When I got there,
She made me take off all my clothes, she said I smelled.
She put my clothes out in the garden, in the rain.
Then she threw me into the shower and
Scrubbed me like I was a horse. Romantic, huh?
I thought it was romantic.

VOICE FROM OUTSIDE THE CIRCLE: Was it fun?

NAOMI FAST TRACKS: Yeah, it was fun. I finally made it with a woman!

(Mesi Tuli Omai walks out of the circle, disgusted. Obsidian Woman appears in the arch. Naomi Fast Tracks and Mesi Tuli Omai sit downstage left. Owl Messenger comes into circle.)

scene 21

IN THE BEGINNING/OWL STORY

OWL MESSENGER: Owl. I, owl, eat mice to live. I must know and respect the life habits of mice. I must know when, where, how they live. Respect mice.

(She looks into the circle as into a mirror. She walks around the circle then goes upstage center and sits. Obsidian Woman enters at far upstage platform and crouches.)

OBSIDIAN WOMAN: It was yesterday.
No, it was a long time ago.
Trying to remember
Una memoria
Like looking into a mirror
It was today.
In the beginning
Of the beginning
Of the beginning
Of the beginning
There was a seed
Tiny kernel of maize
Gold.
Shone so bright
This kernel of maize.
It grew and it grew
Until it was a young girl.

OWL MESSENGER: I hunt when I am hungry. My large eyes, with extraordinary eyesight in the dark, watching, the opening to the burrows and warrens underground. I watch their comings and goings in order to ensure my next meal. The moon. The night. The mouse, as a tasty dinner.

OBSIDIAN WOMAN: She was different, this little girl.
She was different because she heard,

Saw and felt things.
And these things she heard, saw and felt
Frightened her.
So she would try to stop them from coming out.
She tried to stop them from coming out.

OWL MESSENGER: Tonight I'm watching a particular mouse family. There are seven members: a father, a mother, an older sister, an older brother and triplets—I have not as yet determined their sex. I'm waiting tonight for the older sister. I call her—when I think of her, my mouth waters.

OBSIDIAN WOMAN: As time went on, it got harder and harder
Because these things she heard, saw and felt
Started jumping out when she least expected them.
Faster and faster and faster
She would try to push them back in.
She pushed them back in.
She pushed them back in.

OWL MESSENGER: She is sweet and gentle. She is a poet reciting songs and ballads that she composes herself about family history and legends. She dances and sings in a sweet, clear, bell-like voice.

(All make owl sounds.)

The sound of her voice pierces my ear, as she sings the legends to her sisters and brothers—to help them carry on the next cycle.

OBSIDIAN WOMAN: It was yesterday.
No, it was a long time ago.
Trying to remember
Una memoria
Like looking into a mirror
It was today.
In the beginning
Of the beginning

Of the beginning
Of the beginning.

OWL MESSENGER: I called for her but the entire family heard me and surrounded her to prevent her from coming to me.

OBSIDIAN WOMAN: What shall we do with her the people said?
She's an embarrassment.
She's frightening the other children.
They stared at her
Pointed their fingers,
Laughed and shouted,
Shook her up and down
And turned her upside down.
Get rid of her
Cut out her tongue
Tear out her eyes
Cut off her head
Bury her in the earth
And throw her into the ocean.
Now she won't be able to
See, hear or feel anything.

OWL MESSENGER: I call again. I can feel that she wants to come to me. "Give me your hand, you beautiful young being. I'm your friend. Come sleep in my arms."

OBSIDIAN WOMAN: It was yesterday.
No, it was a long time ago.
Trying to remember
Una memoria
Like looking into a mirror
It was today.
In the beginning
Of the beginning
Of the beginning
Of the beginning.

OWL MESSENGER: She cried out, "Pass me by, pass me by. I'm too young to die!"

OBSIDIAN WOMAN: So, the young girl slept.
And while she slept
She dreamed.
Red moon crying
Locusts flying
Birds falling
Stretches of darkness
Climbing, crawling, flying, running
Walls crumbling
Digging, digging
Birds with human faces
Jaguars with human faces
Serpents with human faces.
(Standing outside the circle, she listens into it) They're
here.
They're here.
They're here.
They're here.
They're here / They're here / They're here. *(She touches all parts of her body)*

OWL MESSENGER: I hear scratching sounds of earth being moved, and she is here. She escaped her family and came to me. Beautiful, tender, succulent. I will have her tonight.

(Stage left, there are two women sitting on stools. They become owls. They capture the mouse. They eat the mouse.)

I know and respect the life habits of mice. Tomorrow I will wait in the dark for her older brother.

OBSIDIAN WOMAN *(Outside circle, hands over her eyes)*: It was yesterday.
No, it was a long time ago.
Trying to remember
Una memoria
Like looking into a mirror

It was today.
In the beginning
Of the beginning
Of the beginning
Of the beginning.
(Beat) Now.

WIND HORSE SPIRIT WARRIOR: I've got you!

scene 22

HONORING SONG

All the goddesses approach the circle slowly. They look into the circle as if looking down into the earth. They make their connections to the human beings.

ALL: Make the offering.
　　Remember.
　　Homage extended.
　　Homage received.

WIND HORSE SPIRIT WARRIOR: There is a growling in your soul
　　Now that we've met
　　Eye to glowing eyes.

ALL: Got you!

(They sing "Honoring Song." They move to all the four corners. They go back through the arch from where they came. The stage is lit with stars.)

END OF PLAY

Lisa Mayo is a founding member of two Native American performing arts groups: Spiderwoman Theater and Off the Beaten Path, with whom she has toured world-wide. A performing member of Masterworks Laboratory Theater of New York, she studied at the New York College of Music, and is a classically trained mezzo-soprano. She has also studied with Uta Hagen, Robert Lewis and Walt Witcover, as well as with Charles Nelson Reilly for musical comedy. Ms. Mayo has received a CAPS Fellowship and a grant from the New York State Council on the Arts for the development of *The Pause That Refreshes*, a piece she created and directed. She has performed and studied with Tina Packer and Kristin Linklater of Shakespeare and Company, taught theatre crafts and acting to young people as part of the Minnesota Native American AIDS Task Force, and has directed the Native American Actor's Showcase at the American Indian Community House, where she serves on the Board of Directors. Ms. Mayo performed in Beijing, China, at the 4th World Women's Conference. She and Gloria Miguel received a Rockefeller grant, as well as funding from the Jerome Foundation to create *Nis Bundor: Daughters from the Stars*, which premiered at Dance Theater Workshop. She is the recipient of a D.F.A. honorary degree from Miami University in Oxford, Ohio.

Gloria Miguel studied drama at Oberlin College, Ohio, and is a founding member of Spiderwoman Theater. She has worked extensively in film and television; toured the United States in *Grandma*, a one-woman show; toured Canada as Pelajia Patchnose in the original Native Earth Performing Arts production of Tomson Highway's *The Rez Sisters*; performed in the Canadian play *Son of Ayash* in Toronto; and performed in *Bootlegger Blues* at the Arbour Theater in Peterborough, New Hampshire. She performed as Coyote/Vitiline in *Jessica*, a Northern Lights Production in Edmonton, Canada, for which she was nominated for a Sterling Award for outstanding supporting actress. Previously, she was a drama consultant for the Minnesota Native American AIDS Task Force, which developed a play on AIDS, and she was a visiting professor and drama consultant at Brandon University in Canada. She performed in Beijing, China, at the 4th World Women's Conference. She and Lisa Mayo received a Rockefeller grant, as well as funding from the Jerome Foundation to create *Nis Bundor: Daughters from the Stars*, which premiered at Dance Theater Workshop. When not on tour she is a drama teacher at the Eastern District YMCA in Brooklyn, New York. She is also a judge and teaching consultant for an annual theatre festival at Greyhills Academy, a Navajo high school in Arizona. She is the recipient of a D.F.A. honorary degree from Miami University in Oxford, Ohio. In 1999, Ms. Miguel will be playing Maria in an adaptation of Louise Edrich's book, *Love Medicine*, in Chicago.

Muriel Miguel is a founding member and artistic director of Spiderwoman Theater. She is also a founding member of Open Theater, Off the Beaten Path, Thunderbird American Indian Dancers and The Native American Theater Ensemble. As a member of Spiderwoman Theater, a company that has toured internationally, Ms. Miguel has been instrumental in the development of over twenty shows in the last seventeen years. The most recent of these is *Power Pipes*, which premiered in the fall of 1992. She originated the role of Philomena Moose Tail in *The Rez Sisters* in Canada. She has worked extensively with Native American youth, developing and directing a project for the Minnesota Native American AIDS Task Force in 1991 and also codirecting *Indian Givers*, a play created by the Native American Youth Council of New York City. She has also taught at Bard College in New York and the Native Theater School in Northern Canada. She performed in Beijing, China, at the 4th World Women's Conference. Ms. Miguel has a one-woman show, *Hot 'n' Soft*, which she developed in 1991, and which has played to critical acclaim in the United States and Canada. In 1998, Ms. Miguel was selected for the Native Women of Hope poster. She is the recipient of a D.F.A. honorary degree from Miami University in Oxford, Ohio. Her newest work is *Trail of the Otter*. Ms. Miguel will perform the part of Lulu in Louise Edrich's adaptation of *Love Medicine* in Chicago.

Deborah Ratelle has been the production stage manager for Spiderwoman Theater for the past eight years, and is the production stage manager for the Aboriginal Dance Program at the Banff Centre for the Arts in Banff, Alberta. She has also worked at Native Earth Performing Arts in Toronto. She most recently returned from Phoenix where she worked as the production stage manager for the Spirits in the Sun, the first annual Canadian Indigenous Arts Festival.

Only Drunks
and Children
Tell the Truth

drew hayden
taylor

author's statement

I like to see myself as a contemporary storyteller. In writing my humble, little plays, I like to think of myself as carrying on the tradition of storytelling that our Elders have shared with us. As the times change, we find ourselves going from telling stories around the campfire to telling stories around the stage. The location may have altered, but it is my sincere wish that the heart and essence of the storytelling experience come from the same place. After all, there is little difference between the two. Much like an actor or writer, a storyteller uses his body, voice and imagination to take the audience on a journey. If that is not the essence of theatre, Native theatre, I don't know what is.

Only Drunks and Children Tell the Truth was first produced by Native Earth Performing Arts at the Native Canadian Centre in Toronto, Ontario, on April 2, 1996. The set and lighting designer was Stephan Droege, the costume designer was Kristen Fahrig and the sound designer was Denise Bolduc. Elizabeth Theobald directed the following cast:

JANICE/GRACE	Carol Greyeyes
BARB	Columpa C. Bobb
RODNEY	Darrell Dennis
TONTO	Kennetch Charlette

In 1997, the play was produced at Firehall Arts Centre in Vancouver, under the direction of Donna Spencer. The play was also produced in 1997 by Two Planks and a Passion Theatre, Nova Scotia Touring Show, under the direction of Ken Schwartz.

characters

JANICE (GRACE) WIRTH, 36, lives in Toronto
BARB WABUNG, 24, her sister, living on the Reserve
RODNEY, 25, Barb's boyfriend
TONTO, 32, Rodney's brother

time and place

Late spring, early summer in 1992. The first act takes place
in Janice Wirth's downtown condominium in Toronto. The
second act occurs in Barb Wabung's house in Otter Lake,
a Reserve somewhere in central Ontario.

Act I

Lights up on an upscale condo. Movie and theatrical posters adorn the walls, with the odd sprinkling of Native art. The place is empty. The quiet is broken by four loud and sharp knocks on the door. There is silence, then more knocks are heard. Again, no response. A doorbell rings repeatedly. Silence. Agitated whispering is heard on the other side of the door, a low-decibel argument. Then the clicking of metal on metal, and jiggling of the doorknob. The door opens to reveal Tonto on his knees in front of the lock. He has picked it.

TONTO: When in Toronto, do as the Torontonians do. Told you it wouldn't be hard.

(He enters, followed by Barb and Rodney.)

BARB: This is a bad idea, Tonto. This is breaking and entering.
TONTO: She's your sister, right? *(Barb nods)* It's not technically a B and E if it's your sister's place. It's a law, I think. Here's your jackknife back.
RODNEY: Cool, look at this city. I told you it was a killer view. You can almost see the Reserve from here.
TONTO: That's Lake Ontario. We're that direction.

RODNEY: I didn't say our Reserve. I meant any Reserve. Six nations must be . . .

TONTO: That direction. Syracuse over there. You can almost see where Tyendinaga would be.

RODNEY: Wow, Mohawks as far as the eye can see.

BARB: Where do you think she is?

RODNEY: Not at the Goodwill, that's for sure. Look at this apartment! Barb, when I grow up can I be an entertainment lawyer, too?

BARB: No wonder she didn't want to stay at our place. After seeing this apartment, I don't wanna stay at our place.

RODNEY: Some of these movie posters are signed. Look, an autographed picture of Al Waxman. Is he still alive?

BARB: Don't touch anything. *(Without thinking, she picks up a piece of abstract sculpture)* What is this?

RODNEY: I think they call it art.

BARB: How can you tell?

RODNEY: It's in the middle of the table, and it's not a bowl.

TONTO: The woman's not as white as you thought. There's some damn good art up here. A Maxine Noel, an Odjig, a Roy Thomas.

RODNEY *(À la Star Trek)*: Damn it, Jim, I'm an Indian, not an art critic.

(Rodney disappears into the bathroom.)

BARB: Think they're originals?

TONTO: Well, they're definitely not prints. So either they're originals or great forgeries. And as much as I like Maxine's work, I don't think there's that great a market for fake Noel's. Someday, maybe.

(Rodney comes out of the bathroom.)

RODNEY: Barb, go look at her bathroom.

BARB: I don't want to look at her bathroom.

RODNEY: Trust me, go look at her bathroom.

(Puzzled, Barb peeks into the bathroom.)

BARB: Wow!
RODNEY: Didn't I tell you?
BARB: I've never seen a bathroom like this. Tonto?

(Tonto investigates.)

TONTO: What the hell is that?
BARB: I don't want to know. It's like an amusement park in there.
RODNEY: Hey, Barb. Take a look at this.
BARB: What now?

(Rodney is standing in front of a photograph on a desk.)

RODNEY: See. She didn't forget.
BARB: She still has it.
TONTO: Still has what?
BARB: The picture Mom gave her last Christmas. Of Dad holding her.
TONTO: I'd forgotten how big your father was. How old was Grace there?
BARB: About three months. The C.A.S. took her a couple months later.
RODNEY: See, Barb. It may not be a wasted trip.
BARB: I miss that picture. Why didn't she return our calls? Couldn't she tell it was important?
TONTO: I don't think she's been here for a while. This plant soil is very dry.
RODNEY: You know, sometimes you're just too Indian.
TONTO: Chi-meegwetch. And check her answering machine. Eleven calls. How many times did we call?
RODNEY: Including the two this morning, ten all together.

BARB: So she's not here. A three-hour drive for nothing.

RODNEY: So, what do you want to do? Hang out here and wait for her to get back, or do you want to head home?

BARB: I'm tired, Rodney. I want to go home.

RODNEY: You got it. Let's go.

(They start moving toward the door.)

TONTO: Provided this godforsaken city hasn't towed my truck.

(Suddenly, the rattle and click of keys in a lock is heard. The trio freeze, panic-stricken.)

BARB: Shit!

RODNEY: Everybody hide!

(They all scramble to find places to hide in the apartment. The door opens and Janice enters with her luggage. She looks tired and worn. Barely glancing at her apartment, she drops her bags and takes her coat off. She opens the closet to find Tonto.)

TONTO: Uh, hi. . . . *(Janice screams)* It's okay! It's okay!

(She goes into a martial arts position (Wendo) and punches him solidly. Tonto goes down in the closet, a flood of coats covering him in an avalanche.)

JANICE *(Screaming)*: 911! 911!

(Tonto crawls out of the closet in pain and half-conscious, only to have Janice start kicking him.)

TONTO *(In pain)*: Barb . . . !

(Barb and Rodney emerge from their hiding position.)

BARB: Grace! Take it easy. It's us!

JANICE: Barb? Rodney?

BARB: Hi, Grace.

JANICE: What are you doing here? In my apartment?

BARB: We had to see you.

JANICE: How'd you get in here?

RODNEY: We, uh, snuck past the security guard and, well, Tonto picked your lock.

JANICE: Who picked my lock?

RODNEY: My brother, Tonto.

(Rodney gestures to Tonto, who is only now getting up off the ground.)

TONTO *(Still in pain)*: Hi. I spent a year working for a locksmith in Peterborough. It's quite easy once you know how they work.

JANICE: What are you all doing here? In my apartment?

BARB: Well, when you didn't return our messages—

JANICE: What messages? Will someone tell me what's going on here?

BARB: Grace, Mom passed away four days ago.

JANICE: Anne . . . Oh, Barb, I'm sorry. What happened?

BARB: She went in her sleep.

JANICE: Four days ago?

BARB: The funeral was yesterday. I wanted you to be there.

JANICE: Oh, Barb, I'm so sorry. I've been away and—

BARB: I think you should come back and say good-bye, you know, to her.

JANICE: Go back. *(Realizing)* Go back?! Barb, I can't.

BARB: What do you mean you can't? You owe it to her.

JANICE: I'm sorry about Anne, I really am. And I'll do what I can if you need any help. But going back . . . I can't.

BARB: You have to go back. She's your *mother*. Our *mother*. I don't care if you just drive up, put some flowers down, say good-bye, hop back in, and drive away afterwards.

RODNEY: You really should, Grace. It's the proper thing to do.

JANICE: Sorry, but I'll determine what's proper for me to do. Anne was a lovely lady. . . .

BARB: Your biological mother.

JANICE: I knew her for one hour, that was all.

(Beat.)

BARB: I don't believe you.

TONTO: What have you got against Otter Lake? That's where you come from, that's your people.

JANICE: My people live in London.

TONTO: No, your caretakers live in London, your family lives in Otter Lake.

JANICE: I love my parents.

TONTO: I'm sure you do. Look, I worked for a year as a counselor at the Youth Centre. I met kids all the time, and adults, too, who were trapped between one culture and another. It can do weird things to some people. But I found it can help if you have a sound understanding of where you come from. Then you'll have a better understanding of where you're going. Got me?

JANICE: That's really wonderful.

(To Barb) I realize you're going through a rough time right now, Barb, but I really don't think it would be in anyone's best interest for me to go back to Otter Lake. The last time I left there, I was a mess. I'm still trying to get ahold of myself. I do not want to go through that again.

BARB: Okay, you don't want to come home and say good-bye to the woman who gave birth to you. I'm not surprised, but I am disappointed. I hoped you'd been born with some of Mom's compassion.

JANICE: Don't take this personally. It's me, not you. Now, if there's anything else I can do to help. . . .

RODNEY: Um, yeah, as a matter of fact there is, Grace.

JANICE: Please, my name is Janice.

RODNEY: Okay, Janice. Um, we need a place to crash. Got any room?

BARB: What? I don't want to stay here.

RODNEY: Sweetheart, essence of my existence, we need some place to stay for the night. It'll be dark in an hour, and Tonto can't drive because of his night blindness. . . .

BARB: You have night blindness?

TONTO: It's a personal thing.

RODNEY: I don't have my license since that little altercation with the O.P.P., for which I still think that breathalyzer was rigged. You don't like to drive on the highways. Kind of limits our alternatives.

BARB: I don't want to stay here!

JANICE: All of you? Here?

RODNEY: We're housebroken.

BARB: Listen to me, I don't want to stay here.

JANICE: But Barb doesn't want to stay here.

RODNEY: Listen, honey, do you want to walk home? Sleep in the truck, or, better yet, sleep on the streets? It's early spring, so the chance of getting frostbite is practically nonexistent.

BARB *(To Tonto)*: How bad is your night blindness?

RODNEY: Trust me, it's very bad. We don't have a choice.

BARB: Well . . .

RODNEY: It's decided. Can we?

JANICE: Well, I guess. You're all welcome to stay if you want. It's the least I can do.

BARB: Can't get much more "least" than that.

RODNEY: I think that's a yes. *(To Tonto)* Shall we go get our stuff?

JANICE: I'm supposed to be on vacation.

TONTO: Why bother, you've got a natural tan.

(Rodney and Tonto walk to the door.)

(To Rodney): How long have I had night blindness? Is it fatal?

RODNEY: Shh!

(They exit as the lights go down.)

scene two

It is several hours later. Janice is in the kitchen making coffee. Barb comes out of the bathroom drying her hands. They spot each other and there is an instant note of tension. Barb backtracks into the bathroom. There is silence for a moment.

JANICE: You might as well come out of the bathroom. There's only so much you can do in there. I've made some coffee. Would you like some?

(There is a pause before Barb comes out.)

BARB: Thank you.

JANICE: How long do you think Rodney and Tonto—I can't believe I'm calling him that—will be? *(Barb shrugs, unwilling to talk)* Is the bedroom fine? *(Barb nods)* You're a little old to be giving me the silent treatment.

BARB: Milk, please.

JANICE: That's a beginning.

BARB: You wanna talk? Okay then, I have a question for you. Why are you being so nice all of a sudden?

JANICE: Fair enough. I suppose from your perspective I do deserve a bit of a cold shoulder. I wasn't exactly the warmest of hosts earlier. But you have to admit, it's a little unusual for the three of you to be waiting in my apartment. I just about had a heart attack.

BARB: Back in Otter Lake, if somebody's not home, we wait inside.

JANICE: This isn't Otter Lake. But I guess you had a valid reason for coming here. I understand that.

BARB: How nice of you.

JANICE: And I don't see any point for animosity between us. We are, as you keep pointing out, sisters of one nature or another. I'm not a bad person, Barb.

(Again, there is an awkward silence between them.)

Do you come to Toronto often?

BARB: Last time was Christmas.

JANICE: It's quite the difference, isn't it?

BARB: As Rodney says, "It's a nice place to visit, but I wouldn't want to put a land claim on it."

JANICE: He's got a very interesting sense of humor.

BARB: He's a goof. But he's my goof. This is good coffee.

JANICE: It's a Kenyan blend. Would you like some more?

BARB: Yeah, that company makes good coffee I hear. I need a good jolt. Long car trips put me away.

JANICE: It's decaffeinated.

BARB: Decaffeinated?! Then what's the point? Got any real stuff?

JANICE: You'd drink caffeinated coffee at this hour of the night?

BARB: Yeah?

JANICE: I'd be up all night. Not that it matters. I don't have any what you might call "real stuff" in the apartment. Better warn you, no salt or butter either.

BARB: Boy, we'll be outta here real early tomorrow. The more I talk to you, the more I realize there's nothing to talk about.

JANICE: The subject of coffee is hardly the thing to base a relationship on.

BARB: Sometimes it's all you got. Mom always wondered what kind of place you lived in. I always thought it would look something like this. Certainly better than our old house.

JANICE: But that old house had character. This is just a condo.

BARB: I know a lot of people who would trade some character for a condo like this. Nice art. Even some Native ones, I see. Tonto was impressed.

JANICE: They were gifts.

BARB *(To herself)*: Figures.

(There is an awkward silence between the two.)

JANICE: So when do you think the boys will be back?

BARB: In a little while, I guess. Tonto wanted to see if there was a social tonight at the Native Centre. He's into things like that.

JANICE: That's on Spadina right? Driven by it many times.

BARB: Did you ever go in?

JANICE: Never had the time. I notice I've picked up your habit of calling them boys. They must be on both sides of thirty.

BARB: Yeah, but a boy is always a boy, even in the nursing home. I suspect Rodney will still be climbing trees in his wheelchair. Tonto won't be far behind him.

JANICE: What a bizarre name—Tonto.

BARB: Goes with his character.

JANICE: What does he do?

BARB: Anything and everything. Basically, he survives off of various employment programs, apprenticeships, training incentives, stuff like that. He also drums a bit.

JANICE: Oh, he's a musician. I used to date this jazz guitarist for a while. He—

BARB: He's not exactly a musician. He sings traditional Ojibway songs.

JANICE: Really? That must be interesting. He can make a living off of that?

BARB: I think you're missing the point, dear sister.

JANICE *(Occupied)*: Sorry, didn't catch that.

BARB: I was just thanking you again for taking us out to dinner. That was very nice of you—

JANICE: —For a change. Is that what you were thinking?

BARB: Maybe.

JANICE: That always seems to be it, doesn't it? Always this, what would you call it, tension between us. All through dinner you barely said a word. It doesn't have to be this way, Barb. We could be friends.

BARB: You're the one who doesn't want to say good-bye to our mother. I'm sorry if that makes me a little sensitive. We shouldn't have come here. With all due respect, Miss Wirth, maybe we shouldn't stay here.

JANICE: Little late for that, you're here now. Contrary to what you might believe, I have nothing against you or Otter Lake.

BARB: You'd never know. You haven't even asked how the funeral went.

JANICE: Fine, Barb, how did the funeral go?

BARB: Fine as far as funerals go. Everyone was there, even the people she didn't get along with. Flowers everywhere, people. It was the first time I'd seen some of my uncles in suits since Dad died. Nothing quite like seeing a group of overweight middle-aged men in mismatching, twenty-year-old suits, all standing in a row.

JANICE: Was it a traditional funeral?

BARB: Yeah, Catholic.

JANICE: I was raised Anglican.

(There is another silence between them.)

There's that awkwardness again.

BARB: So much for the saying "Blood is thicker than water."
       (Pause) Nice view. Bet it cost a fortune.

JANICE: What doesn't these days?

BARB: True.

JANICE: Your house has a nice view. I remember that beau-
         tiful willow tree hanging over the lake. The view from
         your kitchen window was quite special.

BARB: You saw it in December. Now there are leaves on the
       willow, and the lake has thawed. Looks even better.
       Except for the cottages.

JANICE: What cottages?

BARB: The band office has leased out land all along the
       southern shore of the village to cottagers from the city.
       They're everywhere, like a bad cold.

JANICE: That's a little harsh.

BARB: Sorry if I offended you. I didn't think you'd take it
       personally.

JANICE: I didn't, and we were talking about the house. Anne's
         house. Are you going to keep it, now that Anne has . . .

(Janice doesn't know how to finish the sentence.)

BARB: I don't know. It all hasn't sunk in yet. The house is a
       mess right now. Mom hired the boys to renovate the
       place with the money she won in that lottery. Add an
       extension, a sewing room, just off her bedroom. I don't
       know what I'll do with it when it's finished. I don't sew
       much. I don't even know what I'll do with Mom's room.

JANICE: How are you holding up?

BARB: I don't have a choice.

JANICE: Everybody has a choice.

BARB: Not me. When Dad died, I held the family together.
       When Paul died, I held the family together. I'm used to
       this now. I never had the luxury of being able to run away.

JANICE: Most people would consider seeing their family for the
         first time in thirty-five years an emotional experience.

BARB: Most people would have stayed for dinner. Most people would have called in six months. She loved you, you know. She did, even after you walked out on her on god-damned Christmas Eve. She still loved you. Thirty-five years of waiting and she was willing to wait some more.

JANICE: I explained—

BARB: Even when she cried, she still loved you. I knew you wouldn't be back, but I couldn't tell her that. Her whole life had been built on hope, even after you left she still hoped. And as her daughter, I had to help keep that hope alive.

JANICE: Barb, please—

BARB: Last March, when she sent you a birthday card, your polite little thank-you card said it all to her.

JANICE: I was leaving on a business trip. I didn't have time—

BARB: Neither did Mom. It was on her night table the morning I found her. You were always beside her. Always.

JANICE: I had no control over that.

BARB: Neither did I. I guess it's all Mom's fault then.

JANICE: That's not fair.

BARB: Surprise, surprise. I'm the one who failed classes in high school, who got drunk, rolled the car, who made her cry. But you were never there to disappoint her. You were the ideal, I was the reality.

JANICE: I don't need this.

BARB: Gonna run away again? Where this time? We're in your place. Or maybe your other family, your white family in London.

JANICE: Leave them out of this. They have nothing to do with this.

BARB: Nothing? Are we having the same conversation?! The government took you away from Mom and gave you to them. Did they ever once try to find your home, take you somewhere where there were Indians? Have you ever been to a powwow? *(No answer)* Just once I'd like to know what's going on in that beautified head of yours.

You've always got those walls around you. Me and Mom spilled our guts to you, but not the immaculate Grace.

JANICE: I told you about my life, how I found you.

BARB: You told us the facts. I don't know one damn thing about you, the person.

JANICE: Oh, you're being ridiculous. Barb, this is my home. You're welcome to stay here, spend the night, whatever, but I hope you'll do me the courtesy of respecting me in my own home.

BARB: Like you said, it's your home. *(Pause)* I wonder where those boys are?

JANICE: Look behind you, in the corner. *(Janice points to a picture hanging by itself. Barb walks over to it and examines it)* I kept it. That picture means everything to me, even though I never knew him.

BARB: Paul's picture. God, I can't get over how much you look like him.

JANICE: Yes, I've been told that. I have two other brothers but it's not the same. They were born to the Wirths. I know we don't see eye to eye, but I do acknowledge who you are and where you came from. I really wish you would do the same for me.

(Suddenly the buzzer for the front door goes off. Janice goes to answer.)

That must be them. Hello.

RODNEY *(His voice comes over the buzzer intercom)*: Aye, Captain, two to beam up. Energize.

(Janice buzzes them in.)

JANICE: Does he ever give up?

BARB: Don't worry, tomorrow we'll be out of your life.

JANICE: I wish we could be friends.

BARB: I wish we could be sisters.

JANICE: Friends are easier.

BARB: Sisters are blood.

(There is a knock, and Janice opens the door. The boys come in.)

RODNEY *(À la Ricky Ricardo)*: Lucy, we're home. Boy, was it rough at the club tonight! Where're my bongos?

TONTO: Is that coffee I smell? I knew there was something about this woman I liked.

BARB: So did you make it to the Native Centre?

RODNEY: Yeah, but judging by some of the people we met, they're more off center.

TONTO *(Fake laugh)*: Nobody was there, so we took a look around downtown.

BARB: You weren't hanging around in lingerie shops again, were you?

RODNEY: He wouldn't let me. But, Barb, look what we found.

(Rodney holds up a hardcover book.)

BARB: Not another one of your books. We got enough as it is.

RODNEY: No, you'll like this one. It's the latest biography of Amelia Earhart.

BARB: Really? Let's see.

(Rodney hands it to Barb, who looks it over excitedly.)

TONTO: We haven't had time to read it yet, but they're always good for a hoot.

BARB: Oh, cool, I love that picture. She looks so young.

TONTO: I can't wait to show her.

JANICE: Show who what?

BARB: This one has her dying in Saipan, a prisoner of the Japanese, in 1937.

TONTO: Give me a break. White people will find a conspiracy anywhere. Wait a minute, turn back. There's the plane. Ugly thing, eh?

RODNEY: She never liked flying the Lockheed 10-E Electra—
too clumsy.

JANICE: Who are you talking about?

TONTO: Amelia Earhart. Who'd you think? This coffee tastes
funny.

BARB: It's decaffeinated.

TONTO: Yuck. The savages. How could they do that to an
innocent little bean?

RODNEY: Geez, when you think about it, another half an
hour and she'd have made Howland Island.

JANICE: Amelia Earhart, the pilot?

RODNEY: You know another? My favorite theory of theirs is
that she was captured by aliens and forced to breed
with Elvis and Jim Morrison to create television evan-
gelists. That would explain a lot, wouldn't it?

JANICE: But how come you know so much about her?

RODNEY: It's common knowledge back home.

JANICE: What, her fan club is located in Otter Lake?

BARB: Not quite. Remember the brown, brick house about
two hundred feet from our place?

JANICE: Yeah, I remember. I almost turned into that driveway by mistake.

BARB: That's where she lives. Just saw her yesterday at the
funeral.

(To Tonto) Maybe we should buy some regular coffee.

TONTO: Definitely.

BARB: There's no salt or real butter either. If she tells me
she's a vegetarian too—

JANICE: What is this? Some kind of joke?

BARB: What joke?

JANICE: Amelia Earhart! In Otter Lake.

BARB: Oh that. Yeah, she and Mom used to be good friends.
Used to baby-sit me and Paul when we were young.

RODNEY: Me, too. Christ, she could swear better than any
of us.

JANICE: Amelia Earhart is dead.

BARB: She's in her nineties, but I wouldn't call her dead.

JANICE: You're all not serious are you? Amelia Earhart? *The* Amelia Earhart?!

RODNEY: Except now she goes by the name Amy Hart. The cutest little, wrinkly, white woman you ever saw. Looks like one of those dried-up apple dolls.

BARB: It is Amelia Earhart, Grace.

JANICE: Janice!

BARB: Okay, Janice.

JANICE: Amelia Earhart's been missing for over fifty years.

TONTO: Fifty-five, isn't it?

RODNEY: Did the big belly flop July 3rd, 1937. Had her first bowl of corn soup in Otter Lake November 21st, 1937.

BARB: It's true.

JANICE: If this is all true, then this is fantastic! Incredible. How'd she get there?

TONTO: That's another long story. You see—

JANICE: And everybody in the village knows this? I mean about Amelia Earhart?

RODNEY: Yeah, it's not as if it's a secret. Almost every kid from the Reserve has done some essay or project on her in school. After a while the teachers were getting suspicious, so we had to make up a story about Indians having a special affinity for her, respecting her because she personifies the feminine presence of the eagle as it flies across Grandmother Moon. One guy even equated her with a legend of "The Woman Who Circled Turtle Island," which he made up during lunch hour.

TONTO: That was me. White people buy all this kind of stuff.

JANICE: This is incredible! Amazing. The media will go crazy. This is the biggest story since—

BARB: Now wait a minute. Don't get carried away.

JANICE: But why? This could be—

BARB: —Wrong. She doesn't want publicity. Her first husband was a publisher and she got sick of all the publicity. She came to Otter Lake to get away from it all.

JANICE: But you said everybody in the village knows.

RODNEY: Yeah, in the village. Because we're her family now. It's her secret, but it's also ours.

TONTO: Telling other people would be like turning in a friend. No can do.

JANICE: Then why are you telling me?

BARB: Contrary to what you think, you are still family, whether you care or not.

JANICE: Then you're taking one hell of a risk.

RODNEY: Not really. So what if you tell somebody else? You'd look cute on the cover of the *National Enquirer*, but then it would just fade away.

JANICE: But I'm a respected lawyer. With connections. If I wanted—

BARB: Yeah, if you wanted. But I'm hoping you don't want to. No matter how long you've lived out here, I think you still have some Otter Lake in you.

JANICE: This is all so crazy.

RODNEY: Yeah, but it kinda makes life interesting, don't you think?

BARB: You're not going to tell anyone, are you?

JANICE: I don't understand you. Not more than fifteen minutes ago you were criticizing me about Anne, now you entrust me with this "precious" secret of yours. What's the game?

BARB: No game. This is who we are. Family, friends—we stick together.

RODNEY: Except during band elections.

BARB: Shut up, Rodney. At our place, we always have people dropping in, visiting, calling, whatever. You, yourself, said our place felt like a home. Sorry, but this place doesn't feel like a home to me.

TONTO: Yeah, bit cold to me, too.

BARB: The walls look so white my eyes hurt. Nobody has called, doesn't look like you get many visitors. You seem kinda alone here.

JANICE: I have friends. I've been away for a while, remember?

BARB: Alone?

JANICE: What's that got to do with anything?

BARB: Where we come from, you have to try, I mean really work at it, to be alone.

RODNEY: Yeah, and I've tried.

JANICE: I feel like I'm being cornered by the three of you. I have my life, and you have yours. Why don't we just leave it at that?

BARB: There's always this barrier you put up. Rodney used to be that way, after Paul died.

RODNEY: But I'm much better now.

JANICE: The bottom line is, I'm happy with my life. That's all that's important. It's getting late, and I've had a long day. I would like to go to bed, if it's okay with you?

BARB: Your apartment.

TONTO: But it's not even eleven yet. I'm just waking up.

JANICE *(To Barb)*: You and Rodney have the guest room. It's already made up.

RODNEY: Great.

JANICE: And I guess Tonto can have the couch.

TONTO *(Less enthusiastically)*: Great.

(Janice exits to bedroom.)

RODNEY: Come on, it will be just like when you lived with Marie. You spent half your nights on the couch anyway.

TONTO: That couch was a lot warmer place, let me tell you, than Marie ever was. The things I do for you two.

RODNEY: Yeah, like you care.

(Janice comes back into the room carrying blankets and a pillow. She puts them on the couch.)

JANICE: This should be okay. Anything else I can get you?

BARB: A cure for night blindness?

JANICE: Help yourselves to the towels on the shelf in the bathroom if you want to shower in the morning.

RODNEY: Oh, look, her towels match. Come, my little crab, into the seafood salad of love.

BARB: I hate it when you talk like that. See you in the morning. We're leaving bright and early.

(Rodney and Barb disappear into their bedroom.)

RODNEY: So, did you bring the trapeze?

(The door closes, leaving Tonto and Janice alone for an awkward moment.)

JANICE: Well, if there's nothing else, I'll be off to bed.

TONTO: What kind of bed do you have?

JANICE: Pardon?

TONTO: Your bed. What kind is it?

JANICE: A queen-size King Koil, why?

TONTO: Awfully big bed. Awfully small couch.

JANICE: Nice try, Tonto. You'll fit on the couch. Bigger and better men than you have slept there.

TONTO: It was worth a try.

(Janice sees her luggage sitting by the front door and carries it to her bedroom.)

TONTO: Need any help carrying those big, heavy suitcases all the way to your room?

JANICE: I got them here from B.C., another few feet won't kill me. Good night . . . Tonto.

(With her luggage, Janice walks awkwardly to her room as Tonto watches.)

TONTO: Good night . . . Kemosabe.

(Her door closes leaving Tonto on stage alone. He starts to make his bed on the couch.)

The big, beautiful city, a big, beautiful Indian, a big, beautiful bed. Now you'd think all those things would go together, wouldn't you? *(He flops down on the couch)* We ain't through yet.

(He pulls the blankets up over his head.)

scene three

Tonto, a sock draped over his eyes, wakes up the next morning to the sound of Janice, in a housecoat, making coffee and a snack for herself. He watches her for a moment.

JANICE: I know you're watching me. *(Tonto doesn't say anything)* Still want to play games, huh?

TONTO: Since when is watching you a game? It's a free country, almost.

JANICE: Do you want some coffee?

TONTO: That would be good. *(Tonto gets up off the couch, dressed only in a T-shirt and underwear)* Here, try this. *(Tonto tosses her a small package)*

JANICE: Hey, what's this? Coffee! Where'd you get this?

TONTO: About six-thirty this morning the sun came streaming in through that big window of yours. Hard to sleep when there's a spotlight on you.

JANICE: I had to pay extra for a southern exposure.

TONTO: When I worked construction for a year, I had to get up at that godforsaken hour. I swore never again. Except for sunrise ceremonies, of course. But even those are getting harder and harder to get up for. Anyway, I went to make coffee, found that decaf stuff of yours and thought, "The hell with this." So, I went out and got some real, good stuff an hour ago.

(Janice examines the package closely, surprised.)

JANICE: I have traveled the world, shopped most of my life in every type of store possible, and I have never, ever, come across any coffee anywhere labeled "Extra-caffeinated." Where did you find this?

TONTO: I worked in a coffee shop for half a year, so I know a little about coffee. Always remember, where there's a will, there's a way.

JANICE: Is this the Otter Lake way?

TONTO: If I wasn't afraid of needles, I'd take it with a syringe. We'll make an Indian of you yet.

JANICE: Is that all it takes? Strong coffee?

TONTO: That and a fine appreciation of good-lookin' aboriginal men.

JANICE: Well, I will say, you do have nice legs.

TONTO: You should see the rest of me.

JANICE: Thank you, but no. Your coffee will be ready in a few minutes.

TONTO: I suppose I should get dressed.

JANICE: Please.

TONTO: An almost-naked Indian scares you?

JANICE: Just my reputation. *(She points to the window. Tonto reacts with embarrassment and quickly tries to dress)*

TONTO: Holy mackerel, three million white people lookin' at me in my undies. Might start a riot.

JANICE: The city of Toronto scare you, Tonto? Tonto. How'd did you ever get a name like Tonto?

TONTO: It's a nickname, my real name is Eli Albert. Now given a choice between Eli Albert and Tonto, which do you think has more character?

JANICE: I think Eli Albert is a nice name. But why Tonto?

TONTO: My dad used to work steel in the city a lot when I was a kid. He'd always be going off to work for days at a time. When I asked where he was, I was told, "Your dad is in Toronto." Only I couldn't say Toronto, I kept pronouncing it "Tonto." The name kinda stuck.

JANICE: I think that's sweet. Do you have a horse named Scout?

TONTO: No, but I have a Bronco called the "Anti-Christ."

JANICE: You're a funny man.

TONTO: How often do you work out?

JANICE: Who? Me?

TONTO: Yes, you. That shot you gave me yesterday was a professional one if I ever felt one. And I'm ashamed to say I've felt a few in my younger days. That punch went right through me.

JANICE: I took a Wendo course at my club. It's a type of self-defense for women. I thought it might come in handy some day.

TONTO: You're lucky you didn't break your hand on my kidney stones.

JANICE: It wasn't that hard. Was it?

TONTO: You could kiss it and make it better.

JANICE: I could make it worse.

TONTO: I'll settle for breakfast.

JANICE: I'd better warn you, you eat at your own risk. I'm not much of a cook.

TONTO: Well, what have you got?

JANICE: Yogurt, I think . . .

TONTO: Boy, this is really a fun house. I'll stick with the coffee. Is it ready yet?

JANICE: Another few minutes.

(Tonto picks up the bag of decaffeinated coffee.)

TONTO: I tried this decaf stuff once. Sort of like kissing a relative. Tastes the same but no spark.

(He drops the coffee into the garbage.)

JANICE: Hey, that's good coffee!

TONTO: That's like buying beer with no alcohol.

JANICE: Ah, one of those real men who doesn't drink non-alcoholic beer.

TONTO: One of those real men who doesn't drink beer, period.

JANICE: I thought all Indian men drank.

TONTO: I thought all women could cook.

JANICE: Touché. Stereotypes everywhere. Sure you don't want the yogurt?

TONTO: Pass.

JANICE: If you don't mind me asking, Why don't you drink?

TONTO: My mother died of the stuff. That can sort of turn you off it.

JANICE: Oh, I'm so sorry. I shouldn't have asked. Rodney never mentioned anything about that.

TONTO: Why should he?

JANICE: You're brothers, aren't you?

TONTO: I was raised by his family after my mother died. We sort of became brothers. I've lived with his family longer than he has. I was there the day he was born. Looked like a worm with legs.

JANICE: You were adopted? Like me?

TONTO: Yeah, except I stayed on the Reserve. Saw my real dad a lot when he was home. He worked in the city all the time and couldn't look after me, so the Stones took me in.

JANICE: That's Rodney's parents?

TONTO: Rufus and Lillian Stone. Good people. Been with them as long as I can remember. Actually, you're one of the reasons I ended up with the Stones. God knows where I'd be if it weren't for you and Anne.

JANICE: Anne! What does Anne have to do with this?

TONTO: It's too bad you never knew your mother better. From what I heard, she really kicked up a fuss after you were taken, once she stopped being afraid of the authorities. I guess taking your child away can really change that fear to anger. Well, whatever, it worked. She rattled some cages.

JANICE: Yes, she told me.

TONTO: But did she tell you that because of her fuss, the Province decided to try a new program to foster Native kids on the Reserve? I was an experiment. I was placed with the Stones at the age of five and—bang, here I am twenty-seven years later, a fine human being. I hear they do that kind of thing in a lot of places now.

JANICE: You got to stay on the Reserve, and I was sent away.

TONTO: Yeah, but my case came eight years after you. A lot changed in that time. And things are still changing. Just think, Miss Wabung, you changed Native history. Not a lot of people can say that. Your mother saved my butt. If it weren't for her, God knows where I'd be now.

JANICE: Only eight years . . . And my name is Wirth.

TONTO: Wirth, Wabung, whatever. The truth is, we're kinda related. Both being raised by other people. Sort of brother and sister. And whatever Barb may say, you look like you've got a good head on your shoulders. I've seen some doozies out there. Next time you're driving around this city, take a good look at those people sleeping on the sidewalks. Our people. A lot of them are you and me, sister. We were lucky.

JANICE: And you got to see your father.

TONTO: Oh yeah, every month or so. It was all cool.

JANICE: That must have been wonderful.

TONTO: Ever been hugged by somebody who chews tobacco? *(Pause)* I heard your new parents were rich.

JANICE: Yes.

TONTO: There you go. Everybody got something.

JANICE *(Lost in thought)*: . . . Something.

TONTO: Rodney's cool for a brother. A little too book smart though. Sometimes you can't make head nor tail of what he's saying. He once spent an hour making a comparison of, get this, the colonization of North America based on the two sci-fi books: *The Martian Chronicles* and *Cat's Cradle*. That guy needs to spend a little more time on this planet. He needs to know tradition.

JANICE: And you can teach him this "tradition"?

TONTO: I listen to the Elders. It's all really obvious. The trouble with Rodney is he thinks like a white person. His heart's Native, but that brain of his needs a good tan.

JANICE: Why do you say that?

TONTO: There! Boom! You just said the magic word. The whole difference between Native people and white people can be summed up in that one, single, three-letter word. "Why?" White people are so preoccupied with why everything works. Why was the universe created? Why is the sky blue? Why do dogs drool when you ring a bell? "Why?" is their altar of worship. Their whole civilization is based on finding out why everything does everything.

JANICE: And Native people are different? What is your answer to "Why?"

TONTO: "Why not?" That's it. That's the answer. Why was the universe created? Why not? Why do leopards have spots? Why not? Why do Indians and religious people play bingo? Why not? You keep asking why you should go home to Otter Lake. Instead of asking yourself "Why?" you should try "Why not?"

JANICE: Why should I listen to you?

TONTO: Why not? Makes sense, huh?

JANICE: I've been in therapy. It's not that easy.

TONTO: People always want to make things difficult. The world was made a certain way. Accept it. It's like this whole concept white people have with, oh, what's that term . . . "finding your Inner Child." Now why would they want that? I mean children are great and all that, but seriously, would you want to start wetting the bed again?

JANICE: I never wet the bed.

TONTO (*Uncomfortably*): A lot of kids did. Anyway, moving on. That's the "white, Caucasian, let's go back to the beginning and try to get it right again" approach. Instead, they should do what Native people do, try to find their Inner Elder. It's a hell of a better payoff. A kid can only appreciate being young. An Elder can appreciate the young and the old, and everything in between. A Child would be afraid to go to Otter Lake. An Elder would interpret it as a necessary learning experience.

JANICE: You make it all sound so easy. Flip a switch and your life is explained.

TONTO: I didn't have to come here, you know. You're Barb's luggage and Rodney's, too, I guess, by association.

JANICE: Then why are you here?

TONTO: Simple. On occasion, life can be a simple math problem. There are more reasons for me to be here, in this apartment, than somewhere else. I had more to learn from coming to meet you than from staying at home. I hate Toronto, but sometimes the pain can be worth it. Basically, the positive outweighed the negative.

(This sinks into Janice for a moment.)

JANICE: You have some interesting theories.

TONTO: It's more than that. It's practice. I never preach anything I don't practice.

JANICE: I'll remember that. You're an interesting fellow. Certainly not what you seem to be. A bit of a closet philosopher, perhaps?

TONTO: Nah, as Rodney would say, I came out of the closet years ago. The philosophy closet that is. So are we gonna get breakfast?

JANICE: Oh, yes, I suppose we should. There's a charming place just down the street.

TONTO: Sounds great to me. Let's go.

JANICE: I think we should wait for the others. They might want to eat, too.

TONTO: Good point. Then let's get them up. Leave it to me. *(He marches over to the door and bangs heavily on it)* Okay, you two. Up and at 'em. I'm hungry.

(There is some mumbling and giggling in the other room and Rodney shouts out:)

RODNEY: Okay, we'll be out in . . . five minutes.

BARB: No, ten minutes.

RODNEY: Yeah, yeah, ten minutes.

TONTO: I'll handle this. *(Tonto opens the door and barges in. There is a scream, then Tonto comes out dragging the blankets)* If I'm not getting it, nobody is. And I said I'm hungry. Move it. *(To Janice)* What are big brothers for?

(Rodney stumbles out as he does up his jeans. He's angry.)

RODNEY: Do you mind? We were . . . busy.

TONTO: You've got the rest of your life for that. We only have this morning to eat. It's a long drive back, remember?

JANICE: Um, Rodney, we're going to get breakfast down the street. You better dress for it.

TONTO: You heard the lady.

RODNEY: And to think I could have been an only child.

(Barb comes out of the bedroom, also angry, and buttoning up her shirt.)

BARB *(To Tonto)*: There you are.

TONTO: You still may become an only child. *(He hides behind Janice)* Now, Barb . . .

BARB: Come here, Tonto . . .

TONTO: Barb, I was just a little hungry, that's all. Rodney?

RODNEY: You're on your own, pal.

TONTO: Janice?

JANICE: I don't believe you three. Barb, take it easy. He was just joking around.

BARB: You're defending him! What did you do to her?

TONTO: Nothing!

JANICE: Everybody just calm down and take it easy, okay?

BARB *(To Tonto)*: You're living on borrowed time, buddy.

TONTO: Respect your elders, I'm older than you, remember.

BARB: Then act it.

TONTO: I got real coffee.

(Pause.)

BARB: You're forgiven.

RODNEY: Ah, coffee has charms to soothe the savage breast.

TONTO: Help yourself.

(Rodney pours himself a cup of coffee.)

RODNEY: I love the smell of Nabob in the morning. Somebody mention something about breakfast?

TONTO: Yeah, down the street.

JANICE: When you're all ready, we'll grab breakfast before we leave.

BARB: What do you mean "we"?

JANICE: I mean *we*. I changed my mind. I'm going with you.

BARB *(To Tonto)*: What *did* you do to her?

JANICE: Now if you'll excuse me, I'll get my things. *(She exits)*

BARB *(Repeating the words)*: She's coming back with us? She's coming back with us?!

(Rodney and Tonto give each other the thumbs-up signal. The lights fade.)

Act II

The scene opens on the Otter Lake Reserve in an old, lived-in house. There is a missing wall at one end due to ongoing renovations. The house is empty until Janice appears in the doorway, alone and silent. The implications and memories of this house flood her. Finally, she enters and slowly glides through the room, taking in the texture and atmosphere of the house she was born in. She stops at a large photograph of Anne and Barb. Her solitude is interrupted when Rodney, in full song, enters, carrying a duffel bag, odds and ends, and the book about Amelia Earhart.

RODNEY:

> Country roads, take me home,
> to the place I was born,
> Otter Lake, mountain mama,
> take me home, country roads . . .
>
> Thank you. Thank you. Please, hold your applause.

JANICE: Was that song for my benefit?

RODNEY: I don't do benefits.

JANICE: Do you have an off button? Traveling in a car with you for three hours is like a cheap trip to Vegas. How does Barb put up with all your high energy all the time?

RODNEY: Best recipe for a solid relationship: good food, good sex, good times. Not necessarily in that order. I do what I can to keep my little Indian princess happy. I give her the surreal, she gives me the real. Not conventional, I'm sure, but it works for us.

(Barb enters.)

BARB: Boy, you really made Tonto's day by letting him park your Saab.

JANICE: He seemed so taken with it.

RODNEY: He spent a year as a mechanic, so he has a fondness for good-quality cars.

JANICE: He will be careful with it, won't he?

RODNEY: He'll treat it like his own. I think he's in love. You're the first woman he's ever met with a car better than his.

JANICE: I don't go anywhere without my car.

RODNEY: Neither does he. Which makes sense considering there's no place to go in, or around, Otter Lake without a car.

BARB: The place hasn't changed much, has it?

JANICE: The refrigerator was over there, wasn't it?

BARB: Good memory. Mom moved it until the renovations are finished. Do you want to go to the graveyard now?

JANICE: Not right now.

BARB: You're not backing out, are you?

JANICE: Barb, I just got here. I need to rest and adjust first. Not everybody runs on your timetable.

BARB *(To Rodney)*: Did we bring everything in?

RODNEY: Yep.

BARB: Anybody want anything to drink?

JANICE: Ah, yes, the quintessential pot of tea. I remember that from my last trip. Do you have any herbal tea?

BARB: What do you think?

JANICE: Of course not. I'll pass for now.

BARB: Think meat and potatoes. That's us. I was nineteen years old before I had lasagna. Twenty-two before I had a stir-fry.

RODNEY: This is sort of like *Dynasty* meets *The Dukes of Hazzard.*

(Tonto enters, holding a car part.)

TONTO: Hey, Grace . . .

JANICE: Please, my name is—

ALL: Janice.

TONTO: Okay, Janice. Do you know what this is?

JANICE: It looks like a car part!

TONTO: It is, but I've never seen anything like it. I got it out of your car. I don't know what it does. I was hoping you would know.

JANICE: You took it out of my car?! Why did you do that?

TONTO: Why not?

BARB: Tonto, put it back.

TONTO: I intend to. Just curious, that's all.

BARB: Rodney, go help him.

TONTO: It's not that difficult.

BARB: Then go work on the house. There's a hell of a draft coming through the wall over there. Do something. Just get out.

RODNEY: Barb, what are you trying to say?

TONTO: Hey, little brother, let's go. I think there's something happening here.

RODNEY: Oh, women stuff. Okay then, let's go out and do something manly. Bet I can spit farther than you can.

TONTO: Gra—Janice, if you want, I can take you up to the graveyard when you want.

JANICE: Thank you. Maybe later. After you put the part back.

TONTO: Okay.

(He and Rodney exit.)

JANICE: Tonto is so different from Rodney. Hard to believe they consider themselves brothers.

BARB: I know, but Rodney has his serious side. He doesn't like to show it, but it's there. Last Christmas when you left, Mom was in a terrible state. I'm not telling you this to make you feel guilty or anything, just Mom sort of went to pieces. Goddamn if Rodney wasn't in here trying twice as hard to make us laugh. At first, we weren't in the mood, but I'll say this for the guy, he's quite infectious. Normally, Rodney doesn't like that sort of family thing. After Paul died—they were really close—he couldn't handle the heavy emotional stuff and tended to run away from it. But not that time. He stayed the weekend, did most of the cooking, chopped the wood. Everything. While I looked after Mom.

JANICE: I'm glad somebody was there for you.

BARB: So am I. Enough of this depressing stuff. Like I said earlier, wanna drink? And I'm not talking about tea.

(Barb pulls out a case of beer and drops it with a thump on the table in front of Janice.)

Have a drink.

JANICE: I'm really not a beer drinker.

(Barb opens a cupboard door, revealing rows of liquor bottles.)

BARB: Fair enough. How about some vodka, rye, rum, gin or tequila?

JANICE: No, thank you. If I was in the mood for a drink, I would prefer a white wine.

BARB: Figures you'd prefer white.

(Barb grabs a bottle of white wine out of another cupboard and puts it on the table.)

JANICE: Barb, I don't mean this to sound critical, but do you have, by any chance, a drinking problem?

BARB: With a mother like Anne, I don't think so. The only liquor she would allow in this house was in rum cakes.

JANICE: Then why . . . ?

BARB: Later. This bottle fine?

JANICE: I'm partial to Chardonnay.

(Barb pulls another bottle out and puts it on the table in front of Janice.)

BARB: French?

JANICE: Wonderful.

BARB: Any particular year you're fond of?

JANICE: Barb, it's barely four o'clock, and I don't feel like a drink.

BARB: Oh, yes, you do. *(She finds a corkscrew and attacks the wine bottle)*

JANICE: What are you up to?

BARB: I bought all this stuff the other day, hoping we could talk you into coming up here.

JANICE: Why?

BARB: Because, big sister, I want to get to know you.

JANICE: You can do that by getting me drunk? Isn't that a little cliché?

BARB: Mom had a saying, and I think it's true: "Only drunks and children tell the truth." I want the truth, and you're a little tall to be a child. So, drink up.

(Barb hands Janice her mug of wine. Janice reads the mug.)

JANICE: "Today is the first day of the rest of your life." *(She reads the opposite side of the mug)* "Provided you're not dead already." That's uplifting.

BARB: A birthday present from Rodney. Sorry, no fancy wine glasses, but I do have some Tupperware, if you—

JANICE: This will be fine. You actually brought me up here to get drunk?

BARB: And say good-bye to Mom. *(With a physical gesture, she urges her to drink)*

JANICE: I'm having a problem understanding this. If Anne was against drinking in this house, then—

BARB: —Why all this? Mom used to say, "God works in mysterious ways, and so does Barb." Why should the mystery stop with Mom's being gone? You know, you've really got to quit asking why. Especially when it comes to hospitality.

JANICE: Please, I've had this lecture.

BARB: Tonto?

JANICE: The same. Quite an interesting man. Has he ever been to university?

BARB: He painted the residences at Trent University one summer, but that's about it. That's our Tonto.

JANICE: I bet if he really applied himself . . . Rodney, too.

BARB: Don't underestimate Rodney. He's taken more university and college courses than there are pearls in your necklace. They're both kind of the same. They just learn what they want to know, then move on.

JANICE: Some would consider that a waste of time and money.

BARB: Not everybody wants to be a lawyer. Some people are happy being who they are.

JANICE: What if who they are is a lawyer?

BARB: Then God help them. Cheers.

(Barb forces a toast with Janice, and they drink, though Janice is still unsure. Barb refills the slightly drained cup and she continues to do this at every opportunity.)

Lighten up there, Janice-Grace. Sit down, put your feet up, suck it back. Make yourself at home.

JANICE: You do this often?

BARB: Nah, can't drink like I used to, not like when I was a kid. Takes days to recover now. And besides, Rodney acts the fool enough for both of us, the entire Reserve, maybe the country.

JANICE: I see.

BARB: This is an example of what I mean about me spilling everything, but not you. You just sit there so prim and proper, keeping quiet while the world around you blabs on.

JANICE: If you remember correctly, the last time I was here, I left in tears. I'd hardly call that prim and proper.

BARB: Yeah, but you didn't tell us why you were crying.

JANICE: Wasn't it obvious?

BARB: Maybe, maybe not. The point is you ran away when you started crying, like it was a weakness. Families were created for weaknesses.

JANICE: Barb the philosopher.

BARB: Barb the realist.

JANICE: Reality is what you make it.

BARB: No, reality is what it makes of you. Oh, my God, I sound like Tonto.

JANICE: Can we do something about all this liquor? I feel like a drunken businessman will try to pick me up any moment.

BARB: You got it.

(They both get up and move the liquor to the counter.)

JANICE: So what is the case with you and Rodney? Is he going to move in with you now?

BARB: He's been here almost constantly since Mom . . . you know. He's been very good. Even been sleeping on the couch at nights. When Mom was alive, we had too much respect to do anything in the house. Then, well . . . last night at your place was the first time we'd slept together since it happened.

JANICE: Remind me to wash those sheets. You haven't answered my question. Is Rodney going to be moving in with you?

BARB: Why do you want to know?

JANICE: Discovery is a two-way street.

(Beat.)

BARB: I don't know what we're gonna do. Maybe we'll build a new house and shut this one down. It's that room.

JANICE: What room?

BARB: Mom's room. I can't go in there. Even after four days it makes me feel too weird. I just hope it doesn't turn into one of those dust-covered shrines weird old people have.

JANICE: Tell me about her. About Anne. I knew her for less than an hour. I want to know more.

(Barb goes to the doorway of Anne's room.)

BARB: Let me show you something. *(She hovers in the doorway)* I can't go in. Grace, you'll have to.

JANICE: For the thousandth time, my name is—

BARB *(Pointing)*: Right there. That package. Get it.

(Barb returns to the table, and Janice enters the room. She returns carrying a wrapped box.)

JANICE: What's this?

BARB: Your birthday present from March. Mom was hoping some day you'd show up and she could give it to you in person. That's the kind of mother she was. And, like everything else, that responsibility now falls to me.

JANICE: I don't like that attitude. Quit making me out to be a villain. I'm not.

BARB: Are you going to open the present or not?

JANICE: In a minute.

BARB: "In a minute"!? Your first present from your birth mother and you say "in a minute"?!

JANICE: These are unfamiliar waters for me. I want to take it slow and calm. That's why I left last time. It was too much too soon. I crumbled. Thirty-five years stuffed into an hour.

BARB: We did a little crumbling ourselves.

JANICE: Was she buried beside Paul?

BARB: Of course. And Dad. The funeral even made the local papers. Wanna see?

JANICE: Please.

BARB: Most of the Reserve came, and quite a few from town. The only time she ever made the papers: when she won that lottery money and when she died.

JANICE: I recognize the church from the drive-in. I take it she was well respected.

BARB: Respect isn't the word. Mom was . . . Mom. Everybody knew her.

JANICE: Who's that old woman in the wheelchair?

BARB: Oh, that's Amy—Amelia Earhart.

JANICE: Not that again. I'm sorry, I don't buy it.

BARB: You don't have to buy it. Look out the window. Go ahead.

(Hesitant but defiant, Janice goes to the window.)

See the brown brick house way down there?

JANICE: Yeah?

BARB: That's where she lives.

(Beat.)

JANICE: Amelia Earhart, who has been missing for over fifty-five years, the focus of one of the greatest, continuous

245

searches in history, lives in a small, brown brick building on the Otter Lake Reserve in Ontario, Canada?

BARB: Why not? Elvis could be making lacrosse sticks in Six Nations for all we know.

JANICE: If that is her, how the hell did she get here?

BARB: Easy. Her plane went down in the ocean. The plane sank in eight minutes with her navigator. She was picked up the next day by a Filipino fishing boat. Nobody spoke English, and they didn't know who she was. Two weeks later, she arrives at some small fishing port in the Philippines, traveling, what's that word, incognito. All that time in the sun had made her very dark. She dyed her hair black. Bought passage on a boat to the States. A month later, she's here. Simple.

JANICE: But why? It makes no sense. What's the motivation? Why here? This little out-of-the-way jerkwater Indian Reserve in the middle of nowhere.

BARB: She was in love. We had a lot of ironworkers come from around here. A lot worked in New York for months at a time. She met Adam Williams, the man who owned that house.

JANICE: But wasn't she married?

BARB: To some publisher-type guy, but it wasn't much of a marriage.

JANICE: So you're telling me Amelia Earhart ran off with an Indian ironworker. Just like that?

BARB: You haven't seen our ironworkers. It was a perfect opportunity. She was supposed to be dead. She was tired of all the publicity and headaches. Hello, Otter Lake. She liked what this place had to offer. It became home.

JANICE: This is too weird.

BARB: This is Otter Lake.

JANICE: I still don't believe you.

BARB: Wanna meet her?

JANICE: What?

BARB: Wanna meet her? I know she's home right now. We could go visit. I know she wants to meet you. Mom told her all about you.

JANICE: I don't know. . . .

BARB: Afraid of the truth? It is Amelia Earhart. And I'm going to prove it to you. *(She goes to the window and yells)* Hey, you two, come here. *(To Janice)* Get your shoes on.

JANICE: Do you think we should?

BARB: Definitely.

(The boys enter.)

RODNEY: You yelled, sweetness?

BARB: I want you or him to drive us down to Amy's, okay, sweetie?

TONTO: Sweetie? Have you been drinking?

(The boys see all the liquor.)

Holy mackerel! Where'd all that come from?

RODNEY: Must be a Chiefs' Convention in town.

BARB: You leave that stuff alone. That's for Grace and me.

TONTO: You got a stomach pump to go with it?

BARB: Just drive us, okay? We'll take care of the rest. Let's go.

(Barb and Janice get up to leave.)

JANICE: Oh, Barb, I'm out of wine.

BARB: No problem, got more, lots more. It ain't a Chardonnay, but around here we have a saying: "Beggars can't be choosers." You'll just have to force down this Beaujolais.

JANICE: Philistines. No more Chardonnay. I'm going to complain to the manager.

BARB: Rodney, grab me a couple beers. I'm running low.

(The women walk out giggling.)

TONTO: What the hell was all that?
RODNEY: Be afraid, be very afraid.
BARB *(Offstage)*: Rodney!
RODNEY: Coming, dear. *(He grabs some beers)*
TONTO: You know what's going on, don't you?
RODNEY: Relax, things are going smoothly. Just as I planned.
TONTO: Any smoother they'll be unconscious.

scene two

It is approximately an hour later and a bit darker. The door opens and Tonto enters, supporting Janice, who is extremely drunk.

TONTO: Easy going. Right in here.
JANICE: Hey, I've been here before. Thirty-six years ago.
  (She bursts out laughing drunkenly)
TONTO: Yeah, yeah, you're hilarious.

(Rodney and Barb enter in the same state.)

BARB: I love you, Rodney.
RODNEY: So do I.

(The two men dump the women at the seats.)

TONTO: What now?
JANICE: Barb, wine?
BARB *(Whining)*: Okay.

(The women burst out laughing.)

TONTO: You realize this was one of the reasons I gave up drinking.

(Barb looks up at the boys.)

BARB: Are you two still here?

RODNEY: Yeah.

BARB: Why?

JANICE: Why not? *(She laughs at her own joke)*

BARB: Girls' night out. Out! *(To Tonto)* You, too.

TONTO: Maybe, like, you two should cut down a bit.

JANICE: It's Barb's idea. We're celebrating Anne.

TONTO: Yeah, well, I don't think it's right.

BARB: Just like a man. Just when you're having a good time, they go and pull out.

(Confused, Tonto looks at Rodney.)

RODNEY: Hey, she's not talking about me. You think maybe they're bonding a little too much?

TONTO: Was that your idea?

RODNEY: My idea was to get them together alone, by themselves somewhere.

TONTO: Maybe they can share a room at the detox center.

BARB: OUT!

(The men exit quickly.)

BARB: Okay, straighten up. It's time to get serious.

JANICE: Well, for two people who don't drink much, we're sure doing okay.

BARB: Rodney is so cute, isn't he?

JANICE: Yep, cute, that's the word I was thinking. Cute. Cute Rodney. Rodney the cute. Sir Rodney the Cute. Barb, what's he like in bed? Is he any good?

BARB: Let's find out. *(Yelling)* Hey, Rodney, come here. *(Rodney sticks his head in the doorway)* Grace wants to know if you're any good in bed?

(Beat.)

RODNEY: Um . . . Uh . . .

(For once Rodney has no snappy retort. He quietly disappears back outside. They burst out laughing again.)

JANICE: He is cute. Want another one?

BARB: You betcha. I thought you didn't drink beer.

JANICE: Like you said: "Beggars can't be choosers."

BARB: I haven't done this in years.

JANICE: Barb, do you think it was proper for us to go over to Amy's like this? In this condition, I mean?

BARB: Oh, Amy could throw them back with the best of them. If anything I think she found us funny. I wonder why? So what did you think of our little Amy Hart?

JANICE: My Lord Christ, you were right. That is her. I can't believe it!

BARB: Believe it. And I can't believe you offered to represent her as her lawyer! That is so tacky.

JANICE: I know, I know. It just sort of popped out. The lawyer runs deep, I guess. What was that she said to me in that language?

BARB: It's called Annishnawbe, Ojibway for Christ's sake. Will you get these things straight? This isn't kindergarten.

JANICE: Amelia Earhart speaks fluent Annishnawbe Ojibway. It gets stranger and stranger.

BARB: Why wouldn't she? She's been here over fifty years. Her and Mom used to rattle on for hours.

JANICE: So what did she call me again?

BARB: Wawasquaneh sim.

JANICE: What does it mean?

BARB: My little flower.

JANICE: Amelia Earhart called me her little flower?

BARB: No. That's what Mom used to call you when you were a little baby. "My little flower." Times were poor, so your first bed was made from old pillowcases patterned with flowers. So Mom started calling you her little flower. Wawasquaneh sim.

JANICE: That's sweet.

BARB: Isn't it.

JANICE: I like Amy.

BARB: I'm so happy.

JANICE: This has got to be the greatest story of the decade.

BARB: What is? That Mom called you her little flower? Talk about a slow news day.

JANICE: No. Amelia. Here, in Otter Lake.

BARB: Oh, but that's our story, the village's.

JANICE: I can't believe you won't let me tell anybody this. It's not fair.

BARB: She's a part of this community. This whole Reserve is like a family. You don't go telling secrets on family.

JANICE: And you consider her family?

BARB: She was one of Mom's best friends. And, remember, she's your godmother.

JANICE: I know! My godmother! Amelia Earhart is my god-mother. I gotta tell somebody. That is so cool.

(Janice knocks over her bottle of beer, spilling it.)

BARB: That wasn't.

JANICE: Barb, this is unbelievable.

BARB: What's so hard to believe?

JANICE: Barb, think about it. I was born here, but I don't feel at home here, and Amelia Earhart does. She's family and I'm not because the Children's Aid Society took me away. Doesn't all this seem a little weird to you?

BARB: After this many beers everything seems weird. *(Testing Janice)* Are you gonna tell on Amy?

JANICE: I don't think anyone would believe me.

BARB: Then, Grace, you gotta problem.

JANICE: I really wish you wouldn't call me Grace.

BARB: Why not? It's your name.

JANICE: No, it's not. My name is Janice. I didn't know about "Grace" until six months ago. I don't feel comfortable being addressed that way. It's like somebody calling you Susan or Victoria all of a sudden. It doesn't feel right.

BARB: Fine, *Janice.*

JANICE: I've made you mad again, haven't I?

BARB: You're just so white.

JANICE: You make that sound so bad.

BARB: It is. You're not white. You're Indian—Ojibway. Go look in a mirror.

JANICE: I know what I am. I've spent most of my life trying to figure that out. I don't need you telling me what I am and am not.

BARB: I don't have to tell you anything. Like I said, looking in the mirror will tell you everything.

JANICE: I've been looking in the mirror for thirty-five years. Tell me what makes an Indian then, Barb? Come on, tell me. What is an Indian? Is an Indian someone who drinks? Look, Barb, I'm drinking. *(She takes a swig of beer)*

BARB: That's bullshit, and you know it.

JANICE: Do you speak this Ojibway language?

BARB: Yeah, kinda.

JANICE: Then if it's so important to you, teach it to me.

BARB: When?

JANICE: Right now. I'm pretty good with languages. What do you call this? *(She holds up a bottle of beer)*

BARB: You're crazy.

JANICE: No, I want to know. What do you call a bottle of beer?

BARB: It isn't that easy. . . .

JANICE: If you try hard enough, anything can be easy. Beer!

BARB: Beer. Let's see. *(Thinking)* Shinkopiiwaabo. That sounds like it.

JANICE: Shinki . . . Shinki . . .

BARB: Shinkopiiwaabo.

JANICE: Shinkopiiwaabo. Wine.

BARB: Um, wine is Zhoominaabo.

JANICE: Zhoominaabo. Shinkopiiwaabo and Zhoominaabo. Window.

BARB: Waasechikan.

JANICE: Waasechikan. How about that lake out there?

BARB: Saakaikan. Is any of this sinking in?

JANICE: Don't rush me. Saakaikan. So far so good. What's next?

BARB: Ahneen, hello. Co-waabmen, I'll be seeing you.

JANICE: Ahneen, co-waabmen. Next.

BARB: Numbers. Want your numbers?

JANICE: Shoot.

BARB: Okay, repeat after me.

(Janice tries very hard to mimic each word.)

BARB:	JANICE:
One	Pashig
Two	Niish
Three	Nswi
Four	Niiwin
Five	Naanan
Six	Koodswaswi
Seven	Niizhwaaswi
Eight	Niizhwaaswa

(Janice stumbles over the Ojibway number eight.)

JANICE: Nishwash. *(Barb bursts out laughing)* Nishwash. What? What did I say?

BARB *(Through the laughter)*: Nishwash!

JANICE: What?

BARB: You said Nishwash. That means a guy's crotch.

JANICE: Nishwash?! *(She bursts out laughing, too)* Maybe I should wait till I'm sober.

BARB: Oh, I wish the boys were here for that one. That was funny.

JANICE: Hey, maybe I can teach you something. I can speak French fluently, some Italian, and I'm still pretty good with Latin. A holdover from my school days.

BARB: An Indian who speaks Italian and Latin. How do you say, "Want another beer?" in Italian?

JANICE: That would be, "Vuole un'altra birra?"

BARB: Forget it. I won't even try that.

JANICE: And the correct answer would be, "Si, certamente." Certainly. Wanna learn some French?

BARB: No, thanks. Four years of high school French taught me all I'd need to know. Ou est la salle de bain? I figure with that under my belt, I can survive just about anything.

JANICE: Then I guess I have nothing to teach you.

(Barb is silent for a moment.)

BARB: You could do me a favor.

JANICE: Me? What?

BARB: You know about money, right? I mean you obviously aren't hurting. . . .

JANICE: Barb, are you hitting me up for a loan?

BARB: Don't flatter yourself. It's all that money we got from the lottery Mom won.

JANICE: If you want, I can set you up with some good investment consultants.

BARB: You. Why don't you look after it for us?

JANICE: It would be better if you had a professional—

BARB: It would be better if we had family looking after family.

JANICE: It would make me feel uncomfortable.

BARB: And giving all our money to some white stranger will make me feel comfortable?

JANICE: You asked for my opinion, I gave it.

BARB: Never mind. I'm sorry I asked. This is not the kind of conversation you would hear on your typical Indian Reserve. Maybe we could start a whole new Reserve for people like you, where you could talk about investment counselors and jazz guitarists and Saabs and stuff.

JANICE: Are you trying to hurt me?

BARB: I can get a car out of a snow-covered ditch. I can chop wood, clean a fish. Not much call for those talents in the big city, huh?

JANICE: I guess Tonto would have to join me on that Reserve.

BARB: No, Tonto's as Indian as they come. It has nothing to do with being adopted. It has to do with being taken away. Some are taken away but never leave. You had a whole family waiting to accept you, and you ran. You took yourself away. That's the difference. And unfortunately, that's the truth of the matter.

JANICE: For you. I have my own truth.

BARB: Truth is truth. You're just playing lawyer again.

JANICE: You wanna play lawyer? You wanna play fucking lawyer? Your honor, my client, one Janice Wirth, was taken into custody by the Children's Aid Society in 1955 in the false belief that her mother, Anne Wabung, was not maintaining a proper and adequate home environment for the infant. It appeared the father had abandoned the family when, in fact, the father had secretly enlisted in the army as a means of providing financial assistance for his family. Flash-forward thirty-five years. After many years of soul-searching and trepidation, my client seeks out her birth family, to put the final piece in the puzzle of her life together. Satisfied with what she's learned, she returns to the world in which she was raised. However, finding herself under severe emotional stress due to her visit, my client is unable to resume work. She decides to take two months off, to deal with the bouncing around in her head. She finally gets herself back together when she finds herself right back where she began. In the same kitchen, with the same people, with the same problems. That, your honor is our case.

(Silence.)

BARB: Wow, you're good at that.

JANICE: It's the truth.

BARB: I guess this is what Mom meant when she said, "Only drunks and children tell the truth."

JANICE: Maybe.

BARB: Mom had a lot of sayings like that.

JANICE: My mother didn't.

BARB: No?

JANICE: She was quite practical, serious. She didn't have much use for cute little sayings. I wonder what I would be like if I had grown up here.

BARB: Probably fatter.

JANICE: Wonderful. When I was a little girl, I always dreamt my mother was somebody like Pocahontas or Saca-jewea. I used to read all about them. Did you know Saca-jewea was a Shoshoni word meaning Bird Woman?

BARB: Binshii-kweh. That means Bird Woman in Annish-nawbe, Ojibway.

JANICE: Binshii-kweh. I must remember that. I also used to dream I had a sister.

BARB: But probably not like me.

JANICE: I seem to remember canoes and buckskin. I don't remember why, though.

BARB: Couldn't have been me then. Never had a buckskin dress in my life. And I hate canoeing, my legs cramp.

JANICE: I wonder if that's why I bought that white fur coat of mine, my heritage coming through.

BARB: Doubt it. You're the only Indian I know who has one.

JANICE: I wanted to belong here so bad. When I drove up that driveway, it seemed like I had prepared my whole life for that meeting. But from the moment I arrived, I knew I didn't belong. You didn't even like me.

BARB: I didn't like you because I knew you were going to hurt Mom.

JANICE: How could you know that?

BARB: Easy. You weren't real to her. You couldn't possibly be everything she dreamed. Somewhere down the line, she would realize you weren't a dream, weren't perfect, and her world would come crashing down. And as usual, I would be there to cry with her. It wasn't you I didn't like, it was the bomb I knew was waiting to go off. I didn't personally start to dislike you until you walked out. The minute that door closed behind you, I knew it was over. *(Beat)* You killed her, you know? As sure as you put a gun against her head. She died because of you.

JANICE: That's not fair.

BARB: No, it's not, is it? I loved Mom, she loved you, and you killed her.

JANICE: Quit saying that.

BARB: When you left, you took her spirit, her will to live, with you. She was dead long before last Tuesday. It just took a while for her body to catch up. Drink up, Janice.

(Janice punches Barb. She goes flying across the room, creating a loud crash.)

JANICE: Don't you dare hang all of that on my head. If you want to hate me then hate me. But you have no goddamn right to blame me for Anne's death. I'm part of this whole fucking picture, too.

(Tonto and Rodney come running in, alerted by the noise.)

(Yelling) Get out!

(Startled, the boys quickly do as they're told. Barb picks herself up slowly.)

I am so sorry for Anne's death, but I am not responsible for what happened to her. I can't be. I can't handle more guilt. Why do you think I didn't want to come here? I've got scars of my own. I know I walked out of here, and I have to live with that fact. You don't think I realize that she's gone and that I'll never know what kind of woman she was or what could have happened between us? I grew up wanting to hate this woman, thinking my whole life was her fault. That's why I ran out of this house. I was all prepared to dislike and pity some old Indian woman that lost me because of alcohol. Instead, I find this wonderful, sweet, caring woman that had her baby taken away by the system for no good reason. A baby she loved and fought to get back. I began to feel it all. I started to care, Barb, but I didn't want to care. If I care, I'll realize what I've lost.

BARB: Mom always said you couldn't miss something you never had.

JANICE: She was wrong.

BARB: I guess. Grace, you're all I've got left.

JANICE: I thought you didn't like me.

BARB: My brother's dead, my father, my mother. I'm an orphan. I don't wanna be alone.

JANICE: You've got Rodney.

BARB: It's not the same.

JANICE: No, I guess it isn't. I don't feel well.

BARB: Neither do I.

JANICE: Oh, your poor face. What did I do?

BARB: Not my face. My stomach.

JANICE: I thought I hit you in the face.

BARB: You did. I think. But my stomach . . . Can you help me sit down?

JANICE: Okay.

(Janice puts her arm around Barb and helps her over to a chair. Once Barb is sitting, Janice takes her arm away, but Barb grabs it.)

BARB: Thank you.

(Barb passes out, her arm knocks the birthday present onto the floor. Janice goes to make her more comfortable.)

JANICE: Poor Barb. I'm so sorry for your face, Anne, every-thing.

(Janice trips over the present on the floor. Drunkenly she picks it up. Fighting tears, she opens the present, revealing a large dreamcatcher.)

What the hell is this? *(She notices a tag attached. She struggles to read it)* ". . . Good dreams pass through the webbing, bad dreams are caught and dissolved by the early morning light. Usually given to newlyweds to hang over the window in their bedrooms or to the mother of a newborn baby, to ensure her baby will only have pleasant dreams." . . . Newborn baby . . .

(Janice starts to cry. Slowly she lays her head down on the table and passes out. The men enter tentatively, checking out the territory. Tonto lifts Janice's head, but it falls with a thud.)

TONTO: Normally that should hurt.
   (Tonto examines the present) What's all this stuff? Nice dreamcatcher. Do you mind telling me what's going on here?

RODNEY: It worked.

TONTO: What worked?

RODNEY: The plan. Barb's plan. With a little coaching from yours truly.

TONTO: Oh, God, what have you two done this time?

RODNEY: They needed to bond. And nobody bonds like a couple of drunks.

TONTO: But it's a false bonding. Drunks will kill each other over the last mouthful of booze. You're playing with fire.

RODNEY: Firewater?!

TONTO: Damn it, Rodney, this is serious. Alcohol doesn't solve problems, it creates them.

RODNEY: I know, I know, but the system fucked them up royally. Something equally screwy had to fuck them back down. Fight fire with fire.

TONTO: I used to work in a detox center, you didn't. Two wrongs don't make a right.

(Rodney approaches Barb.)

RODNEY: Look at her. Sleeping peacefully. She just got drunk with her adopted sister for the first time. I'm sure there's a country song in there somewhere.

TONTO: Rodney, why did you do this?

RODNEY: I told you . . .

TONTO: Uh-uh. You told me what you did, but not why. There's something going on in that book-clogged head of yours. Let me have a peek.

RODNEY: Anne.

TONTO: Yes?

RODNEY: The car accident, when Paul died. She never blamed me for that.

TONTO: Why should she? Wasn't your fault.

RODNEY: He was coming to pick me up at the bar. I phoned him, remember? He wouldn't have been on that road if it hadn't been for me. Half the village was giving me dirty looks, but, God bless her, she never thought a single bad thing about me. What a woman.

TONTO: And all this? . . .

RODNEY: I took part of her family away. I had to return another part. Barb planted the idea, but I cultivated it. Remember the stuff with the night blindness?

TONTO: Oh, Rodney, man . . .

RODNEY: It's okay now. Really.

(Barb moans and wakens.)

BARB: Rodney?

RODNEY: Right here, Barb.

BARB: I love my mother.

RODNEY: I know you do, sweetie. And she loves you.

BARB: Put me in her bed. I want to sleep there.

RODNEY: Sure thing.

(Rodney helps the almost unconscious Barb toward the bedroom.)

TONTO: Okay, genius, what do I do with this one?

RODNEY: Put her in Barb's room. And Tonto, better get some buckets out of the back room.

TONTO: Good idea. Oooh, are you gonna be in pain tomorrow, Kemosabe.

scene three

The scene opens on a graveyard. All four enter the grounds. Again, the women are leaning quite heavily on the men. Barb and Janice are in pain.

BARB *(Squinting)*: Rodney, do something about that sun, please?

JANICE *(To Tonto)*: Not so fast. Easy. Slow down. Never again.

BARB: Rodney, Rodney, if you love me, you'll kill me right now.

JANICE: I may never eat again.

RODNEY: Boy, I wish we had a camera.

(They arrive at Anne's grave.)

TONTO: Here we are.

JANICE: So this is it.

TONTO: You sure you're up to this?

JANICE: No time like the present.

TONTO: Still, it is kinda tacky visiting your mother's grave hungover.

RODNEY: That's my Barb, tacky all the way.

BARB: Okay, you guys, get away. Go wait at the car. This is daughter stuff.

RODNEY: You sure? You look a little unsteady.

BARB: It's okay. We'll be fine.

RODNEY: We'll be over here, if you need help.

(The men exit.)

JANICE: God, I feel awful. Maybe this wasn't such a good idea.

BARB: Mom used to say, "Self-inflicted wounds don't count." Janice, hold me up.

JANICE: I can barely hold myself up.

BARB: Okay. I'm okay.

(Barb walks to the tombstone.)

Mom, look who I brought. It's Gra—It's Janice, Mom. You were right. She did come home again.

JANICE: I don't know what to say, Barb.

BARB: You'll think of something. I got to go. I'm not feeling well. *(She hobbles away in obvious pain. Calls plaintively)* Rodney!!

(Janice is left alone at Anne's grave.)

JANICE: Hello, Anne. Wherever you are, I hope you're feeling better than I am. The last time you saw me, I was a mess. Confused. In great emotional pain. Now it's physical pain. I don't know which one is better. *(Pause)* Yes, I do. The physical pain will go away. The emotional pain will take longer. If at all. I'm sorry I left the way I did. It must have been a horrible Christmas for you. But you must understand I didn't walk out on you. I walked out on me. To everybody I was Grace, but to me I'm Janice. I don't know if I can ever be the Grace you wanted, or the Grace Barb wants. I don't know anything anymore. I'm hungover. I've met Amelia Earhart. And I'm standing at your grave, a woman I barely got to know. What a town this Otter Lake of yours. I guess the reason I'm here is to seek forgiveness for the bad thoughts I had about you. I couldn't help it. I needed a reason, some excuse for what happened to me, what I went through. You were all I had. Growing up in the home I did, looking the way I do, the schools I went to, the jokes I heard. I had to blame somebody. I feel so ashamed. You were so kind to me, so nice. And all I wanted was evidence, proof to justify my anger. And there you were, so sweet and accepting. My whole life fell away. Everything I had wanted to believe was gone because of you. That made me even more angry. I hate myself now. I'm tired of being angry. I'm tired of mistrusting you. I'm tired of everything. I just don't want to fight it any more. I'm sorry. You deserve better. . . .

(Janice collapses. Tonto comes running up to her side.)

TONTO: Yo, Janice, are you okay?

JANICE: I don't know anymore.

TONTO: Know what?

JANICE: Anything.

TONTO: That's an awful lot to forget after one night of drinking. Trust me, you know everything you need to know. People may learn a few facts or stories over the years, but all the real important things in life we know at birth.

JANICE: I don't need graveside therapy right now. You had it easy, you grew up here. You knew everything.

TONTO: That has nothing to do with it. Janice, have you ever heard of a bird called a cowbird? *(Janice shakes her head)* Interesting bird, the cowbird. They lay their eggs in other birds' nests, then fly off.

JANICE *(Sniffling)*: Cuckoos.

TONTO: What?

JANICE: Cuckoos. The English have a similar bird called a cuckoo.

TONTO: Whatever. Anyway, the robins or starlings, whichever the nest belongs to, they raise the baby cowbird as a robin or a starling or whatever. But when it grows up, the cowbird is still a cowbird. It lays its eggs in another bird's nest just like any other cowbird. Somewhere, deep inside, it knew it was a cowbird. No matter how it was raised or what it was taught. What are you, robin or cowbird?

JANICE: I don't know.

TONTO: Well, let's go find out.

JANICE: What do you think I've been trying to do all these years?

TONTO: Yeah, but you've been doing it alone. Two, three, four, eight, ten heads are better than one.

JANICE: But it's not your problem.

TONTO: I'm a cowbird, too, remember. Let me help, okay?

(Beat.)

JANICE: Why not?
TONTO: Are you done here?
JANICE: Not yet. Go ahead, I'll be down in a moment.

(Tonto exits. Janice turns around and looks at the grave one last time. She sees a daisy growing off to the side. She picks it and gently places it against the headstone.)

Co-waabmen, Mom, from your daughter, Grace.

(Janice walks toward the car, exiting. The lights go down.)

END OF PLAY

During the first thirteen years of his professional career, Drew Hayden Taylor has written, directed or worked in some way on approximately seventeen film and video documentaries about Native issues. During an experimental journalism phase, Mr. Taylor spent a year and a half with CBC Radio as a Native affairs reporter, and later dabbled with *Macleans*, *This Magazine*, *Southam News* and other periodicals.

Mr. Taylor has worked for television in various capacities on the *Spirit Bay* television series, as a publicist for the made-for-TV movie *Where the Spirit Lives*, and as a writer for *The Beachcombers*, *Street Legal* and *North of Sixty*. One of Canada's first Native scriptwriters, he has story-edited numerous writing workshops for well-known minority writers. He is currently working on two movie projects.

Mr. Taylor's more recent passion has been in the theatre, thanks to a stint as Playwright-in-Residence for Native Earth Performing Arts in the late 1980s. (From 1994 to 1997, Drew proudly served as Native Earth's Artistic Director.) In the last eight years, he has received thirty-two professional productions of his plays. His play, *Girl Who Loved Her Horses*, was nominated for a Chalmers Award. *Only Drunks and Children Tell the Truth*, the sequel to his play *Someday*, was nominated for four Dora Mavor Moore Awards, winning Outstanding New Play in June 1996. In the summer of 1997, "The Baby Blues" was produced by Pennsylvania Centre Stage. It won first prize at the University of Alaska Anchorage Native Playwriting Contest, and was produced in Toronto in the fall of 1998. His volumes of plays are: *Toronto at Dreamer's Rock/Education Is Our Right* (for which he won the Chalmers Canadian Play Award for Best Play for Young Audiences), *The Bootlegger Blues* (for which he won the Canadian Authors Association Literary Award for Best Drama) and *Someday*. His fourth book, an anthology he co-edited with Linda Jaine, titled *Voices: Being Native in Canada*, was published by the University of Saskatchewan Press.

Mr. Taylor has also written short stories for various anthologies and satirical commentaries for the *Globe and Mail*, *This Magazine*, *The Toronto Star*, *CBC Radio* and various Native newspapers. In 1997, a collection of these pieces was published in book form: *Funny, You Don't Look Like One: Observations of a Blue-Eyed Ojibway*. Next on his plate is a collection of short stories.

The Woman
Who Was
a Red Deer
Dressed
for the
Deer Dance

diane glancy

author's statement

I want to connect with the land to find placement for the words I write, which is a vital aspect of storying. In Indian communities, you can actually tell a story by mentioning various places in the landscape, and the hearers will remember what took place on that land, and therefore know the story. So connecting words to the land on which they happen is a necessary act for Native writing.

Native American storytelling is also an act of gathering. It takes many voices to tell a story. Many points of view. One voice alone is not enough because we are what we are in relationship to others, and we each have our different way of seeing. Native American writing is also a placement or balancing or alignment of voices so that the story may come through. A relational stance is the construct of Native American writing. In my short stories, poems and creative nonfiction, I can follow the rules of conflict/resolution, one point of view, plot, chronological order and the usual, but there is something essential in Native storying that is not included in the above, which is hard to define. It's a migratory and interactive process of the moveable parts within the story. It's also the element of Native American oral tradition told with what it is not—the written word—then returned to what it is by the act of the voice.

I think *The Woman Who Was a Red Deer Dressed for the Deer Dance* is an example of Native spoken-word art. The poetic piece is an intermixing of ethnographic material (the story of *Ahw'uste*), with pieces of the old language (Cherokee), and with contemporary materials (the granddaughter's life in the soup kitchen and dance bars).

I would like to take the process a step further, and extend ethnographic monologue to ethnopoetic dialogue in a new mix of oral tradition with the sound of more than one voice.

I want to work more with experimental poetics in a combination of fiction, poetry, myth/magic/ethnography, and the drama of Indian life in the harsh reality of poverty and commodities in the urban/reservation life.

I think writing exists, in part, for healing, not only in the writer, but also for the reader/hearer. For instance, in Navajo and Hopi sand paintings, the painter aligns the design in the sand to the hurt in the one needing healing, and the alignment draws the hurt into the painting, and the painting is destroyed, and the ailment along with it. Thus, there is healing. Storying should do the same. It is much needed in a culture with a ninety percent alcoholism rate, poverty, purposelessness and low racial esteem. It is through art that healing has a chance. I suppose there's an analogy between Native storying and sand painting. During storytelling, you come together in a tribal gathering. You hear the words. They align with the feelings inside you. The feelings are pulled to the surface where they can be dealt with. When the words are over, you have worked the renewal process into your life.

The Woman Who Was a Red Deer Dressed for the Deer Dance was created in part with commissioning support from the Walker Art Center, Minneapolis, Minnesota. It was presented September 14, 1995 at the New Dramatists/Mutt Rep Native American Playwriting Festival in New York City, and was performed by Siouxson Monson (director) and Barbara Kidd Calvano. It was performed at the Walker Art Center on November 11, 1995, with Diane Glancy (Grandmother) and Carolyn Erler (Girl). The play received a production at American Indian Communtiy House in New York City on December 7, 1995, and was performed by Margarita Promponas and Siouxson Monson (director).

My deer dress is the way I felt,
transformed by the power of ceremony.

This dramatic/poetic piece is an intermixing of ethnographic material (the story of *Ahw'uste* was taken from Doi on Ahu'usti and Asudi on Ahw'usti in *Friends of Thunder, Tales of the Oklahoma Cherokees* (Frank and Anna Kilpatrick, eds., University of Oklahoma Press, Norman, 1995), pieces of the old language (Cherokee), and contemporary materials (the granddaughter's life in a soup kitchen and dance bars). It is a dialogue/monologue between a grandmother and her granddaugther, each arguing against the other for her own way of life. The grandmother talks about stories and the spirits and the red deer dress she has made to feel more in tune with *Ahw'uste*, a mythological spirit deer. The granddaughter talks about the problems of a contemporary life, including her experiences with several men. The grandmother continues talking about *Ahw'uste* and the spirits, who in the end, she realizes, let her down. "Damned spirits. Didn't always help out. Let us have it rough sometimes," she says as she talks of hunger and the uncertainty she faced in her life. The granddaughter says she has to look for work, which she can't find, and says she doesn't have time for the *Ahw'uste* and the spirits, and longs for more practical help from her grandmother. In the end, the granddaughter enters some of her grandmother's world and says, "You know, I've learned she told me more without speaking than she did with her words."

In this I try. Well, I try. To combine the overlapping realities of myth, imagination and memory with spaces for the silences. To make a story. The voice speaking in different agencies. Well, I try to move on with the voice in its guises. A young woman and her grandmother in a series of scenelets. Divided by a line of flooring. Shifting between dialogue and monologue. Not with the linear construct of conflict/resolution, but with the story moving like rain on a windshield, between differing and unreliable experiences.

GIRL: Have you heard of *Ahw'uste?*
GRANDMOTHER: I have, but I've forgotten.
GIRL: They said they fed her.
GRANDMOTHER: Yes, they did.
GIRL: What was she?
GRANDMOTHER: I don't know.
GIRL: A deer?
GRANDMOTHER: Yes, a deer. A small deer.
GIRL: She lived in the house, didn't she?
GRANDMOTHER: Yes, she did. She was small.
GIRL: They used to talk about her a long time ago, didn't they?
GRANDMOTHER: Yes, they did.
GIRL: Did you ever see one of the deer?

GRANDMOTHER: I saw the head of one once. Through the window. Her head was small, and she had tiny horns.

GIRL: Like a goat?

GRANDMOTHER: Yes, like that.

GIRL: Where did you see her?

GRANDMOTHER: I don't know. Someone had her. I just saw her. That's all.

GIRL: You saw the head?

GRANDMOTHER: Yes, just the head.

GIRL: What did they call her?

GRANDMOTHER: A small deer.

GIRL: Where did you see her?

GRANDMOTHER: What do they call it down there?

GIRL: Deer Creek.

GRANDMOTHER: Yes, that's where I saw her.

GIRL: What did they use her for?

GRANDMOTHER: I don't know. There were bears there, too. And larger deer.

GIRL: Elk maybe?

GRANDMOTHER: Yes, they called them elk.

GIRL: Why did they have them?

GRANDMOTHER: They used them for medicine.

GIRL: How did they use them?

GRANDMOTHER: They used their songs.

GIRL: The deer sang?

GRANDMOTHER: No, they were just there. They made the songs happen.

GIRL: The elk, too?

GRANDMOTHER: Yes, the elk, too.

GIRL: And the moose?

GRANDMOTHER: Yes, the moose.

GIRL: It was like talking to myself when I stayed with her. If I asked her something, she answered flat as the table between us.

Open your deer mouth and talk. You never say anything on your own. I could wear a deer dress. I could change into a deer like you. We could deer dance in the woods under the red birds. The blue jay. The finch.

U-da-tlv:da de-s-gi-ne-hv'-si, E-li'-sin

Pass me the cream, Grandmother.

My cup and saucer on the oilcloth.

How can you be a deer? You only have two legs.

GRANDMOTHER: I keep the others under my dress.

GIRL: It was a wordless world she gave me. Not silent, but wordless. Oh, she spoke, but her words seemed hollow. I had to listen to her deer noise. I had to think what she meant. It was like having a conversation with myself. I asked. And I answered. Well—I could hear what I wanted.

When I was with her, I talked and never stopped because her silence ate me like buttered toast.

What was she saying? Her words were in my own hearing?

I had to know what she said before I could hear it?

GRANDMOTHER: I don't like this world anymore. We're reduced to what can be seen and felt. We're brought from the universe of the head into the kitchen full of heat and cold.

GIRL: She fought to live where we aren't tied to table and fork and knife and chair.

It was her struggle against what happens to us.

Why can't you let me in just once and speak to me as one of your own? You know I have to go into the *seeable*—live away from the world of imagination. You could give me more.

GIRL: You work the church soup kitchen before? You slop up the place, and I get to clean up. You night shifts think you're tough shit. But I tell you, you don't know nothing. I think you took my jean jacket. The one with Jesus on the cross in sequins on the back. Look—I see your girl wearing it, I'll have you on the floor.

Don't think I don't know who's taking the commodities—I'm watching those boxes of macaroni and cheese disappear.

I know it was you who lost the key to the storeroom, and I had to pay for the locksmith to change the lock. They kept nearly my whole check. I couldn't pay rent. I only got four payments left on my truck. I'm not losing it.

———

GIRL: She said once, there were wings the deer had when it flew. You couldn't see them, but they were there. They pulled out from the red deer dress. Like leaves opened from the kitchen table—

Like the stories that rode on her silence. You knew they were there. But you had to decide what they meant. Maybe that's what she gave me—the ability to fly when I knew I had no wings. When I was left out of the old world that moved in her head. When I had to go on without her stories.

They get crushed in this *seeable* world.

But there're still there. I hear them in the silence sometimes.

I want to wear a deer dress. I want to deer dance with *Ahw'uste.* . . .

———

GIRL: What does *Ahw'uste* mean in English?
GRANDMOTHER: I don't know what the English was. But *Ahw'uste* was a spirit animal.

GIRL: What does that mean?

GRANDMOTHER: She was only there for some people to see.

GIRL: She was only there when you thought she was?

GRANDMOTHER: She had wings, too. If you thought she did. She was there to remind us—you think you see something you're not sure of. But you think it's there anyway.

GIRL: Maybe Jesus used wings when he flew to heaven. Ascended right up the air. Into holy Heaven. Floating and unreachable. I heard them stories at church when I worked the soup kitchen.

Or maybe they're wings like the spirits use when they fly between the earth and sky. But when you pick up a spirit on the road, you can't see his wings—he's got them folded into his jacket.

GRANDMOTHER: They say rocket ships go there now.

GIRL: The ancestors?

GRANDMOTHER: Yes, all of them wear red deer dresses.

GIRL: With two legs under their dresses?

GRANDMOTHER: In the afterworld they let them down.

GIRL: A four-legged deer with wings—wearing a red deer dress with shoes and hat? Dancing in the leaves—red maple, I suppose. After they're raked up to the sky? Where they stay red forever only if they think they do?

Sometimes your hooves are impatient inside your shoes. I see them move. You stuff twigs in your shoes to make them fit your hooves. But I know hooves are there.

Why would I want to be a deer like you?

Why would I want to eat without my hands?

Why would I want four feet?

What would I do with a tail? It would make a lump behind my jeans.

Do you know what would happen if I walked down the street in a deer dress?

If I looked for a job?

I already know I don't fit anywhere—I don't need to be reminded—I'm at your house, Grandma, with

my sleeping bag and old truck—I don't have any place
else to go. . . .

GIRL (*Angrily*): OK, dude. Dudo. I pick you up on the road.
I take you to the next town to get gas for your van, take
you back when it still won't start. I pull you to town
'cause you don't have money for a tow truck. I wait two
hours while you wait. Buy you supper. I give you love,
what do you want? Hey, dude, your cowboy boots are
squeaking, your hat with the beaded band. Your CB's
talking to the highway, the truckers, the girls driving
by themselves, that's what you look for. You take what
we got. While you got one eye on your supper, one eye
on your next girl.

I could have thought you were a spirit. You could
have been something more than a dude. . . .

GRANDMOTHER: The leaves only get to be red for a moment.
Just a moment, and then the tree grieves all winter
until the leaves come back. But they're green through
the summer. The maple waits for the leaves to turn
red. All it takes is a few cold mornings. A few days left
out of the warmth.

Then the maple tree has red leaves for a short while.

GIRL (*Angrily*): I can't do it your way, Grandma. I have to
find my own trail—is that why you won't tell me? Is
that why you won't speak? I'm caught? I have no way
through? But there'll be a way through—I just can't see
it yet. And if I can't find it, it's still there. I speak it
through. Therefore, it is. If not now, then later. It's
coming—if not for me—then for others.

I have to pass through this world not having a place, but I'll go anyway.

GRANDMOTHER: That's *Ahw'uste.*

GIRL: I'll speak these stories I don't know. I'll speak because I don't know them.

GRANDMOTHER: We're like the tree waiting for the red leaves. We count on what's not there as though it is, because the maple has red leaves—only you can't always see them.

GIRL: You'd rather live with what you can't see—is that the point of your red-leaf story?

GRANDMOTHER: I was trying to help you over the hard places.

GIRL: I can get over them myself.

GRANDMOTHER: I wanted you to look for the red leaves instead of the dudes on the highway.

GIRL: A vision is *not* always enough—

GRANDMOTHER: It's all I had.

GIRL: You had me—is a vision worth more than me?

GRANDMOTHER: I wanted to keep the leaves red for you.

GIRL: I don't want you to do it for me.

GRANDMOTHER: What am I supposed to do?

GIRL: Find someone else to share your silence with.

GIRL: I was thinking we could have gone for a drive in my old truck.

GRANDMOTHER: I thought we did.

GRANDMOTHER: *Ahw'uste's* still living. Up there on the hill, straight through *(Indicating)* near Asuwosg' Precinct. A long time ago, I was walking by there, hunting horses. There was a trail that went down the hill. Now there's a highway on that hill up there, but, then, the old road divided. Beyond that, in the valley near Ayohli Amayi,

I was hunting horses when I saw them walking and I stopped.

They were this high *(Indicating)*, and had horns. They were going that direction. *(Indicating)* It was in the forest, and I wondered where they were going. They were all walking. She was going first, just this high *(Indicating)*, and she had little horns. Her horns were just as my hands are shaped—five points, they call them five points. That's the way it was. Just this high. *(Indicating)* And there was a second one, a third one, and a fourth one. The fifth one was huge, and it also had horns with five points. They stopped a while, and they watched me. I was afraid of the large one! They were turning back, looking at me. They were pawing with their feet, and I was afraid. They were showing their anger then. First they'd go *(Indicates pawing)* with the right hoof and then with the left, and they'd go: *Ti! Ti! Ti! Ti!* They kept looking at me and pawing, and I just stood still.

They started walking again and disappeared away off, and I wondered where they went. I heard my horses over there, and I went as fast as I could. I caught a horse to ride and took the others home.

There was a man named Tseg' Ahl'tadeg, and when I got there, at his house, he asked me: What did you see?

I saw something down there, I told him.

What was it?

A deer. She was just this high *(Indicating)*, and she had horns like this *(Indicating)*, and she was walking in front. The second one was this high *(Indicating)*, and the third one was this high *(Indicating)*, and the fourth one *(Indicating)*—then the rest were large.

It was *Ahw'uste*, he said.

GIRL: I thought you said *Ahw'uste* lived in a house in Deer Creek.

GRANDMOTHER: Well, she did, but these were her tribe. She was with them sometimes.

GIRL: She's the only one who lived in a house?

GRANDMOTHER: Yes.

GIRL: In Deer Creek?

GRANDMOTHER: Yes, in Deer Creek.

GIRL: Your deer dress is the way you felt when you saw the deer?

GRANDMOTHER: When I saw *Ahw'uste*, yes. My deer dress is the way I felt, transformed by the power of ceremony. The idea of it in the forest of my head.

GIRL: Speak without your stories. Just once. What are you without your deer dress? What are you without your story of *Ahw'uste*?

GRANDMOTHER: We're carriers of our stories and histories. We're nothing without them.

GIRL: We carry ourselves. Who are you besides your stories?

GRANDMOTHER: I don't know—no one ever asked.

GIRL: OK, bucko. I find out you're married. But not living with her. *You aren't married in your heart*, you say. *It's the same as not being married*. And you got kids, too? Yeah, several, I'm sure. Probably left more of them behind to take care of themselves than you admit. You think you can dance me backwards around the floor, bucko?

GRANDMOTHER: Why would I want to be like you?

GRANDMOTHER: Why can't my granddaughter wait on the spirit? Why is she impatient? It takes a while sometimes. She says, *Hey spirit, what's wrong? Your wings broke down? You need a jumper cable to get them started?*

My granddaughter wants to do what she wants. Anything that rubs against her, well, she bucks. Runs the other way. I'm not going to give her my deer dress to leave in a heap on some dude's floor. It comes from long years from my grandmother. . . .

I have to live so far away from you. Take me where you are—I feel the pull of the string. *(She touches her breastbone)* Reel me in. Just pull. I want out of here. I want to see you ancestors. Not hear the tacky world. No more.

GIRL: You always got your eye on the next world.

GRANDMOTHER: I sit by the television, watch those stupid programs.

GIRL: What do you want? Weed the garden. Do some beans for supper. Set a trap for the next spirit to pass along the road.

GRANDMOTHER: The spirits push us out so we'll know what it's like to be without them. So we'll struggle all our lives to get back in—

GIRL: Is that what life is for you? No—for me—I get busy with day-to-day stuff until it's over.

I told 'em at church I didn't take the commodities—well not all those boxes—I told 'em—shit—what did it matter?

Have you ever lost one job after another?

GRANDMOTHER: Have you eaten turnips for a week? Because that was all you had in your garden. In your cupboard. Knowing your commodities won't last because you gave them to the next family on the road? They got kids and you can hear them crying.

GIRL: Well, just step right off the earth. That's where you belong. With your four deer feet.

GRANDMOTHER: Better than your two human ones. All you do is walk into trouble.

GIRL: Because I pick up someone now and then? Didn't you know what it was like to want love?

GRANDMOTHER: Love—ha! I didn't think of that. We had children one after another. We were cooking supper or picking up some crying child or brushing the men away. Maybe we did what we didn't want to do. And we did it every day.

GIRL: Well, I want something more for my life.

GRANDMOTHER: A trucker dude or two to sleep with till they move on? Nights in a bar. The jukebox and cowboys rolling you over.

GIRL *(She slaps her)*: What did I do? Slap my grandmother? That felt good!

You deserved it. Sitting there in your smug spirit mode. I don't curl up with stories. I live in the world I see.

I've got to work. Christ—where am I going to find another job?

GRANDMOTHER: You can't live on commods alone.

GIRL: You can't drive around all day in your spirit mobile either.

GIRL: I been paying ten years on my truck, bub. You think I need a new transmission? 'Cause I got 180,000 miles on the truck and it's in the garage? You think you can sell me a new one, bubby? My truck'll run another hundred thousand. I don't have it paid for yet. You think you can sell me a used truck? You couldn't sell me mud flaps. Just get it running—try something else or my grandma'll stomp you with her hooves. My truck takes me in a vision. You got a truck that has visions? I don't see it on the list of options, bubby.

GRANDMOTHER: *Gu'-s-di i-da-da-dv-hni.* My relatives—I'm making medicine from your songs. Sometimes I feel it. But mostly I have to know it's there without seeing. I go there from the hurts he left me with—all those kids and no way to feed them but by the spirit. Sometimes I think the birds brought us food. Or somehow we weren't always hungry. That's not true. Mostly we were on our own. Damned spirits. Didn't always help out. Let us have it rough sometimes. All my kids are gone. Run off. One of my daughters calls from Little Falls sometimes. Drunk. Drugged. They all have accidents. One got shot.

What was that? *E-li'-sin*—Grandmother?

No, just the blue jay. The finch.

Maybe the ancestors—I hear them sometimes—out there, raking leaves—or I hear them if I think I do.

Hey—quiet out there, my granddaughter would say.

Just reel me in, Grandmother, I say.

GIRL: So I told 'em at my first job interview: No, I hadn't worked that kind of machine—but I could learn.

I told 'em at my second interview the same thing. . . .

I told 'em at the third . . .

At the fourth I told 'em—my grandmother was a deer. I could see her change before my eyes. She caused stories to happen. That's how I knew she could be a deer.

At the fifth I continued—I'm sewing my own red deer dress. It's different than my grandma's. Mine is a dress of words. I see *Ahw'uste* also.

At the rest of the interviews I started right in—let me talk for you, that's what I can do.

My grandma covered her trail. Left me without knowing how to make a deer dress. Left me without covering.

But I make a covering she could have left me if only she knew how.

I think I hear her sometimes—that crevice you see through into the next world. You look again, it's gone.

My heart has red trees. The afterworld must be filling up with leaves.

You know, I've learned she told me more without speaking than she did with her words.

END OF PLAY

Diane Glancy is Associate Professor of English at Macalester College in St. Paul, where she teaches Native American literature and creative writing. She had four books published in 1996–97: *Pushing the Bear*, a novel about the 1838 Trail of Tears (Harcourt Brace, New York); *The Only Piece of Furniture in the House*, a contemporary novel (Moyer Bell, Wakefield, Rhode Island); *War Cries*, a collection of nine plays (Holy Cow! Press, Duluth, Minnesota); *The West Pole*, a collection of her essays (University of Minnesota Press, Minneapolis). Her first collection of essays, *Claiming Breath* (University of Nebraska Press, Lincoln, 1991), won an American Book Award and the American Indian Prose Award. Her latest books are *Flutie*, a novel (Moyer Bell, Wakefield, Rhode Island, 1998), and *The Cold-and-Hunger Dance*, a collection of essays (University of Nebraska Press, Lincoln, 1998). In 1998, Ms. Glancy was chosen for the Sundance Native American Screenwriting Workshop. She is currently at work on the script of *Flutie*.

The Story
of Susanna

victoria nalani
kneubuhl

I am a playwright because I believe the theatre provides the possibility of a communal experience which is at once both artistic and intensely human. It is a conduit into our everyday world through which mystery and magic may still enter. At the same time, theatre can serve as a powerful platform for examining the social and political issues of our time. I am extremely proud to be part of a craft that is forceful yet transitory and fragile. I love theatre which is above all theatrical, multidimensional, lively and risky.

I hope my work has encouraged both adult and young audiences to appreciate our island home and the unique community in which we live. Having lived nearly all of my life in either Hawaii or American Samoa, I feel an unbroken connection between my self, my work and the Pacific. My sense of who I am and the visionary focus which has guided my writing are inextricably woven together with my experiences of island life. I have been fortunate as an artist in having a rich wellspring from which to draw.

production history

In 1996, *The Story of Susanna* received readings at the Women's Community Correctional Center in Kailua, Hawaii; the University of Hawaii for T. J. Mahoney, Transitional House for Women, Honolulu, Hawaii; and the Kumu Kahua Theatre in Honolulu. In the fall of 1998, the play received its first full production at the Kennedy Theatre of the University of Hawaii, Honolulu. In 1997, *The Story of Susanna* received a Jane Chambers Playwriting Award honorable mention.

The author thanks
Dr. Juli Burk for her help
as dramaturge on this play.

time and place

Prologue: Babylon, B.C.
Act I: Different times, imaginary places
Act II: Contemporary time, a transitional house

the set

Three intersecting offset circles. The Upper Circle is center back and the smallest circle. The Middle Circle is two steps lower, larger and extends forward and stage right. Two steps down, the Lower Circle, delineated at stage level, is the largest circle and extends forward and stage left. The use of these areas changes between acts and within the acts themselves. The circles are supplemented by minimal movable props.

prologue

Dreamlike. Dim lights. Distant music. Masked dancers move like shadows in a stylized dance/pantomime as Player 1 and Player 2 recount story.

PLAYER 1: This is the story of Susanna as it comes to us from the Greek Bible and the Vulgate.

PLAYER 2: There once lived a man in Babylon whose name was Joakim.

PLAYER 1: Joakim was rich, and he had a fine house, and adjoining his house was a fine garden.

PLAYER 2: He married a wife named Susanna, the daughter of Hilkiah.

PLAYER 1: And Susanna was pious and beautiful and well raised in the law of Moses.

PLAYER 2: Two of the elders of the people were appointed judges, and came constantly to Joakim's house.

PLAYER 1: And all who had cases to be decided came there.

PLAYER 2: And it happened that when the people left at midday—

PLAYER 1: Susanna would go into her husband's garden.

PLAYER 2: So the two elders saw her every day.

PLAYER 1: And they conceived a passion for her.

PLAYER 2: They were smitten with her.

PLAYER 1: Their thoughts were perverted.

PLAYER 2: And they could not look up to heaven—

PLAYER 1: or consider justice in giving judgment—

PLAYER 2: so great was their desire for her.

PLAYER 1: And they said one to another:

PLAYER 1 AND PLAYER 2 (*To each other*): "Let us agree to try to find her alone."

PLAYER 2: And it happened one day that Susanna went to the garden with her two maids.

PLAYER 1: But as the day was very hot, she said:

PLAYER 2: "Bring me olive oil and soap so I might bathe in the garden."

PLAYER 1: So the maids went back to the house not seeing the elders who were hidden.

PLAYER 2: And when the maids left, the elders ran after Susanna in the garden and said:

PLAYER 1: "We are in love with you, so you must lie with us."

PLAYER 2: "If you do not, we will testify against you."

PLAYER 1: Susanna gave a loud scream.

PLAYER 2: But the two elders shouted against her.

PLAYER 1: And the next day—

PLAYER 2: full of their wicked design to put Susanna to death,

PLAYER 1: the two elders told their story:

PLAYER 2: "As we were walking by ourselves in the garden,"

PLAYER 1: "This woman came, shut the doors of the garden and dismissed her maids."

PLAYER 2: "And a young man, who had been hidden, came to her and lay down with her."

PLAYER 1: "We were in the corner of the garden, and when we saw this wicked action,"

PLAYER 2: "we ran up to them, but we could not hold him,"

PLAYER 1: "because he was stronger."

PLAYER 2: "And he opened the doors and rushed out."

PLAYER 1 AND PLAYER 2: "This is our testimony."

PLAYER 1: Everyone believed them, and as they were the elders and the judges of the people,

PLAYER 2: they condemned Susanna to die.

PLAYER 1: As she was being led away to the place of death, the Lord heard Susanna's cries.

PLAYER 2: And the Lord stirred the holy spirit of a young man named Daniel who shouted out:

PLAYER 1: "You Israelites are such fools. Go back to the place of trial, for these men have borne false witness against a daughter of Israel."

PLAYER 2: And Daniel separated the elders widely, one from another and he went to the first elder and said:

PLAYER 1: "Now you, if you saw this woman, under which tree did she lie with the young man?"

PLAYER 2: "Well . . ."

PLAYER 1: replied the elder.

PLAYER 2: "Under the mastic tree, we saw them."

PLAYER 1: And Daniel went to the second elder and asked:

PLAYER 2: "So you, now tell me under which tree did you catch them?"

PLAYER 1: "Why under the live oak tree!"

PLAYER 1 AND 2: "The angel of God, has heard these lies,"

PLAYER 2: said Daniel.

PLAYER 1 AND PLAYER 2: "He is waiting to saw you in two and destroy you both."

PLAYER 2: So innocent blood was saved that day. And Hilkiah and his wife praised God for their daughter Susanna.

PLAYER 1: And so did Joakim her husband, and all her relatives, because she had done nothing immodest.

PLAYER 2: And from that day onward, Daniel had a great reputation in the eyes of the people.

(Blackout. All exit. Musical transition.)

Act I

scene 1

Lights rise slowly on Susanna in the Upper Circle.

SUSANNA: Like a body entombed in a crypt, I've been here for all these years. You know why, Daniel. You know why I locked myself up behind these walls. You know as well as I all the things that happened so long ago. At first, when the trouble was over, everyone seemed so happy for me. "Susanna, Susanna . . ." Remember how they shouted out my name, threw flowers at my feet and covered me with praise and kisses? For a moment, I almost believed in their affection. My family *pretended* to be concerned about me hiding myself, but of course, it was a great relief to them, a great relief to have me swept under the carpet like a dirty little secret. And by then, I was past caring. *(Pause)* Time never touches me here. The past and the future grow in and out and all together. But lately, Daniel, things have grown thick with another kind of yearning. I feel the pressure—the wanting of shape and form, and the wanting of words, words to describe it. I'm telling *you*, Daniel. I'm asking *you* because you were the first and final witness to

everything, everything that came before and after I
passed on to you—to your dreams and visions, to your
voices in the night.

scene 2

*Lower Circle. Annie, Kim, Pam and Barbie play jump rope. Sus-
anna enters, watching.*

ANNIE, KIM, PAM AND BARBIE:
Not last night, not last night, not last night
But the night before
Twenty-four robbers came knocking at the door
As I ran out

(Susanna runs in and jumps rope.)

They ran in
I hit 'em on the head with a rolling pin
I asked 'em what they wanted
This is what they said:
Spanish dancer shake your hips
Spanish dancer do the splits
Spanish dancer turn around
Spanish dancer touch the ground
Spanish dancer get outta town.

*(Susanna runs out of the jump rope. Annie, Kim, Pam and
Barbie put down the jump rope and move to the Middle
Circle. Susanna follows. The girls cut out pictures from
magazines with shiny, silver scissors.)*

ANNIE: Fruits.
KIM: And vegetables.
PAM: Dairy products.

BARBIE: Fish and poultry.

KIM: Bread and grain.

SUSANNA: That's what I like, bread.

PAM: Yeah, with nuts and raisins.

SUSANNA: Plain bread, sometimes with butter.

ANNIE: Ugh! Why do we have to do this?

BARBIE: Because the teacher said we have to. And we don't want our kids to get rickets or scurvy.

ANNIE: So what?

BARBIE: It's school. We have to.

KIM: Vitamin C prevents scurvy. It is found in fruits, oranges, lemons.

BARBIE: Vitamin D, found in fish oil.

SUSANNA: And sunlight!

BARBIE: Sunlight isn't food.

SUSANNA: Found in fish oil and sunlight from the sky!

KIM: Here's a tomato for the vegetables.

PAM: Actually, the tomato is a fruit.

BARBIE: How do you know?

PAM: I looked it up.

BARBIE: I think it's a vegetable.

PAM: Look it up.

ANNIE: I still don't see why we have to do this.

KIM: So we'll know how to feed our families.

BARBIE: Properly.

SUSANNA: But I'm hungry, *now*.

BARBIE *(Looking at a magazine picture)*: Look at this lady, isn't she pretty?

PAM: I heard heels like that can ruin your back.

ANNIE: They make your legs look good.

KIM: Can you pass the glue please?

SUSANNA: How do they get their hair to go around like that?

BARBIE: The lady turns around and around until she looks perfect.

PAM: Then they take the picture.

KIM: Could you pass the glue please?

BARBIE: Sometimes, the models get to keep the clothes. Look, Kim.

KIM: Perfect, just perfect, now give me the glue!

ANNIE *(Tossing it)*: Here, take as much as you like.

scene 3

Susanna in the Upper Circle.

SUSANNA: There are places on this earth, Daniel, places of freedom and solitude. There are worlds we make, gardens for the performance of miracles. There are scenes we pass through, scenes in which we know ourselves, by being part of something great and fragile and full of wonder, and that garden was *mine*. They snapped things off that were meant to bloom. They trampled things that, for the first time ever, had a chance to grow. And who? Who has ever answered for that? *(Pause)* I could hardly say when it started. First, I just noticed that little things had changed. Then, I had a feeling that eyes were watching me. But I'd turn around and nothing—I would see nothing. Only I could always feel the eyes on me, on the back of my neck, on my waist, my lips, my breasts. All the time, like someone was tracing me with a pencil. I could feel the point of it on my skin. I could feel the terrible eyes, staring. Fear spread like a rapacious weed. It covered everything.

scene 4

In the Lower Circle, the girls are setting up for musical chairs and putting on party hats. Annie opens up a child's record player.

ANNIE: We're going to have a party now—girls only. So Susanna, what about you?

(Susanna enters Lower Circle.)

SUSANNA: What?
ANNIE: When you grow up, do you want to be married?
SUSANNA: I dunno.
PAM: I might marry my father.
KIM: Me, too.
BARBIE: Or someone like my father.
ANNIE: You dummies, you can't marry your father!

(The music starts. The girls walk around.)

PAM: Why not?
ANNIE: Cause he's already married.
KIM: Maybe my brother.
SUSANNA: Mine's a turd.
ANNIE: Don't you know anything? You can't do it with your father or your brother.
BARBIE: Now what are you talking about?

(Music stops. Barbie is out. She stands outside circle. Same for the others.)

ANNIE: I found out where babies come from.
SUSANNA: I know where babies come from. They come from God. That's how we know there really is a God. Proof. He looks down and sees when a man and woman are married and then he sends a baby inside the mother.

(Music starts.)

PAM: Yeah.
BARBIE: That's right.

ANNIE: No, you turkeys, don't you know?
KIM: Know what?

(Music stops. Kim stands outside circle.)

ANNIE: Listen to this, my sister just told me.
SUSANNA: What? Tell us.
ANNIE *(Darkly)*: Are you sure?
PAM: Yeah!

(Music starts.)

ANNIE: You know the hole in girls, right behind the peepee one?
PAM: Yeah.
SUSANNA: Yeah.
KIM: Yeah.
BARBIE *(Lying)*: No!
ANNIE: Well it's there, Barbie. Go look for it!

(Music stops. Pam stands outside circle.)

PAM: Go on. Tell us.

(Music starts.)

ANNIE: Well, the husband sticks his, you know, his dick in there, and that's how the baby gets in.
PAM: OOOO, sick!
SUSANNA: Who would do that?
BARBIE: You're lying. She's always lying.
ANNIE: No! And when the man forces a woman it's rape.
SUSANNA: Rake?

(Music stops. Susanna stands outside circle.)

ANNIE: RAPE! Haven't you read the newspapers. R-A-P-E. Rape!

PAM: Who would ever want to do it?

SUSANNA: My father wouldn't do that to my mother.

KIM: I bet it would hurt.

ANNIE: I saw all the pictures in my sister's book. I swear it's true.

SUSANNA: Only married women do it?

ANNIE: My sister said when you get older, all the boys try to get you to do it.

SUSANNA: Are you sure?

ANNIE: Yeah. And you know that word that's written all over the bus stop? F-U-C-K? That's what it means, getting a guy's thing inside you.

KIM: I don't feel good.

BARBIE: Yeah, shut up about that stuff now. Let's play something else.

(Kim and Barbie move aside.)

KIM AND BARBIE *(Doing hand clapping routine)*:
Johnny and Janey up in a tree
K-I-S-S-I-N-G.
First comes love,
Then comes marriage,
Then comes Janey with a baby carriage.

(Susanna in the Upper Circle.)

SUSANNA: Then came the mirrors. They said *I* put them in the garden. Why should I want a mirror in the garden? But I began to find them there, almost every day, placed somewhere where I was sure to see myself, as if whatever it was wanted me to join in the watching. First, they spied on me because it gave them pleasure. Then, they ruined my garden with mirrors because they thought it would give them *more* pleasure to look at me looking at myself, and later, they accused me of vanity.

scene 5

The girls in the Middle Circle getting ready for a dance.

ANNIE: Lace bras!
KIM: Matching underwear!
BARBIE: Real silk stockings.
PAM: For smooth shaved legs.
KIM: Lotion, deodorant, perfume.
ANNIE: And nail polish.

(Susanna moves into Middle Circle.)

SUSANNA: Lipstick, eye shadow, powder, mascara.
ANNIE: It's a lot of stuff.
BARBIE: To look pretty. No one wants to dance with you unless you look pretty.

(Susanna picks up a mirror, moves aside.)

SUSANNA *(As if giving a demonstration)*: Makeup should be applied with the greatest care and look as natural as possible. Start with a liquid base as close to your own coloring as you can find. Distribute evenly for a smooth foundation.
PAM *(To Kim)*: Ouch! I cut myself shaving.
SUSANNA: Next apply the facial powder which should match the foundation.
ANNIE: I wanna use that eye shadow with the glitter.
BARBIE: It's too flashy.
ANNIE: So what? What do you think, Kim?
KIM: I don't know. I guess its okay.

SUSANNA: Blush should highlight your cheekbones and give your face a flushed, excited look. Make sure you blend in the edges.

ANNIE: I'm gonna use it.

PAM *(Dabs the cut with tissue; to Kim)*: I wonder if razor cuts get infected easily.

KIM *(To Pam)*: I think so.

PAM: It keeps bleeding.

SUSANNA: Use eye shadow to create dramatic effects and to give yourself that aura of mystery.

BARBIE: Annie, you already have on glitter nail polish.

ANNIE: So what if I do?

KIM *(To Pam)*: My cousin knew a girl who cut herself shaving once.

PAM: Yeah?

BARBIE *(To Annie)*: With a sweater and a short skirt, I think it's too much.

ANNIE: Too much what?

KIM *(To Pam)*: Yeah, and she didn't take care of it and keep it clean, and it got all infected and stuff.

PAM: Did it get bigger?

KIM: Yeah, real big.

SUSANNA: Start the eyeliner under your eye so that it begins at the center of your pupil and take the line out to the edge. This will make your eyes look bigger, doe-like and more inviting.

BARBIE *(To Annie)*: Well, I don't want to tell you what to wear, but if you overdo it, you might attract attention.

ANNIE: Isn't that what we want? What the hell!

BARBIE: Swearing—you're always swearing.

KIM *(To Pam)*: One day, she noticed this red vein going up her leg, and she had to go to the hospital.

SUSANNA: Mascara will make your lashes look long, soft and velvety.

BARBIE *(To Annie)*: Of course we do want attention, but not the wrong kind.

PAM *(To Kim)*: Did she get a fever?

KIM: Yeah, she got a really high fever and the infection turned into gangrene.

PAM: Gangrene?

BARBIE: We just don't want to look too available.

ANNIE: But we are! We want to! That's what we're doing!

BARBIE: But it has to be a certain way!

KIM *(To Pam)*: Yeah, and they had to cut off this big part of her leg!

PAM: Oh shit! Where's the alcohol???

SUSANNA: Lips, the lips are very important. Outline them with a darker pencil and fill them in with color. Full, they should look full.

ANNIE: Look, Barbie, you do it your way, and I'll do it my way. But I bet my way is faster!

(Fadeout. Girls exit. Susanna is alone.)

SUSANNA: I'm sitting here looking at myself in the mirror, and this strange feeling comes over me that I'm not real. I'm looking at my reflection, but it's like I've left my body and I'm looking at an empty thing. And what I want to know is—if I'm not here, who's watching?

scene 6

Susanna moves to Upper Circle looking in the mirror. She puts the mirror down.

SUSANNA: Years and years went by, but they couldn't leave me alone. Of all the stories they had to choose from, they sought out that humiliating scene, and over and over again set it down for everyone to remember—as if they couldn't stop looking, as if they wanted to keep

me forever in an image of exposure, as if my violation
was a public pleasure, and they called it "art, " spelled
with an "a" for absolution.

Once in my garden
there was no watching.
In this garden,
no webbing of desire,
no feeding on images,
no glossy destinies.

Unlocked, the gate
describes a shining arc and
closed behind me
as I enter, the sun
flashes on feathers, on wings.
In flight I come to the pool
spreading clear and
the nightingale sings
in my garden.

Once, twice,
I hear the gate groaning
on its hinges.
A dangling hunger
covers the sun.
They appear behind me
like decaying clouds,
fatherly.
Robed by the prophets
they speak and a foul mist curls the flowers:

"You, made in our image
you, made for our wanting."

I watch the leaves wither and drop.

"So simple."
They are smiling as the pool tilts
 and slides into mirrors.
"Open up our sister,
our love, spread out ."
The bird falls and falls through glass.
"Refuse and shame,
shame and death will be your lovers."

(Pause, build.)

Silent, spinning sharpness
choking on slivers and
fragments I bleed out the
words I will not the
words I will not are
rushing out, they scream:
"We have found her in the garden."
It's dying and they scream and scream:
"We accuse her, Susanna, the whore, the whore of
Babylon."

DANIEL: This is what they wrote down about me: "And the
Lord stirred the Holy Spirit of a young man named
Daniel." But I didn't need a holy spirit to see what was
happening. It was so easy to unravel their story, so simple to prove them wrong—corroborating evidence, witnesses examined separately, and then they proceeded to
make sure I was never forgotten. I was the chosen one.
They always get it wrong, don't they? They picked me
to put in their canon, to put in the holy book of Daniel.
But I know, I have always known, it's *your* story. It's
your story we all should have paid most careful attention to.

scene 7

The girls at a dance in Lower Circle.

ANNIE: This dance sucks.

BARBIE: You are so crass.

ANNIE: I wanna dance with Johnny Rook.

BARBIE: You've already danced with almost everyone else.

ANNIE: Must be the glitter, Barbie.

BARBIE: I think it's the way you drape yourself around.

ANNIE: You've just danced with that geek.

BARBIE: James isn't a geek.

ANNIE: The chess club?

BARBIE: Johnny's a greaseball.

ANNIE: He's got a car.

BARBIE: And everyone knows what he uses it for!

ANNIE: Shut up!

SUSANNA: Will you two stop?

KIM: Look, Susanna, there's Lee.

SUSANNA: I don't care.

PAM: Liar.

(Pause.)

SUSANNA: What's he doing?

ANNIE: He's looking over here.

BARBIE: Smile at him.

SUSANNA: I hate this.

BARBIE: If you want to dance with him, smile.

ANNIE: Yeah, you better, or I will.

SUSANNA: Okay, okay, here goes.

BARBIE: Good, that was good.

ANNIE: Don't look too long—

BARBIE: Yeah, kind of look away, and then look back for a second.

SUSANNA: He's not looking, and he'll never ask me.

ANNIE: Shut your face, I bet he does.

SUSANNA: I feel like a cow.

BARBIE: Be cheerful, they like cheerful.

ANNIE: Susanna, here he comes.

BARBIE: Remember, act a little shy—

ANNIE: But not too shy.

BARBIE: Make him feel like you admire him.

(Lee enters. He is clean, smooth, innocent looking and charming. The girls fade back except Susanna.)

LEE: Would you like to dance, Susanna?

SUSANNA: Okay.

LEE: So how are you?

SUSANNA: Fine.

(Lee and Susanna dance for a few beats. Lee can dance like Fred Astaire. She can't keep up. Lee stops.)

LEE: I think we're having a little trouble here. Listen, when we're dancing, all you have to do is to try and feel what I'm doing? I mean, I'm leading and all you have to do is follow me closely, okay?

SUSANNA: I'm sorry, I guess I'm not very good.

LEE: It's all right. Just follow my lead. We can look good out here, you want to look good, don't you?

SUSANNA: Oh sure.

LEE: Then just stay close to me, Susanna.

(They dance well. The girls stand and clap.)

That was pretty good, you seem to pick it right up.

SUSANNA: You think so?

LEE: Maybe we could practice together, would you like that?

SUSANNA: Yes, I would.

LEE: I'll come and get you sometime.

SUSANNA: Okay.

LEE (*After a beat*): Listen, is that your boyfriend over there or something?

SUSANNA: No.

LEE: He keeps looking at you.

SUSANNA: I don't even know him.

LEE: Are you sure?

SUSANNA: Positive.

LEE: I thought I saw you looking at him during the last dance.

SUSANNA: Well, I wasn't looking *at* him, I mean, I just saw him there.

LEE: You know, Sue, when I dance with a girl, I really want to feel like she's with me, or I can't really get into it.

SUSANNA: I'm with you.

LEE: I mean only with me.

SUSANNA: I'm not with anybody else.

LEE: What I mean is, I don't want to feel like you're looking over my shoulder at other guys.

SUSANNA: I wasn't. I just looked in that direction.

LEE: Yeah, well, guys can think you're fishing around, like one guy isn't enough.

SUSANNA: I wasn't doing that, honest.

LEE: I mean, a guy can notice how pretty my girl is, but he has to definitely get the idea she's with me. Get it?

SUSANNA (*Flattered*): Sure.

LEE: So just keep looking at me, when we dance, even if I look away or something.

SUSANNA: Okay, Lee.

LEE: Or sometimes, you could close your eyes.

SUSANNA: Close my eyes?

LEE: Yeah.

SUSANNA: Like this?

LEE: Yeah, that's it, like you're in a really great dream.

(Lee whirls Susanna away and lets her go. Susanna dances to the Upper Circle.)

scene 8

The music changes to something slower, more rhythmic and sensuous. Susanna dances in a different way.

SUSANNA: Once, Daniel, I had a dream. I dreamed I was not raised in the law, a pious woman, Hilkiah's daughter, but instead, a nomad's child, those wanderers from the south. In the dream, I am a nomad's child in my sun-rinsed clothes, insulting Babylon with insolent lips that twitch and laugh at the laws of Moses. Wanderers have no need of laws for we keep secrets instead, secrets grown from bones, from the marrow of bones and secrets from the voices of songs. Somewhere we meet, and I sing you away, away from the judges, away from the kings of Babylon, away from dragons and lions. I sing you only: the wide floating islands of the desert, a sea woven from the sky, and I make you a shimmering garden, on my shoreline of dreams.

scene 9

Girls in the Middle Circle.

ANNIE: Come on Susanna.

(Susanna enters the Middle Circle.)

SUSANNA: What?
BARBIE: Come on, say it.
SUSANNA: But I wouldn't dream of saying that!

ANNIE: Why not?

SUSANNA: Would you, Pam?

PAM: Well, I say it in a different way, several different ways.

KIM: I said it once. I couldn't believe how it worked.

SUSANNA: But did you really mean it? Was it true?

KIM: I did it anyway.

ANNIE: It's what they want to hear.

BARBIE: If we keep thinking it's true, that's a way of telling ourselves, and then we believe it, and it *is* true.

ANNIE: You get used to it.

PAM: Practice! I said it over and over again in the mirror, staring at my face until it came out naturally.

BARBIE: Yeah, and watch the way the women in the movies say it.

KIM: They're really good at it.

PAM: Try it.

SUSANNA: Now?

ANNIE *(Hands her a bottle in a brown paper bag)*: Here, this helps.

SUSANNA *(She drinks)*: Okay, here goes. "What I want to tell you . . . what I mean to say, Lee is . . ." Wait, I need more. *(She drinks again)*

ANNIE: Courage.

(Susanna drinks again, a beat, then very sincerely:)

SUSANNA: What I mean to say, what I really mean to say is that I love you so much. You just don't know how, how you're my whole universe.

(Pam and Kim move aside.)

PAM: Did you see that movie on TV last night?

KIM: What movie?

PAM: It was all about a woman who would fall asleep and wake up in this same creepy hotel room, always having

this same conversation with her husband, but every
time she woke it was a different man!

KIM: What happened?

PAM: She couldn't figure anything out, and so she finally
went crazy.

scene 10

Daniel and Susanna in the Upper Circle.

DANIEL: The great wheel turns and for each gossamer life, a
shifting. Faces twist in the turn of a sigh, from one
thing to another, reshaping forms, and we never know
the next moment. Fate is fixed in this endless spinning.
The great wheel turns night into day, resurrects our
saviors, burns our Jews, sends plagues to Egypt, makes
flowers spring from dung.

SUSANNA: When I asked them to believe, they all hid their
faces. When I told my story, they covered up their ears.
When my eyes filled with fear, they laughed. When I
begged for their mercy, they picked up stones. Let me
tell you this, in one breath, his loving hand across your
cheek so easily becomes a hard fist on your mouth

scene 11

*Middle Circle. Lee is working out with two large dumbbells. He
has a box. Susanna enters.*

SUSANNA: What are you doing?

LEE: I have to be strong.

SUSANNA: What for?

LEE: This makes you really strong.

SUSANNA: For a contest?

LEE: If you're strong then they'll leave you alone.

SUSANNA: Is someone after you?

LEE: If you're strong, you don't lose control.

SUSANNA *(Looks in the box)*: What's in the box?

LEE: China.

SUSANNA: Real china?

(Lee stops lifting, puts down weights and goes over to the box. He carefully lifts one of the pieces out of the box.)

LEE: Bone china, English, early nineteenth century.

SUSANNA: It looks so delicate.

LEE: My mother gave it to me.

SUSANNA: To *you*.

LEE: Isn't it beautiful? She doesn't want my father to break anymore of it. It's up to me to keep it safe.

SUSANNA: It must mean a lot to you.

LEE: It's a family thing. Carry it home for me, would you?

SUSANNA: Me?

LEE: It's so fragile. I have to carry these weights.

SUSANNA: Is it heavy?

LEE: You can handle it.

SUSANNA: Okay.

LEE: And when we get to my place, do you think you could arrange it in the cabinet?

SUSANNA: You have a china cabinet?

LEE: Yes. It's a cabinet with glass doors and shelves and hooks for the cups and a lock. I was hoping you would arrange it for me in a pretty way. The way women do it.

SUSANNA: If you like.

LEE: Would you be so kind?

SUSANNA: It is very nice china.

LEE: I wanted you to be the one.

(Lee picks up the box and carefully puts it in Susanna's arms like a baby. Girls in the Lower Circle playing jump rope.)

GIRLS:

Cinderella
dressed in yella,
went upstairs
to kiss a fella.
By mistake
she kissed a snake.
How many doctors will it take?
1, 2, 3, 4, 5, 6 . . .

(Lights fade as the rope goes faster and faster.)

scene 12

Susanna in the Upper Circle.

SUSANNA: Imagine, if you will, being frozen alive while the bright sun shines above like a shimmering disc. You feel a cold, icy sharpness moving down the rivers of your veins, moving like the steady ocean tides toward the heart, the heart which just sits there beating like it has all the time in the world. The beautiful heart with all of its irregular contours—round, smooth, dense, deep, so full of life, is the shape, yes, the perfect shape for a glacier. Dear Daniel, I am very cold, it's so very cold here this time of year.

(Susanna moves to Middle Circle.)

scene 13

Enter Lee.

LEE: Who are you talking to?
SUSANNA: No one.

LEE: That's a waste of time.

SUSANNA: I like to imagine.

LEE: It's just stupid.

SUSANNA: I want to—

LEE: This is the way things are here.

SUSANNA: I want to say that—

LEE: You don't need to. You have me.

SUSANNA: I do?

(He hugs her.)

LEE: Yes.

SUSANNA: I really do?

LEE: Yes, and I'm real. I'm part of reality. You want to live in the real world don't you?

SUSANNA: Of course I do.

LEE: I'm here and this is it for you. You know that, don't you?

SUSANNA: I do.

LEE: So you know you'll have to forget all that other stuff, okay?

SUSANNA: I will, I do, yes, I do.

(Susanna, looking at Lee, freezes in a sculptured pose.)

scene 14

Daniel enters the Upper Circle. He looks at Susanna and speaks.

DANIEL: That is how I first saw her—numb, vacant and oblivious to what lay before her. The way animals look when they know there is nowhere they can go. And this is what she wants me to tell you, things that pain has torn away from her voice: they dragged her in front of a mob of people. They stripped her. The two elders accused her. They said they watched as she sent away her women. They said they saw her enter the garden and call to a young man who secretly came to her. In lurid detail, they described her making love to him. They said they raised a cry and the young man got away before they saw his face. Then, with her sitting there, in front of the town, naked, exposed to all violating eyes, the elders began their questions: Don't you like to feel men's eyes on you? Do you return their smiles? When a man smiles at you, do you smile back? Do you speak in pleasing tones to men? Do you? Do you not behave in an inviting way when they are in your husband's house? Make them feel welcome, don't you? Do you not laugh in front of men? Throw back your head in a certain way? That way, that free way? In truth, don't you do these things to excite men? You know it excites men when you do that. You like that, don't you? Knowing you excite men. Don't you like it when you excite your husband? Hasn't he heard you groan with pleasure? Don't you think about those moments during the day? Don't you think of them whenever a man is around? Whenever you smell one? When you're alone, don't you wish for it? Even now aren't you thinking of having it, even now this very minute of having it with a man, any man? *(Pause)*

And I stood there and watched and saw Susanna folding away.

scene 15

Lights to Annie and Susanna in the Middle Circle.

ANNIE: Where have you been? We all do it.

SUSANNA: Everyone?

ANNIE: Not Barbie of course, but Kim does and Pam once and a while and me—love it.

SUSANNA: Well, what does it feel like?

ANNIE: I really get into it. First, you just start to feel kind of lazy like, and then this warm feeling starts to spread through your body. I mean this really good warm feeling. And pretty soon, you just forget, forget about the outside world and all the ugly things out there.

SUSANNA: He wants me to do it with him.

ANNIE: Well, if you don't want to, I know a few girls who would be happy to take your place.

SUSANNA: He keeps asking me.

ANNIE: You just have to be careful, about wanting it all the time.

SUSANNA: I guess everyone's scared who hasn't before. Does it hurt?

ANNIE: I'm telling you. It's so good. You won't feel any pain.

scene 16

Daniel in the Upper Circle.

DANIEL: At night sometimes I dream about you, and I am young again. I live in a garden and at the center is a pool—deep, clear and cool. I'm waiting for you. I am very patient. *(Pause)* There is a certain cycle in the seasons when we must put everything away, when we bury things, pack them down underground and smooth over the top like no one's ever been there. Then, there is nothing left to do but wait. I could sing you those songs about spring, but you would know better. Nothing's for sure, so we wait.

scene 17

Lee and Susanna in the Middle Circle.

LEE: You were so scared the first time, and now you want it all the time.

SUSANNA: Well, maybe not all the time.

LEE: But you haven't been a very good girl lately.

SUSANNA: Don't tease, Lee.

LEE: I'm not the tease. Hey, look at me when I'm talking to you.

SUSANNA: Sorry.

LEE: Last week you made me break a china teacup.

SUSANNA *(Moves close to him)*: I didn't mean to make you mad.

LEE: No?

SUSANNA: No, I mean, I really love you so much. You just don't know how, how you're my whole universe.

LEE: Really?

SUSANNA *(Seductive)*: Please, let's do it now.

LEE: First let's dance like I taught you. Turn around.

(Lee dances with her roughly, pushing her and spinning her around and having a great time.)

SUSANNA: Lee!

LEE: Turn around until you look perfect. Still want to?

SUSANNA *(Begging)*: Please.

LEE *(Sexy)*: We'll have to do it how I like.

SUSANNA: Anything.

(Lee gets something from a box. He stands facing Susanna with his back to the audience. The girls enter and line up in a soft spot of light. Like Susanna, they obey Lee.)

LEE: Get down on your knees. Put out your arms, straight out. Look, look up at me.

(Lee ties a small piece of rubber hose around her right arm and holds up a needle and syringe.)

Now say it. Say it like you mean it.

SUSANNA: Please, do I have—

LEE: Say it.

SUSANNA AND THE GIRLS:

> Our father, who art in heaven,
> Hallowed be thy name.

LEE: Wait a minute, stop, let's just stop all this—way too dramatic. It's yesterday's news. You girls can leave. That's right, would you just leave. It's absolutely too much.

SUSANNA: It is?

LEE: Yeah, see, it's different. We don't even do things this way anymore.

(Lee puts away the needle, unties her arm and throws her a small bag.)

SUSANNA *(Looks in bag)*: How shall we do them?

LEE *(Tenderly)*: We? We? You don't need me anymore, Susanna. You're a big girl now. You can do things all by yourself.

(Exit Lee. Susanna takes out a small vial from the bag and looks at it. Blackout. The girls in the Lower Circle play jump rope.)

ANNIE, PAM, KIM AND BARBIE:

> Mother, Mother I am sick.
> Call the doctor
> quick, quick, quick,
> call for the doctor, call for the nurse,
> call for the lady with the alligator purse.
> Doctor, Doctor will I die?
> Yes, my dear and so will I.

Act II

Daniel and Susanna in the Lower Circle.

DANIEL: This is how they wrote it down: "And Hilkiah and his wife praised God for their daughter Susanna and so did her husband Joakim, because she had done nothing immodest." But Susanna didn't praise anyone, not her mother, her father, her husband Joakim and least of all God. She locked herself in the garden and never came out. Although they all shook their heads and pretended to be concerned, they were secretly relieved. No one ever knew what happened to her after that, no one at all except a young man who would come to her, when the afternoon sunlight dappled the garden.

SUSANNA: Daniel, I want you to go away now.

DANIEL: I don't want you to do this.

SUSANNA: It's how things happen.

DANIEL: I'm afraid for you.

SUSANNA: You'll have to take them.

DANIEL: What?

SUSANNA: These dreams and visions.

(Susanna hands Daniel a small wooden box.)

DANIEL: Please, don't.
SUSANNA: Visions and dreams, that's what you're famous for,
  isn't it?
DANIEL: What if someday you want them back?
SUSANNA: I'll call you.
DANIEL: What if they want *you* back?

(Susanna exits.)

I'm confused about what happened next, about time and
place, but after a while they did want her, or she wanted
them and everything began to feel thin and risky as if it
had been pulled on so much it was about to tear.

(Exit Daniel.
  Upper Circle. Susanna sits up in a bed. In a dream state,
she talks to a Man. The Man has a pair of silver scissors that
he ominously clicks open and shut.)

MAN: I'm not trying to hurt you, Susanna. I just want to
  know why you did it.
SUSANNA: Why?
MAN: Yes.

(Silence.)

Did you know what you were doing?
SUSANNA: He was blind.
MAN: I mean at the time, do you feel you knew what you
  were doing?
SUSANNA: His eyes were open, but he was blind. Yes. He
  looked like he could see, but he couldn't see at all.

MAN: Yes, but at the time, how did you feel?

SUSANNA: I don't know.

MAN: Were you conscious?

SUSANNA: I couldn't say.

MAN: Were you firmly in control of your thoughts and actions, or did you feel yourself driven by passion?

SUSANNA: I just couldn't say.

MAN: You know why I'm asking you this, don't you?

SUSANNA: Because you're not sure which place to lock me up in.

(Susanna lies down as the Man fades away. Waking, Susanna finds an open jewelry box near her bed with jewelry strewn around.)

Not again! *(Calling)* Marina!

scene 2

Middle Circle. Adele writes at a desk and speaks as if recording her thoughts in a journal.

ADELE: October eleventh. It is hard to believe that nearly ten years have passed since I came to Threshold. When we opened, people gave us a year before some breach of trust on the part of the women would cause us to close. Extremists predicted we would be murdered in our beds, and now, we are what some consider a model institution whose "enlightened" methods are entering the mainstream. I attribute our success to our integrity. If I did not have absolute faith in that integrity, how could I possibly ask for the trust of the women here? And why should they be expected to give it? No, what heals here as much as any therapy, is a knowledge that there is some kind of stability to life, a truthful and honest way of living with ourselves and others, and this is just where Molly has become infinitely clever. I was warned about her manipulative behavior. I can see her ability to exert power over others. She seems to have developed a sixth sense about my vulnerability. She's found the thing that means the most to me and picks away at it. She wants to make me angry. A new person came to us today— *(Enter Hazel. She sits. Adele closes her journal)*

HAZEL: —So, I figured this bourgeois booby hatch was better than the farm.

ADELE: Hazel, this is hardly a bourgeois booby hatch.

HAZEL *(Fingers Adele's sweater on her desk)*: Nice sweater, Doctor, cashmere?

ADELE: Yes.

HAZEL: Can I try it on?

ADELE: If you like.

HAZEL *(Puts on sweater)*: Okay, an exclusive halfway house, then.

ADELE: Closer, but not in the conventional sense.

HAZEL: One of the guards in prison really had the hots for me.

ADELE: Really?

HAZEL: She was nice to me. I didn't mind.

ADELE: I see.

HAZEL: So what's to stop everyone from running?

ADELE: Nothing but the consequences. If *you* get caught, you go back to where you came from, but not everyone came from prison.

HAZEL: Does my presence help you get grant money?

ADELE: Are you always so cocky?

HAZEL: Almost.

ADELE: Hazel, the board, according to the terms of the trust, carefully selects women from a variety of places.

HAZEL: Some rich geezer left his money to wayward women?

ADELE: *Her* money, and I don't know what you mean by wayward.

HAZEL: Fuck-ups.

ADELE: Actually, women are chosen who have had extenuating life circumstances to overcome, who've survived against the odds.

HAZEL: What odds?

ADELE: The odds of dying.

HAZEL: Death!?

ADELE: Death. That's *one* of the criteria.

HAZEL: That's what the wacko lady said in her trust?

ADELE: Ummm-hmmm.

HAZEL: Why?

ADELE: Does it matter?

HAZEL: No, it's just bizarre.

ADELE: Or creative, like you, Hazel.

HAZEL: So what exactly goes on here?

ADELE: Sometimes people change for the better.

HAZEL: Just how do they do that?

ADELE: Different ways. First of all, we do all the work ourselves to keep this place going.

HAZEL: You mean housework?

ADELE: This morning you can go and help in the laundry.

HAZEL: Dirty clothes, huh??

ADELE: No, just the general stuff, towels, sheets, things like that.

HAZEL: For a minute I thought I was going to get to go through people's pockets.

ADELE: You'll work with Susanna and Molly, and Marina.

HAZEL: Do they know about me?

ADELE: No one knows anything, unless you tell them or they tell you.

HAZEL: Except you, Doctor.

ADELE: Adele, please call me Adele.

HAZEL: Except you, Adele, you know everything.

scene 3

Lower Circle. Susanna folds and sorts sheets and towels on a big table. Marina sits at a separate, smaller table, sorting red and white beans from a big jar into smaller jars.

MARINA: Ma-nee rid, Suss-anna.

SUSANNA: A red bean day it is then.

MARINA: Rid been dey. *(Pause. She looks at beans, then in perfect English)* I wish I had a diamond for every tear I've seen you cry.

(Enter Molly with a basket full of clean towels.)

Moley.

MOLLY: Hey, Marina, how's the bean business.

MARINA: Rid.

MOLLY *(Looks at Susanna)*: Rid?

SUSANNA: Red, red beans. She just said one of her things again. Something about tears.

MOLLY: I wonder what they mean?

SUSANNA: I think Adele knows, but she wouldn't tell.

MOLLY: Not telling is part of her job.

SUSANNA: I heard there's someone new.

MOLLY: I met her yesterday.

SUSANNA: What's she like?

MOLLY: Young, sassy. Okay, I guess. She'll probably show up soon.

SUSANNA: Good, with another person, we could finish faster.

MOLLY: I'm talking to Adele today.

SUSANNA: Be careful, Molly.

MOLLY: You believe me, don't you Susanna?

SUSANNA: I guess so.

MOLLY: Because you know it's true.

(Enter Hazel.)

HAZEL: So, Molly, I guess this is the laundry, huh?

MOLLY *(Laughs)*: No, it's Tiffany's.

HAZEL *(Slightly defensive)*: Why do you say that?

MOLLY: Joke, it's just a joke.

SUSANNA: I'm Susanna.

HAZEL: I'm Hazel *(Looks at Marina)* What are you doing?

MARINA: Beenzz.

SUSANNA *(Gives her two quarters)*: Marina, would you do me a favor? Could you get me a Coke, a Diet Coke, please?

MARINA *(Exiting)*: Just one more lousy drink in a lousy gin joint.

SUSANNA: Thank you, Marina.

MOLLY *(To Hazel)*: That's Marina. She can't talk very well, except for those things she says that don't relate, like . . . well, you'll get used to them.

SUSANNA: We like them.

HAZEL: Do we have to do this every day?

SUSANNA: Mondays. It doesn't take that long.

MOLLY: *If* we cooperate.

HAZEL: I can cooperate.

MOLLY: Then help Susanna fold these.

HAZEL: So how come she can't talk?

SUSANNA: I don't know. Something happened to her, an accident or something.

HAZEL: So what's with the beans?

SUSANNA: She sorts them out. It makes her happy.

HAZEL: A real lulu, huh?

SUSANNA: Don't call her that.

HAZEL: Sorry.

MOLLY: Look, we all like her. After a while, you will, too.

(Marina returns with a soda.)

SUSANNA: Thank you, Marina.

MOLLY: She understands everything. We think.

HAZEL: She has a familiar face.

SUSANNA: She has those funny habits, like the beans, those things she says, and there's this thing she does with her jewelry.

HAZEL: Jewelry?

SUSANNA: Yeah, every morning—we're in the same room— she gets up and leaves her jewelry all over.

MOLLY: I still don't see why Adele doesn't keep that stuff in a safe. It's valuable.

SUSANNA: She says Marina should keep them. It's some kind of connection.

MOLLY: To what?

SUSANNA: I don't know.

HAZEL: Maybe you should keep them. Finders keepers.

SUSANNA: Yeah, right! Look, we're almost finished. Hazel, you might want to look around the grounds or—

HAZEL: Thanks. I'll check the mail, want me to look for you?

MOLLY: Yeah, Lightfoot, Molly Lightfoot.

HAZEL: Susanna?

SUSANNA: No one remembers I'm alive.

(Exit Hazel, staring at Marina on the way out.)

MOLLY: I'm going to see Adele now.

SUSANNA *(Concerned)*: What are you going to tell her?

MOLLY: I told you, I always tell the truth.

scene 4

Molly walks into Middle Circle. Adele is at her desk.

ADELE: It's all here in the police report.

MOLLY: I *never* threatened him. I never even saw him until that day. They made it up.

ADELE: Why would they do that?

MOLLY: They made it up so he wouldn't be charged with attempted murder.

ADELE: There's a telephone log here from the phone company. It shows all the calls you made to his house.

MOLLY: His family practically owns the phone company.

ADELE: And these notes you sent.

MOLLY: Forgeries.

ADELE: They must be good to get past the handwriting experts.

MOLLY: They're the best.

ADELE: And then there's the testimony of these people—

MOLLY: His family and friends?

ADELE: Who said they saw you watching the house on January 2nd with a gun.

MOLLY: They're lying.

ADELE: And *his* testimony that you approached him a few days later with a knife.

MOLLY: He lied.

ADELE: So you're trying to say that this, all this evidence is falsified, that they're in it together, the family, the phone company, even the police?

MOLLY: I told you, they own the town. You think it's a problem for them to buy off the police?

ADELE: It's just too fantastic.

MOLLY: Don't you get it? Instead of attempted murder, he's found temporarily insane.

ADELE: You're perfectly capable of accepting the truth.

MOLLY: He'll be out of that place before you can bat your eyelashes.

ADELE: Molly, terroristic threatening is a crime.

MOLLY: But *he* shot *me*!

ADELE: Yes, what he did to you was horrible, and I don't for one minute think your actions deserved—

MOLLY: They weren't my actions—

ADELE: Okay, okay! He's locked up now!

MOLLY: Not where he should be!

ADELE *(Short pause)*: You know, you're really lucky the Board voted to assume responsibility for you.

MOLLY: I'm sure money or favors changed hands somewhere along the line.

ADELE: Pardon?

MOLLY: They definitely wanted me out of the way.

ADELE: They could have let you go to jail.

MOLLY: But they didn't want to feel too guilty.

ADELE: This is a pretty good option.

MOLLY: They're keeping me here. It's the perfect place.

ADELE: Now that *is* a fantasy.

MOLLY: Are you afraid I'm right?

ADELE *(Sincere)*: Threshold will only work for you if you begin at the beginning, and that means making an effort to face the truth, even if it's painful.

MOLLY: You *are* afraid, aren't you?

ADELE *(Getting mad)*: You're using this as a smoke screen to deny your rage.

MOLLY: You tell us those things, that you care about us, that you want us to be strong, but you lie to us—

ADELE: I do mean "those things"—

MOLLY: You tell us lies.

ADELE: Let's just call a time-out here.

MOLLY: From now on, I'll call you on your lies.

ADELE *(Loses it)*: Lies? This whole conspiracy theory, that's the lie!

MOLLY: You're part of them, just a mirror image.

ADELE: *I* would *never* be involved with *anybody*, or *any organization* that would set up an innocent person.

MOLLY *(Retreating, smiling)*: And you're the one who always says that sometimes a woman's first impulse is to protect her abuser.

scene 5

Lower circle. Marina sorts beans as Hazel enters.

HAZEL: Where's Molly? I have her mail.

(Marina stares at her and goes back to sorting beans.)

Marina, Molly, where's Molly?
MARINA: Moley?
HAZEL: Yeah, Moley, Molly.
MARINA *(Transforming)*: Sorry sailor, you've missed the boat.
HAZEL: What did you say?
MARINA: Sorry sailor, you've missed the boat.
HAZEL: *Equatorial Crossing*, 1957.
MARINA: No, no, Moley.
HAZEL: *Jejune*, 1959.
MARINA: No Moley here!
HAZEL: *And the Angels Sing*, '61; *It Happened on Tuesday*, '63.
MARINA: No here! No here!
HAZEL: *Autumn Song*—
MARINA: No, no, no!

(Marina, now very upset, spills her beans on the floor as Susanna walks in.)

SUSANNA: What is going on here?
HAZEL: Nothing, I was just looking for Molly, asking her and she got upset.
SUSANNA: What did you say to her?
HAZEL: *Nothing*, I just asked her about Molly.
SUSANNA: Well, could you help me pick up these beans.
MARINA *(Pointing at Hazel)*: No, no, no!
HAZEL: Okay, I'm sorry. She doesn't want me to touch them.

(Marina picks up her bean jar and walks away angrily.)

SUSANNA: God, you really pissed her off.
HAZEL: What a weirdo. Can you give this to Molly?

(Hazel exits.)

SUSANNA: Sure.

(Susanna continues to clean up beans. Enter Molly.)

MOLLY: What happened?
SUSANNA: Marina spilled the beans. There's a letter Hazel brought.
MOLLY *(Helping pick up beans)*: That girl's a thief.
SUSANNA: Did Adele tell you that?
MOLLY: No, I just know.
SUSANNA: Did you talk to Adele?
MOLLY: Have you ever noticed how smug she can be?
SUSANNA: Did she believe you?
MOLLY: Fear can make you blind, Susanna.

(Susanna and Molly exit with sheets and towels.)

scene 6

Lower Circle. Hazel.

HAZEL: Marina Montclair, you know, Marina Montclair! But that wasn't her real last name. Don't you watch old movies? A real star! Yeah, and she married this really rich guy and quit acting and had a kid or something after waiting the longest time. I read something about her a couple of years ago, about the kid dying and the husband up and leaving with a younger woman two weeks after the funeral, and *very Hollywood*, they find Marina Montclair one day overdosed on booze and pills, and I mean pills! They find her lying on the floor in the middle of the room, her head split open from the fall, surrounded by piles and piles of film. She'd taken out all her old movie reels, and unrolled reel after reel until she was surrounded by clouds and clouds of it like a celluloid heaven. I saw a picture. She was beautiful, you know—clothes, money, jewelry, unbelievable jewelry!

scene 7

Middle Circle. Molly, Susanna, Marina and Adele are sewing up the hems of curtains as Adele leads a group meeting. Hazel enters, sits and starts to sew.

HAZEL *(Sticks herself with a needle)*: Shit, I can't do this.

ADELE: You can learn.

HAZEL: What for?

ADELE: Because the rec room needs curtains. Go on Susanna.

SUSANNA: And in public, or with other people, if anyone said anything bad about him, I'd feel angry and defensive, or if they hinted that he was doing the things he was really doing, I'd get even more furious. I just don't understand why I did that. I mean, I hated him so much.

ADELE: It's common for women to protect their abusers. It's directly connected to a woman wanting to keep the shameful, humiliating secret under wraps. Besides, there's little support for exposing the abuser, and sometimes the consequences are much worse.

SUSANNA: Well, I guess I don't have to worry about him now.

ADELE: Hey, come on, he was driving. He had control of the car. He almost killed you more than once. He almost killed you in that car. If we stop being willing to take the blame, it won't always get dumped on us.

MARINA: Maxim, I believe you're wearing my coat.

HAZEL *(Soft, to Marina)*: *Monte Carlo Afternoon* with Ted Day.

ADELE: Hazel?

HAZEL: Nothing.

ADELE: I think that's enough for tonight, but before we finish, I want to congratulate you, Susanna. You've come such a long way, and it hasn't been easy. I want you to know that I believe in you. I believe in your goodness. I believe in your strength. God knows sometimes life asks so much from us, but I think when it gets hard that if we just believe, that somewhere inside of us sits a strong, wise woman—

(Molly starts clapping.)

MOLLY: Bravo, bravo. *(Pause)* We should have brought some flowers for the diva.

ADELE: If you have something to say to me, Molly, you could at least do me the courtesy of saying it straight out.

MOLLY: The way you just tell it to us "straight out," Adele?

ADELE: I won't participate in your covert games.

MOLLY: Ah, *my* covert games? Is it now?

ADELE: Molly, the hostility has to stop. I need to see some cooperation, some adjustment in your thinking.

MOLLY: *Your* thinking needs adjustment.

ADELE *(Angry)*: I could have you transferred *(Snaps her fingers)* like that.

SUSANNA *(Pulling her away)*: Stop it, Molly.

MOLLY: No, I won't. I won't stop because I haven't done anything. She's just afraid because she thinks I might be right. Do you think she'd act this way if she was sure? *(To Adele)* I stood true with my story, and don't you think I'm afraid of you.

scene 8

Adele and Molly move to Lower Circle.

ADELE: This is the tale of Molly Lightfoot and how she stood true with her story. She was working at a place, a place that was once the home of her mother's mother's mothers, a place that was once called home by her father's father's fathers, and in that place she spoke.

MOLLY: In this place, in this very place there once was a night like blue glass, the luminous moon tumbling down on the tanned skins of our dwellings, and the men going down to the river. Once on a night like stars and dark blue glass, the luminous moon gleamed down on the tanned skins of our dwellings and we the women and children sat to sing. Let us sing.

ADELE: Let us sing.

MOLLY AND ADELE: Let us sing.

MOLLY: Sing a song about the river and the reeds, of nets swaying in the water and fish slipping along. A song for men watching in stillness, a waiting song, a gathering song, a song for silvery fish shining in dark waters. Let us sing.

ADELE: Let us sing.

MOLLY AND ADELE: Let us sing.

MOLLY: But once there was a night like stars and dark blue glass with the luminous moon grinning down across the tanned skins as we sat to sing, we heard another kind of song. A song like horses hooves and a deep, pushing breath, a clattering song that killed the luminous moon with flags and swords and glistening guns, brass buttons shining and boots. And the moon turned upside down, pouring out our blood and our bleeding—and our blood you have killed, the tanned skins, you have killed the singers, the elders curled in their blankets and nothing to stop your blood. Let us sing.

ADELE: Let us sing.

MOLLY AND ADELE: Let us sing.

MOLLY: Sing a song of the night like stars and dark blue glass, the luminous moon as it slips away.

MOLLY AND ADELE *(Quietly)*: Let us sing.

ADELE: But that wasn't the story Molly Lightfoot was supposed to tell, no. *(To Molly)* You will tell a brave story, a story of the noble courage of the black boots and shiny buttons. Against all odds and savages you will tell how they, great protectors, preserving the blessed way of life, the only way of life, how they forged a nation. One nation under God.

MOLLY: No, I won't tell that story.

ADELE: Molly said—

MOLLY: That isn't my story.

ADELE: So Molly told the other story instead, and the people came and listened, and some liked it and some didn't, but Molly didn't care because everyone began to wonder which story was really true. And Molly liked that.

MOLLY: One day the man came. He wore a black suit, and he too had shiny buttons, and he listened very carefully to Molly's story, and when it was finished, he stood up very straight and hard and said:

ADELE: "You lie! You lie about the blue glass night. You lie about the singing luminous moon. You lie about women and children and blood in the night. You lie about men who come on horses. Lies, lies! He was brave and courageous. You tell lies about my father's fathers, great men building this great nation. One nation under God."

MOLLY: "No," said Molly. "That is not a true story."

ADELE: Then out came the gun so quick and easy.

(Adele pulls out a gun and shoots Molly once.)

The first shot and white light flashed in Molly's skull.

MOLLY: "No."

ADELE *(Fires again)*: The second shot let blood out all over her blouse.

MOLLY: "No."

ADELE *(Fires again)*: The third shot buckled her legs and brought her to her knees.

MOLLY: "No," said Molly. "That is not a true story."

ADELE: This is the tale of Molly Lightfoot and how she stood true with her story.

scene 9

Lights to Daniel.

DANIEL: Here are some things she wanted me to tell you: awake or asleep, it all comes back when you least expect it. The things that happened come back. Your mind is very strong and can fight with the scenes that try to run like movies over and over, showing you the same reel, but your body, your body is so vulnerable, and there is no way to protect it from the fear imprinted on every cell—the fear of that meticulous, unpredictable scrutiny, that fear which now makes the smallest act, the slightest look, an enormous risk. Awake or asleep, it all comes back and every breath is a prayer for survival.

(Upper Circle. Susanna talks in a dream state to the Man. With the jump rope, the Man fashions a noose.)

MAN: I don't want to persecute you, Susanna, I'm simply trying to understand your train of thought.

SUSANNA: Train of thought?

MAN: Yes, at the time, how you ended up there.

SUSANNA: It *is* like a train—once you get on, you can't get off until the next stop.

MAN: Come on, at any time you could have stopped, called a halt to it.

SUSANNA: And you just can't go back once it starts. Like that one night we were driving back from his friend's. It was just the smallest thing that set it off, about the wife's old boyfriend back in town. And he started telling me how attractive she used to be and how many guys she slept with before. Then he started asking me slowly about who I liked before. When I said I didn't want to talk about it, it made him mad. "And what are you hiding from me anyway?" he yelled. Then came the quizzing and the questions, over and over. And did I think what she did before was okay, and pretty soon I was just like the friend's wife who slept with everyone in town and only thought about what was between her legs. And when I told him to shut the fuck up about me, he jammed on the brakes and smacked me in the face with the back of his hand. But I lost control and just kept screaming, "You fuck you fuck you fuck you . . ." And he kept hitting my face until the blood came all over his hand.

MAN: Yes, but all the time you could have stopped it, you could have.

SUSANNA: How?

MAN: You could have been quiet, you could have stopped, you could have apologized and disengaged his anger.

SUSANNA: Disengaged?

MAN: Yes, you could have.

SUSANNA: What you mean is, I should have just shut up and taken it.

(Susanna wakes up as the Man fades away. She gets up, finds the open jewelry box and jewelry lying around.)

Marina! Marina!

(Susanna picks up the jewelry.)

scene 10

Lower Circle. Marina silently sorts beans while Hazel watches.

HAZEL *(So Marina can't hear)*: I know who you are, Marina
Montclair. On the shiny box, in the cheap, green, TV-
screen light you floated through my childhood. When
even the rats scratched the walls for food and the plas-
ter cracked through our lives, you rang for the soup in
your penthouse. When my mother left at five A.M. with
a paper bag and half of last night's dinner, you filed
your nails on the Riviera. And when she cried and cried
and my father poured another drink, Ted Day sent
flowers to your suite. I watched you sweep out of ele-
vators, down staircases, across ballrooms in a trail of
mink while she curled up in a Goodwill blanket to keep
warm and kissed my fingers, telling me my Cracker
Jack ring was just like the one you got in *Bride to Be*.
Yes, yes, I saw you and you had everything. I loved you
and couldn't get enough of you, and you took me out
and away from what I hated to remember. Yes, I saw
you, and I hated you for everything she'd never have.

(Hazel walks up to Marina.)

I know who you are!

*(Hazel aggressively sweeps up two piles of Marina's beans
and mixes them up. Surprised, Marina screams. Hazel runs
away. Marina patiently looks for any beans that may have
fallen on the floor, when Molly and Susanna enter with a
broom and a dustpan.)*

MARINA: We tried so hard with her, I don't know where we
went wrong.

345

SUSANNA: You okay, Marina?

MARINA: Beenz.

(Molly and Susanna start sweeping.)

MOLLY: Hazel thinks Marina was in the movies.

MARINA *(To herself)*: No, no here.

SUSANNA: Where is she anyway?

MOLLY: She said she didn't feel good.

SUSANNA: Again?

MARINA *(To herself)*: Hey-zell, no here.

MOLLY: How much do you think Marina really understands?

SUSANNA: Sometimes I think a lot, sometimes it seems like not very much.

MOLLY: She concentrates so hard.

SUSANNA: Have you noticed how there's more white beans than red beans?

MOLLY: Yeah, so what?

SUSANNA: Well, watch. When she finds the red ones, she puts them all in a pile. The white ones she just dumps right into the jar, but the red ones, she looks over each one carefully, like it was going to tell her something.

MOLLY: Maybe it does.

SUSANNA: Then she mixes them up and starts again.

MOLLY: I wonder if she can recognize them—

SUSANNA: Certain beans?

MOLLY: Yeah, when she finds them again.

SUSANNA: Molly?

MOLLY: Yeah?

SUSANNA: How come you came down on Adele like that?

MOLLY: She lies to herself.

SUSANNA: Why?

MOLLY: At first, lies are easier than truth.

SUSANNA: I don't think she wants to hurt you.

MOLLY: She can't accept certain things, not like you—

SUSANNA: Like me?

MOLLY: You *know*. But you hide it on purpose.

SUSANNA: Know what?

MOLLY: Don't ask me that, Susanna.

SUSANNA: Why not?

MOLLY: Because I might answer, and I told you, I always tell the truth.

scene 11

Upper Circle. Hazel finds Marina's jewelry.

HAZEL: There you are. Let's have a look. Yes, come out, come out my pretty, pretty children, sparkling and dazzling—my hard, cold, lovely children. Let me put you on, and we can sit back together, just you and I, and watch ourselves move frame by frame like someone in a an old movie. We'll lie back and watch our lives go by so bright and brilliant and far away. Far away from all the hungry and the unprotected people, from every unpleasantness, surrounded by everything they said we couldn't have.

scene 12

Middle Circle. Adele is at her desk.

ADELE: Could you tell me where he's been transferred to? Thank you, good-bye. *(Pause)* Hello, I'd like to speak to Lieutenant Lake.

(Lake Enters behind Adele. He paces around. They never see each other.)

LAKE: Lake here.

ADELE: Lieutenant Lake, I'm Dr. Brown, Adele Brown from the Threshold Institute.

LAKE: What can I do for you?

ADELE: I understand you were in charge of investigating a shooting a while ago. It involved Molly, Molly Lightfoot. *(Silence)* Mr. Lake?

LAKE: Yes?

ADELE: Were you?

LAKE: The case is closed, Dr. Brown. It's all in the police report.

ADELE: Look, I'm a friend of Molly's.

LAKE: Friend?

ADELE: I'm her doctor. I'm in charge of the facility.

LAKE: Kind of like her jailor.

ADELE: I don't like to think of myself that way.

LAKE: Okay then, you're in charge of the facility.

ADELE: Why were you taken off the case?

LAKE: How rude, Dr. Brown, asking such personal questions when we've only been acquainted a few minutes.

ADELE: Are you going to answer?

LAKE: I suppose my superior officer didn't like the way I was handling the case. Why don't you ask him?

ADELE: I did. He said you were overzealous in your investigation of the charges against her.

LAKE: There you have it.

ADELE: Were you?

LAKE: Was I?

ADELE: Overzealous?

LAKE: Look, Dr. Brown, we do what we can, you know? We do what we can. I, like everyone else, probably like you, Dr. Brown, I do what I can up to a point. I'll take the risk and up the stakes to a point, and then, well, then we have to weigh the consequences. Are the risks and the stakes as important as some of the other things we have to consider? Wouldn't you say that's how all of us generally go about things, Dr. Brown?

ADELE: I'd say.

LAKE: All of us except, maybe, Molly Lightfoot. *(Pause)* Well, I'd say you should just look over the police report, the witnesses and evidence against her. Yes, who were the witnesses?

ADELE: I'll do that, Lieutenant.

LAKE: And timing—when evidence turned up, complaints— timing, always important in a case.

ADELE: Yes. I see. I will.

LAKE: Look, that's all I have to say, and it's probably more than I should have.

ADELE: Thank you. Good-bye.

scene 13

Lower Circle. Marina sits with beans in her hand, sorting them into jars.

MARINA *(Straight out)*: Me, me, where me? No words, no me. *(Picks up a red bean)* Me? Me? *(Smiles)* Me. *(Drops it in jar and begins sorting out white beans)* No, no me. Where me? No, no, no, no me. *(Frustrated, she stands and looks out)* Where? Where me? *(Looks at the audience)* Me? No. Me? No. Me? No. *(Dejected)* Me, nowhere. *(Sits)* No words. Nowhere.

scene 14

Lower Circle. Adele, Molly and Susanna enter with vegetables. They chop and peel and put them in a pot. Enter Hazel.

HAZEL *(Straight out)*: I don't mind telling you I've always want- ed what other people had. I was born to covet my neigh- bors' goods, and I love it that I can never be trusted.

ADELE: You don't have to talk if you don't want to.

HAZEL: I don't care what any of you know. I mean, who are you going to tell?

SUSANNA: How did you meet him?

HAZEL: I'd seen him before, and *he* came on to *me*.

MOLLY: Now isn't anybody going to say he was just asking for it?

HAZEL: His wife's in Europe, so we go up to his apartment, fourteenth floor, very la-dee-da.

MARINA: Dry please, two olives.

HAZEL: Anyway, we just finished, well, you know.

SUSANNA *(Smirks)*: No, we don't know.

MOLLY: Yeah, explain it to us.

ADELE: Go on, Hazel.

HAZEL: I would have bet money he was asleep. His eyes were closed, he was snoring and everything. He'd taken off these diamond cuff links. I took those first. Then I cleaned his wallet. I started to go through the drawers. I found some jewelry—his wife must have left it behind. I swear I thought he was asleep.

ADELE: But he wasn't, was he?

HAZEL: No. I was just about to leave, when he grabbed me from behind and started calling me all these names and hitting me. I told him to stop, but he kept hitting me, so I hit him back, and then he hit me really hard and kind of threw me or something, because the next thing I know, I'm up against the railing bent backwards, looking at the sky, and I know he wants to push me off.

ADELE: So what did you do?

HAZEL: Nothing. I did nothing.

MOLLY: What? You didn't keep fighting?

HAZEL: No. I thought if I stopped somehow it would change.

SUSANNA: So did it?

HAZEL: He pushed me over.

MOLLY: Fourteen stories?

HAZEL: In a way, it was such a relief to go over an edge. With everything flying by, there was nothing for me to do. I pictured my mother making waffles in her old robe with the climbing vines, and it made me feel comfortable. Then I hit a tree branch, and another, and a smaller tree. Then I fell in a bush.

ADELE: Broken collarbone, sprained ankle, cuts and bruises.

SUSANNA: Impossible.

MOLLY: True.

HAZEL: But he lied. He said I was a burglar surprising him in his sleep.

MOLLY: He's probably enjoying the view this very minute.

ADELE *(To Hazel)*: And what do you think about all of that?

HAZEL: There are some crazy people out there in the world!

SUSANNA: She means about *stealing*.

MOLLY: Yeah, she's trying to be subtle.

HAZEL *(To Adele)*: Have you ever pinched anything?

ADELE: Not really. I mean I've taken grapes in the supermarket, not returned money I've found—not much money.

HAZEL: No, I mean something worth a lot.

ADELE: No.

HAZEL: Then you just wouldn't know.

ADELE: But can't you see, at least in this instance, where being a thief has taken you?

HAZEL: Of course, it's set me apart and raised me above the ordinary.

scene 15

Susanna in Lower Circle.

SUSANNA: I want you to know, that the reason I tell you these things is because everything adds up. I was just a little girl, but I remember. I remember I had just gotten into the car with my mother and her friends. They were all dressed up in hats and nylons and perfume, when on the sidewalk the lady down the street came walking by.

She was looking down, but we could see her face was bruised, all black and blue. She had this quick, hurried kind of walk, like an animal scurrying back to its burrow. "He beat her up again," one of them said, and they all shook their heads at the evidence of her tawdry life. "Poor thing," said the driver as she started up the car engine and pulled away from the curb. My mother and her friends took me with them to lunch in an extra nice restaurant with little paper umbrellas in the drinks and an indoor fountain. All the ladies laughed a lot with their nails painted in pretty colors that looked so delicate when they held their forks or laid their hands against the cloth napkins. After lunch, they all opened compacts and applied lipstick. On the way home as we drove by the lady down the street's house, they slowed down the car to observe. All the curtains were quietly drawn and the windows shut tight. Weeds grew unchecked along the walk and things were left out, forgotten in the garden—sure signs of dark goings-on within. They all stared hard as if peering over a deep abyss. When we got home, I asked my mother if she was going to visit the lady down the street. "Oh no, dear," she said with her sweet red mouth, "we'll just have to leave her alone. That's none of our business." So you see, if you put it together, things do add up.

(Adele enters.)

ADELE: Stop it, Susanna, you couldn't fix everything. Come outside with me for a minute.

(Adele and Susanna move downstage as lights change to night.)

We get so wrapped up in ourselves and each other here, we forget about the world outside. Look, it's cloudy, but you can see the moon peeking through.

SUSANNA: I had a friend once. His name was Daniel. I can't remember if he was real, or I made him up. I used to think somehow he watched over me, like the stars.

ADELE: Where is he?

SUSANNA: I don't know. I can't remember.

(Susanna turns and exits. Adele turns to face Molly.)

ADELE: I want you to know, Molly—

MOLLY *(Softly)*: I know.

ADELE: But I'm sure they wouldn't knowingly be a part of—

MOLLY: You'll find out—

ADELE: Everything we've ever stood for, all we've worked for.

MOLLY *(Sad)*: How terrible it is to be betrayed.

ADELE: Why do you make me?

MOLLY: You want to know now, don't you?

scene 16

Adele moves to Middle Circle while Molly remains in her place. Board Member enters.

ADELE: I want to know.

BOARD MEMBER: All of us on the Board of Directors read the police report.

ADELE: I think I have to consider the possibility.

BOARD MEMBER: Anything's *possible* but we go by the report.

ADELE: Her threats were never reported until *after* he—

BOARD MEMBER: What else but relentless threats could drive a man of his character to such drastic measures.

ADELE: As if a plea of temporary insanity were only—

BOARD MEMBER: Force an otherwise sane man to act so irrationally.

ADELE: She may be caught in something.

BOARD MEMBER: Instinctively, she meant to paralyze him with fear.

MOLLY:

> Into our small lives
> Comes the web,
> Intricate and glistening
> Like so many words.
> Radiating from an indolent creator
> Custodian,
> And defender.

ADELE: I'm afraid—

BOARD MEMBER: But he had a right.

ADELE: that she was, at the center, defenseless, abandoned to—

BOARD MEMBER: A right to protect himself from her violent threats.

ADELE: the grip of wealth and power.

BOARD MEMBER: Defend his home and family. *They* were the real victims.

MOLLY:

> In my father's house,
> Are many luminous deceiving threads,
> Ready to enfold us
> In their first soft cocoons.

BOARD MEMBER: It's obvious *she* is a deeply disturbed woman.

ADELE *(To Molly)*: If I knew, I would have told you—

BOARD MEMBER: We saw Threshold as the perfect place.

ADELE *(To Molly)*: *I* prepared a place for you.

MOLLY: In my father's house.

(Molly exits as Adele turns to Board Member.)

ADELE *(To Board Member)*: Tell me, is it true?

BOARD MEMBER: We need to just put this behind us and move on.

scene 17

DANIEL: She gets through it by pretending it happened to someone else. You hear about things like that happening to someone else: burned brides, sewn-up virgins, drowned baby girls, daughters sold for prostitution. Now, in Susanna's reality everything happened to someone who looked like her that she now feels very sorry for. Sometimes she would like to do something, to take her out of that place, but every time she's tried to move from the place of watching—and this is her reality—every time, the horrible stench of it hits her in the face and she is frozen by the nausea. And that certain smell engulfs her, and paralyzes her in a way that she cannot convey to you from this reality which is only hers. Everything—fear and guilt, shame and disgust—twists in knots and grows so large that she could never find you, much less tell you about these things, in this place of which you will never know. So you will always think that it happened somewhere else. You too can think that it always happens to someone else.

(Upper Circle. Susanna dreams. The Man enters with a chair and sets it down.)

MAN: I'm talking to *you.*

SUSANNA: Why me?

MAN: I'm not trying to make you suffer, Susanna, but I have to know what your motives were.

SUSANNA: Motives?

MAN: Yes, what moved you, prompted you to do such an unnatural thing.

SUSANNA: It moved naturally through him.

MAN: Him?

(Susanna moves to circle the chair.)

SUSANNA: It moved like a second nature.

(*Man aggressively circles the chair with her.*)

MAN: Listen to me. Listen to me! I'm talking about *you*!

(*During the following speech, Susanna tries several times to sit in the chair, but the Man pushes her, and pulls or moves the chair away rudely.*)

SUSANNA (*Talking down, as if to someone else*): Listen to me! I'm talking to you! You look like a clown in that dress. You're always talking about things you don't know anything about. Don't kid yourself, you're not smart enough. You're not leaving this house like that. Why don't you put on some makeup or something? Look at your hair for God's sake. And just who are you trying to impress? Because I said so, that's why. Who the hell do you think you are anyway? . . .

MAN: Tell me about why you did it!

SUSANNA (*Laughs*): What a stupid thing to say.

(*Susanna sits in the chair. Man yanks her up.*)

MAN: You can really be a bitch, can't you?

SUSANNA: Isn't that what you want?

scene 18

Lower Circle. Hazel and Molly have two seed flats. They are mixing in soil and planting seeds.

HAZEL: This is driving me nuts.

MOLLY: Don't you like gardening?

HAZEL: I don't like to get my hands dirty.

MOLLY: Funny thing for a thief to say.

HAZEL: You should be nicer to me.

MOLLY *(Laughs)*: Why?

HAZEL: Because we're kind of the same.

MOLLY: How?

HAZEL: The way we were under attack.

MOLLY: Night and day, Hazel.

HAZEL: No it wasn't.

MOLLY: You don't need another delusion.

HAZEL: They tried to kill us, but they couldn't.

MOLLY: Look Hazel, he tried to kill me because I stood for something, for a certain truth he couldn't accept. They took something away from me. You were just stealing for—I don't know why—maybe because you don't like to work.

HAZEL: Maybe I want something back too.

MOLLY: Like what?

HAZEL: I'm not sure exactly, but it's something, something I haven't had or really seen—like a language I'm suppose to know that no one can teach me, a lost continent that sunk before I was born, an island home that sailed out of memory. You know what I mean. And all the while, the world distracts me and tries to pretend that it's not real, and even if it was real, tells me I wouldn't deserve it—that I'm just some girl out of the slums, and I should behave, stop stealing, but I can't. Do you hear me? I can't go on like that. I feel the other want under my skin. It meets me around corners when I least expect it, it pushes me screaming and pleading for the thing I can't define. Then I see someone with jewelry. I watch to see who's got the goods and I go after them.

MOLLY: What have jewels got to do with it?

HAZEL: They seem so much like what I want. Clear and colored stones, deep and rich, made underground, little treasures hidden for centuries from intrusive eyes, things unto themselves, and every stone unique and of its own character. And that's the truth, Molly.

MOLLY: Maybe it is, but you can't just keep stealing them.

HAZEL *(Laughs)*: How else can I get what I want?

scene 19

Upper Circle. Marina and Susanna look into an empty jewelry box.

SUSANNA: She stole it.

MARINA: Sheee?

SUSANNA: Hazel.

MARINA: Hay-zell?

SUSANNA: She stole your necklace.

MARINA: No.

SUSANNA: Where, then? Where is it?

(Marina shrugs).

Look, it's gone, not here.

MARINA: Nowhere.

SUSANNA: That little thief.

MARINA: No, mad, no.

SUSANNA: Yes, I'm mad. She can't do this to you.

MARINA: Suss-anna—

SUSANNA: I'm telling Adele.

MARINA: No.

SUSANNA: Yes!

(She exits.)

MARINA: No. *(Pause)* Stop it, Alberta, stop it. There's no oasis there, no city of gold, you're just hot and tired and thirsty. Yes, I think we're all a little thirsty.

scene 20

Lower Circle. Molly and Hazel are folding clothes. Enter Adele and Susanna.

ADELE: Hazel, something is missing.
HAZEL: What's that?
SUSANNA: You know. You better give it back.
HAZEL: Touchy, touchy, Susanna.
ADELE: Look Hazel, this is no time to be coy. It's serious. Now if you want I can go through the formalities. I can ask for help in searching your room or your person. I am still in charge here, and I am still in control. Are you going to cooperate or do I have to drag in the police?

(Hazel fishes in her bra and takes out the necklace, putting it down on the table. Marina enters.)

SUSANNA: You thought she was stupid and you could take advantage of her.
ADELE: I'm very sorry you did this, Hazel. Your residency here at Threshold was a privilege, and you have chosen of your own free will to violate the agreement you made when you came. I'm afraid your stealing the necklace will have serious—
MARINA: Suss-anna, Hay-zell, no. I give Hay-zell.
SUSANNA: What?
MARINA: I . . . give . . . Hay-zell.
ADELE: Marina, you gave Hazel the necklace?
MARINA *(With great compassion)*: Yesss. *(To Hazel)* You Hay-zell need, I give—

(Marina takes off her ring and puts it in front of Hazel.)

More Hay-zell? You need more Hay-zell? More Hay-zell. I have. More . . . I have. All you. I give . . .

(Marina takes off her earrings, her bracelet. She takes jewelry out of her pockets and piles it in front of Hazel. Hazel looks up and places her hand on top of Marina's.)

HAZEL *(Touched; softly)*: Stop . . . Marina, please . . . stop. That's enough.

(Susanna, Molly and Adele exit. Marina moves to her jars of beans and begins to sort them out. Hazel watches her.)

If Marina could talk this is what she would say.

(Marina stands and walks to face the audience.)

MARINA: In a world of illusions, of painted faces and unnatural lights, live pieces of myself, forever imprinted on celluloid. They are waiting somewhere, like a map, and if I stuck them all together, somewhere, you could see me. *(Pause)* I lifted up those disincarnate beings from the pages of scripts, wore them like skins, let my arms and legs be pulled by their strings—my looks and glances saw around their corners. First, I began to discover little bits here and there. Yes, in that movieland whose bedrock is illusion, I began to find small pieces of myself. Then all at once, one day, it all came pouring down on me, lighting my flesh with the mysterious other, a cool flame whose presence I bowed before. And each little time, afterwards, I knew who I was. Do you hear me? I knew who I was. *(Long pause)* Then, came that one part, as the bride, the one I thought I had to take—a character intricately fashioned and cut for centuries. Oh, I had a million-dollar set, a more-than-handsome cast, lavish costumes and all those pieces of myself got lost, lost in the dull plot of every day and the predictable lines of a well-made play. *(Pause)* But there was one saving grace—that beautiful child. I was her star and she was my heroine, and every day I watched her spring up like a vine toward the sun. But that ended, prematurely—it ended badly. A nameless man in a nondescript car with an unknown gun on a passing corner picked her out for his own. I brought her into the world after years of waiting, months of illness and hours of pain. He took her out in a few minutes, so quickly with no fuss. They said she called out three times for help, three times before she said no more. But I couldn't hear her. I wasn't there. I wasn't there and I couldn't hear her. I couldn't hear her. *(Pause)* Now, I just know if I look carefully, if I just recover all those moments, that presence will come again. She *will* be there. We will be there. We will, and we will hear each other's voices.

(Marina returns to her table and silently sorts beans.)

scene 21

Middle Circle. Adele and Molly.

ADELE: I'm sorry.

MOLLY: Are you?

ADELE: Yes, for you, not for me. I want you to know I'll work to see that your case is reopened.

MOLLY: No you won't.

ADELE: I will. I can't just sit by—that would be criminal.

MOLLY: I don't want you to.

ADELE: Why not?

MOLLY: I don't want that. I just wanted you to know.

ADELE: Now I know. Now we should do something.

MOLLY: You'll lose Threshold.

ADELE: That's possible.

MOLLY: I guarantee it.

ADELE: I'll risk it.

MOLLY: And you should stop thinking about resigning too.

ADELE: Why shouldn't I? I've been used.

MOLLY: When I first came here, maybe I thought I wanted those things. Justice established, wrong made right, but it's my choice, whether I want to go on fighting or not, and right now I'd like some rest. I'd like a little rest from the world. (Pause) You know, this place is here and holds together because of you, Adele. I want you to know, I think it's just you who's got to be right. That's why I wanted you to know. What you do about the Board, that's up to you, but believe me, it's you who filters through to us every day, and so it's you who has to stay right.

ADELE: This place can't just depend on one person. That would make it easy to erase.

MOLLY: Places like this exist because someone, some person, has imagined it and made it. They all need you. I do, too.

ADELE: Molly, you shouldn't even be here.

MOLLY: It's not a matter of being charged with something I never did. Do you really think if Lake couldn't stop it, you could?

ADELE: I don't know, I could try.

MOLLY: No don't! Do you hear me? Don't drag it all out again! (Pause) I'm tired, Adele. I told you, I just want to rest here.

ADELE: I'm sorry. I wasn't thinking about you.

MOLLY: No, you weren't. I distracted you, but you had to know . . . before.

ADELE: Before what?

MOLLY: Before you could hear me.

ADELE (Takes Molly's hand): I'm so sorry, Molly.

MOLLY: I carry every hurt that's been done to them, all of them. I take it very personally. I am them. I stood up to tell the truth, and a man shot me. He tried to kill me.

He hated me because I made him hear, hear that we are whole human beings. Why is that, Adele? Do you understand? Why don't they want to hear?

scene 22

Middle Circle. Susanna, Marina and Hazel move to Molly and Adele. They all sew the curtains at a group meeting.

HAZEL: When are we going to finish these?

MOLLY: When you do more sewing than moaning.

SUSANNA: So over and over again people kept saying things to me like, why do you sit around and take that? If you're not part of the solution, then you're part of the problem. We make our own reality. Why don't you just leave?

HAZEL: So why didn't you just leave?

SUSANNA: I did. Once I went to my sister's house, and he followed me. He took a rock and broke her window. He started screaming outside in the street about how if I didn't come out he would take out all the windows, one by one.

HAZEL: So did he?

SUSANNA: No, my sister said she didn't want any trouble, which translated as: "Could you please leave?" Then another time I started to get my stuff together to leave, and as I'm going out the door he grabs my hair and pulls me back, and it all started again even worse than before.

HAZEL: Did you ever call the cops?

ADELE: Wait now, wait just a minute. Do you see what's happening here, Hazel?

HAZEL: Yeah, I'm asking her if she ever called the cops.

ADELE: Why? Why are we always saying these things? Why didn't she do this? Why didn't she do that? Did she deserve it? Why did she stay? Why did she hang around? What in the world is wrong with her? *Why didn't she just leave?* Just stop and think for a minute. Stop and ask yourself why it is we're not saying: You know, something is really wrong with that man, and he'll never be able to get away with this. Now he's charged with a crime and he'll be prosecuted. Thank heaven she and the children are protected from him. Her family and friends are all there to support and reassure her. They've helped to arrange for a place for her to stay and they've offered her financial support too. Everyone wants to help. *(Pause)* I want you to stop and and ask yourself, Hazel, why it is, all the things we *should be* saying are replaced with: *Why didn't she just leave?*

SUSANNA *(Vacantly)*: He wanted to kill me.

ADELE: Susanna?

SUSANNA: The times I tried to leave, he really wanted to kill me.

scene 23

DANIEL:

This is no Eden
this world of ebbing light,
no jeweled serpents folding
thick-tongued promises in your ear,
no gods with passion, jealous,
no red apples full and ripe,
no flaming swords
no naked desires.

Here we approach the final descent:
hot white ashes powder,
the rolling wasteland,

dark clouds boil,
coiling, uncoiling, recoiling,
endlessly seeking a form
your eyes could not bear to see,
but that,
even that kind of meaning would do.

The final signs read:
This is the last gate.
This is your backyard.
This is a cultivated garden.

(Upper Circle. Susanna dreams. The Man enters. He has a pair of silk stockings which he twists around his hands.)

MAN: Look, I've tried to be nice to you, but I've just about had it.
SUSANNA: Have you?
MAN: That's right.
SUSANNA: I see.
MAN *(Mad)*: Are you going to tell me about it now, on your own, or am I going to have to give you some help.
SUSANNA: Haven't you learned anything yet?
MAN *(Yelling)*: I'm serious, quit fucking around with me—
SUSANNA: I wouldn't think of it.
MAN *(Grabs her, twists her arm and holds her in a headlock as if to choke her)*: Goddamn it. Listen, you bitch, I don't want to hurt you. I'm just trying to help now once and for all. I want you to tell me what made you so mindlessly violent.

(The Man throws the silk stockings over Susanna's neck. She struggles as he tries to strangle her. In a violent fight for her life, and with tremendous effort, Susanna fights him off and falls back on the bed. Man backs off into the shadows.)

SUSANNA *(Agitated, tossing)*: Let me go.

MARINA: Suss-anna, Suss-anna.

SUSANNA *(Yelling)*: No! No! No! Don't come near me!

MARINA: Suss-anna.

SUSANNA: I'll kill you. Do you hear me? I'm going to kill you!

MARINA: Suss-anna!

SUSANNA *(Wakes with a start)*: Marina?

MARINA: Suss-anna.

SUSANNA *(After a pause)*: It won't stop, maybe never. You understand, don't you, Marina? I want to . . . I want to tell you. Yes, I want to tell *you*. Listen, Marina, we were driving one night, you see, and the road was slick with rain and the air was full and gray and thick we were—I don't really know where. But he was mad again, and I was frightened, and we were both high on God knows what this time. He was full of some new cruelty, yelling about where or who or what. I can't even remember that now because everything kind of came together in one moment. He reached over and slammed his fist into the side of my head, and I couldn't even think. I was gone. I watched. I watched like I wasn't there. My hand, strong and sure, rising up, coming down, grabbing the wheel in one swift jerk, and then the long scream of tires like a tunnel of sound going on forever, and the body rolling and bumping and tumbling, and the cloud of darkness folding into me like sleep. *(Silence)* I meant it for both of us, you know, but it only took him. I killed him. I just killed him, Marina.

(Marina holds Susanna, rocking her back and forth. Soft light on Daniel.)

DANIEL: Once I asked you this question: "Susanna, what is a garden?" And you said, "A garden is a place where the life in things grows or dies." And because I could never preach to you about never giving up on life, this then, my dearest friend, becomes my prayer: that in your hours of darkness, life will not give up on you.

MARINA: Suss-anna, you good. Cry, cry, very good. Very good. I here. I hear Suss-anna. Yes me here now. I hear you good. *(Pause)* And I told you, I won't leave this place, Colonel, until every single one has safely crossed over.

(Enter Adele and Molly.)

ADELE: What's going on?

MOLLY: We heard screaming.

ADELE: Are you okay, Susanna?

MARINA: Okay, Suss-anna. Safe now . . . safe.

SUSANNA: I guess I was just having a bad dream. You know, another nightmare.

MOLLY: Is that true?

SUSANNA: It was the truth, Molly.

(Enter Hazel.)

HAZEL: What's everyone doing here? Is someone sick?

SUSANNA: No, just me screaming in my sleep.

HAZEL: Maybe you wanted someone to hear.

SUSANNA *(With a laugh)*: Maybe I did.

HAZEL: Well, here we are.

MOLLY: Yeah.

ADELE: All of us.

scene 24

Lower Circle. Molly and Hazel spread a white cloth over ground mats. Hazel places a beautiful lantern in the middle.

HAZEL: Did she say what it was about?

MOLLY: I think it's a birthday.

HAZEL: Whose?

MOLLY: I don't know, not mine.

HAZEL: Not mine.

(Enter Marina and Susanna with a cake and candles.)

SUSANNA: Here's the cake! Whose birthday?

MARINA: No, me.

HAZEL: Maybe she's having a party for herself.

SUSANNA: Who?

MOLLY: Adele.

HAZEL: No, that's not her style.

(Enter Adele with a bottle and glasses.)

ADELE *(Passing out glasses)*: Good evening. Lovely night out, isn't it?

MOLLY: Charming.

ADELE *(Holds up bottle)*: And tonight, we have, direct from France, a bottle of the best.

HAZEL: Against the rules, Adele.

ADELE: The best *white grape juice*. Molly, could you light the candles?

MOLLY: How old are you, Adele?

ADELE: Ten.

SUSANNA: Really, if you're going to lie about your age—

ADELE: We are all ten. Today Threshold is ten years old, and since we are Threshold, it is a birthday for us all.

HAZEL: Quick, wish and blow them out!

(All blow out the candles.)

ADELE *(Toasting)*: And now to us.

(All raise their glasses and drink. Marina looks up at the sky.)

MARINA: Suss-anna . . . *(Points)* Starzzz.

SUSANNA: I see them Marina.

MOLLY: Look, they're all coming out.

HAZEL: Everyone different and of it's own nature.

SUSANNA: Here's to Threshold making it ten more.

ADELE: We did fine today, and we can do it again tomorrow, and that's the truth, Molly.

MOLLY *(Raises her glass)*: To you, Adele.

ADELE: Look at the sky. Do we need anymore right now?

HAZEL: Nope.

MOLLY: Yeah, a story, we need a story.

ADELE: Yes, let's tell us a story.

SUSANNA: What story should we tell?

MOLLY: A true story.

HAZEL: Let's tell the story.

ADELE: The story of Susanna.

(Enter Daniel.)

SUSANNA: Here is the story of Susanna as it comes to us from our own memory.

DANIEL: There was once a woman called Susanna, and for a time, longer than our knowing,

SUSANNA: she lived behind a wall,

DANIEL: in the company—

ADELE: of betrayal.

HAZEL: Anger.

MOLLY: Hurt.

SUSANNA: Fear.

MARINA: Silence.

DANIEL: She sat frozen, in a mirror of cold time.

SUSANNA: And then one day,

DANIEL: the sun found her thoughts reflected in a certain angle.

SUSANNA: As if they had been searching for the very moment.

DANIEL: And she remembered what was forsaken.

SUSANNA: Daniel.

DANIEL: And he appeared before her emerging through a thousand shattered images.

SUSANNA: Daniel.

(Daniel hands Susanna the box she gave him at the start of Act II.)

DANIEL *(Softly)*: What if someday you want them back? What if someday they want you back?

SUSANNA: And Susanna took back the things which were always hers.

DANIEL: And the end of the story has its beginning in the first new day.

SUSANNA: And in honor of the day, Susanna called the women, and together they came into the garden.

DANIEL: And the first dawn rose.

SUSANNA: And this became known as the Time of Planting.

HAZEL: I give this to the earth, that it may grow you a jewel—clear, deep and rich, and of its own nature.

MOLLY: I give this to the earth, that it may grow you a night like stars and dark blue glass, on which there is only peace.

MARINA: I give this to the earth, that it may grow you a place, in which I will always hear your voice.

ADELE: I give this to the earth, that it may grow you a light, by which you will always find your way.

DANIEL: I give this to the earth, that it may grow as a constant prayer, that you suffer no more.

SUSANNA: I give this to the earth, that it may grow you a miraculous garden, where, with each sunrise, arms branch out, unfolding into life.

END OF PLAY

Victoria Nalani Kneubuhl was born in Honolulu of Samoan, Hawaiian and Caucasian ancestry. She holds a Bachelor's degree from Antioch University and a Master's degree in drama and theatre from the University of Hawaii at Manoa. Ms. Kneubuhl has had ten plays produced in Honolulu, primarily by Kumu Kahua Theatre and the Honolulu Theatre for Youth. Her plays, *The Conversion of Ka'ahumanu*, and *Ka'iulani* (co-author), toured Edinburgh, Washington D.C. and Los Angeles. Her children's play, *Tofa Samoa*, was an invited production at the Okinawa International Children's Theatre Festival in 1994. She received the Hawaii Award for Literature in 1994, the highest literary award in the state of Hawaii, and in 1995 she was the first theatre artist in Hawaii to receive an Individual Artist's Fellowship from the State Foundation on Culture and the Arts.

In addition to writing for the theatre, Ms. Kneubuhl is a part-time lecturer in the Department of Women's Studies at the University of Hawaii, Manoa, and also works as a writer and researcher for many historical and cultural programs on the islands. For her historical street pageant, *January 1893*, which was performed to commemorate the one-hundredth anniversary of the overthrow of the Hawaiian monarchy, she was named one of the "10 Who Made a Difference" in the Hawaiian Islands, by the *Honolulu StarBulletin* in 1993. The Hawaii Heritage Center chose her to receive The Keeper of the Past Award in 1994 for her contributions toward the cause of preserving and sharing Hawaii's unique heritage. Ms. Kneubuhl is a member of The Dramatist's Guild.

Epilogue

Elizabeth Theobald

It seems like a simple concept. Today's Native theatre movement is made up of Native people creating plays that are expressions of their lives—their own comedies, their own tragedies. By hiring these playwrights, their directors and production teams, a theatre will be supporting not only a production, but an artistically rich movement that is overflowing with new voices, new stories, new styles.

Often I get a call from an artistic director telling me that his/her theatre company is producing an American Indian play—and then I find out that Native people had nothing to do with writing, directing, designing (and sometimes acting) in the piece. What these producers are telling me is that the play is *about* Indians: maybe an anthropologist meeting Indians, or a pioneer family captured by Indians, or a soldier in the U.S. Cavalry meeting a Great Plains Chief. They usually feel very passionate about these stories—they are powerful, beautiful and speak to the mainstream's hunger for a different way of life. But these are not Native works.

Unfortunately this romantic need to revisit the Wild West of the 1890s has nothing to do with the 1990s or the approaching millennium. Unique Native voices are coming out of places like Minneapolis, Toronto, New York, Santa Fe, Los Angeles, Honolulu, Oklahoma City, Juneau and Winnipeg. (And when I say Native, I'm covering a lot of territory, grasping at a way to give a cohesive name to Native Americans—Native Canadians, Hawaiians, Alaskan Natives, Mexican Natives, Caribbean Natives—over five hundred Nations that call themselves by their own names, and are filled with talented individuals.)

Americans are missing out on the many unique voices of First Nations writers. They are missing out on the creativity of Native directors and designers. They are missing out on the movement.

Native theatre today is everything one wouldn't expect. If you've read all of the plays in this compilation, you'll notice there are no captives or cavalrymen. These plays are written from the inside, from what the writer cares about: their families, the wounds they have suffered in their lives; they care about healing, getting produced, laughing, poking fun; they care about their communities.

So upon the publication of TCG's first volume of plays by North America's Indigenous playwrights, I must ask the question: How do we (as Spokane/d'Alene novelist Sherman Alexie put it) get ourselves "off the cultural reservation"? How do we effect a change in people's minds making it absolutely clear that we're not just romantic subject matter shelved next to the North American history books? How do we get other producers to join the likes of Native Earth Performing Arts, Bill Yellow Robe's Wakiknabe Theater Company, and other more mainstream theatres, such as Seattle's Group Theatre and the New York Theatre Workshop to start producing scripts by Native writers?

The future of Native theatre relies on—well, it sounds like a cliché—but it relies on education—on educating others: audiences, producers, funding sources and teachers.

And in order to educate, people need to talk to each other, listen to each other and develop relationships.

My work as a director and administrator has been to advocate for play development, to see that theatres support Native American writers in developing their pieces—not just have them sitting alone at a typewriter or a computer—but giving them feedback from professionals; providing them the opportunity to see their work on its legs; allowing them a chance to collaborate with a director, dramaturg and actors; and giving them the benefit of developing long-term producer/artist relationships. Native scripts are often stuck in the staged reading revolving door, and don't move on to the intention of play development: full productions.

Besides lack of funding, there are other walls that need to be torn down so that more Native theatre can happen. America's institutional theatres need to actively seek partnerships with Native theatre companies and ensembles. Funders need to be educated about specific needs of the Native communities (one example: our borders aren't your borders). Graduate theatre programs need to actively recruit Native students (and learn how and where to recruit them), and Native organizations need to use new technologies (like the Internet) to make information about our artists available to each other and to mainstream institutions.

Full productions require money—something everyone is short of. But that's not an excuse, nor will it ever be, for overlooking the richness of the work that's out there. The publication of this volume of exceptional plays, by Hanay Geiogamah, William S. Yellow Robe, Jr., LeAnne Howe and Roxy Gordon, Spiderwoman Theater, Drew Hayden Taylor, Diane Glancy and Victoria Nalani Kneubuhl, offers a beginning.

When producers fear that audiences won't buy tickets to Native plays, they need to remember: we are here. Native people don't just live on reservations. We live in cities and suburbs. We drive pickups and station wagons. We have blunt cuts, long hair and short hair. We might not be recognized on the ticket line, but we are buying tickets and reading reviews. We are not just someone's subject. We are here.

Elizabeth Theobald (Cherokee)
Director of Public Programs
Mashantucket Pequot Museum and Research Center
Mashantucket, Connecticut
January 1999

Suggested Bibliography

Plays

Berson, Misha, ed. *Between Worlds: Contemporary Asian-American Plays.* New York: Theatre Communications Group, 1990.

Brougham, John. *Po-ca-hon-tas; or The Gentle Savage.* New York: Samuel French, 1855 (year approx).

Carroll, Dennis, ed. *Kuma Kahua Plays.* Honolulu: University of Hawaii Press, 1983.

Clark, Barrett H., ed. *Favorite American Plays of the Nineteenth Century.* Princeton: Princeton University Press, 1943.

Colorado, Elvira and Hortensia. *1992: Blood Speaks.* In *Contemporary Plays by Women of Color*, edited by Kathy A. Perkins and Roberta Uno. New York: Routledge, 1996.

Custis, George Washington Parke. *Pocahontas; or The Settlers of Virginia.* In *Representative American Plays*, edited by Arthur Hobson Quinn. New York: Appleton-Century-Crofts, 1953.

Elam, Harry J., and Robert Alexander, eds. *Colored Contradictions: An Anthology of Contemporary African-American Plays.* New York: Plume, 1996.

Geiogamah, Hanay. *New Native American Drama: Three Plays.* Norman: University of Oklahoma Press, 1980.

Glancy, Diane. *War Cries*. Duluth, MN: Holy Cow! Press, 1997.

Gomez, Terry. *Inter-tribal*. In *Contemporary Plays by Women of Color*, edited by Kathy A. Perkins and Roberta Uno. New York: Routledge, 1996.

————. *Reunion*. In *Gathering Our Own*, the Institute of American Indian Arts Anthology Series. Berkeley: Small Press Distribution, 1996.

Hatch, James V., ed. *Black Theatre USA: 45 Plays by Black Americans, 1847–1974*. New York: The Free Press, 1974.

Highway, Tomson. *Dry Lips Oughta Move to Kapuskasing*. Saskatoon, Saskatchewan: Fifth House Publishers, 1989.

————. *The Rez Sisters*. Saskatoon, Saskatchewan: Fifth House Publishers, 1988.

Hunter, Kermit. *Trail of Tears*. Tahlequah, OK: Cherokee National Historical Society, 1966.

————. *Unto These Hills: A Drama of the Cherokee*. Chapel Hill: University of North Carolina Press, 1950.

Kopit, Arthur. *Indians*. New York: Hill and Wang, 1969.

Mahone, Sydné, ed. *Moon Marked and Touched By Sun: Plays by African-American Women*. New York: Theatre Communications Group, 1994.

Medoff, Mark. *Doing a Good One for the Red Man*. New York: Dramatists Play Service, 1974.

Mojica, Monique. *Princess Pocahontas and the Blue Spots: Two Plays by Monique Mojica*. Toronto: Women's Press, 1991.

Moody, Richard. *Dramas from the American Theatre, 1762–1909*. New York: World Publishing, 1966.

Moses, Daniel David. *Coyote City*. Stratford, Ontario: William-Wallace Publishers, 1990.

Nichol, James W. *Sainte-Marie Among the Hurons*. Vancouver: Talonbooks, 1980.

Osborn, M. Elizabeth, ed. *On New Ground: Contemporary Hispanic-American Plays*. New York: Theatre Communications Group, 1987.

Riggs, Lynn. *Green Grow the Lilacs.* New York: Samuel French, 1931.

_____. *Russet Mantle and Cherokee Night: Two Plays by Lynn Riggs.* New York: Samuel French, 1936.

Ryga, George. *The Ecstasy of Rita Joe.* Vancouver: Talonbooks, 1970.

Schaffer, Peter. *The Royal Hunt of the Sun.* New York: Samuel French, 1964.

Sergel, Christopher, adapt. *John Neihardt's Black Elk Speaks.* Woodstock, IL: The Dramatic Publishing Company, 1996.

Skinner, Cornelia Otis. *The Vanishing Red Man: A One Woman Show.* Chicago: Dramatic Publishing Company, 1974.

Spiderwoman Theater. *Sun, Moon, and Feather.* In *Contemporary Plays by Women of Color,* edited by Kathy A. Perkins and Roberta Uno. New York: Routledge, 1996.

_____. *Winnetou's Snake Oil Show from Wigwam City.* In *Canadian Theatre Review* 68 (Fall 1991): 56–62.

Stone, John Augustus. *Metamora; or the Last of the Wampanoags.* In *Favorite American Plays of the Nineteenth Century,* edited by Barrett H. Clark. Princeton: Princeton University Press, 1943.

Taylor, Drew Hayden. *The Bootlegger Blues.* Saskatoon, Saskatchewan: Fifth House Publishers, 1991.

_____. *Toronto at Dreamer's Rock* and *Education Is Our Right: Two One-Act Plays.* Saskatoon, Saskatchewan: Fifth House Publishers, 1990.

Uno, Roberta. *Unbroken Thread: An Anthology of Plays by Asian-American Women.* Amherst: University of Massachusettes Press, 1993.

Other Sources

Barba, Eugenio. "Theatre Anthropology." *The Drama Review,* 26 (Summer 1982): 5–32.

Berger, Peter L. *The Sacred Canopy.* Garden City, NY: Doubleday, 1969.

Boal, Augusto. *Theatre of the Oppressed.* Translated by C. A. and M. L. McBride. New York: Urizen Books, 1971.

Braunlich, Phyllis Cole. *Haunted by Home: The Life and Letters of Lynn Riggs.* Norman: The University of Oklahoma Press, 1988.

Brown, Joseph Epes. *The Spiritual Legacy of the American Indian.* New York: Crossroad, 1982.

Capps, Walter Holden, ed. *Seeing with a Native Eye.* New York: Harper and Row, 1976.

Carlson, Marvin. "The Performance of Culture: Anthropological and Ethnographic Approaches." In *Performance,* chapter 1, 13–33. New York: Routledge, 1996.

Case, Sue-Ellen. "Women of Color and Theatre." In *Feminism and Theatre,* chapter 6, 95–111. New York: Methuen,1988.

Clifton, James, ed. *The Invented Indian.* New Brunswick: Transaction, 1990.

Cox, Paul R. "The Characterization of the American Indian in American Indian Plays, 1800–1860, as a Reflection of the American Romantic Movement." (Ph.D. diss., New York University, 1970.)

Crow, Joseph Medicine. *From the Heart of Crow Country.* New York: Crown Publishers, 1992.

D'Aponte, Mimi Gisolfi. "A Sampling of New York's Ethnic Celebrations." *City Lore* 3 (1993–94):16–19.

D'Aponte, Mimi Gisolfi, and Charles Gattnig. "The Route of Evanescence: Sand and Sawdust in Rituals of Transformation." *Centerpoint* (Winter 1975–76): 17–28.

Deloria, Vine, Jr., and Clifford M. Lytle. *American Indians, American Justice.* Austin: University of Texas Press, 1983.

Dog, Mary Crow, and Richard Erdoes. *Lakota Woman.* New York: Grove, Weidenfeld, 1990.

Drucker, Philip, and Robert J. Heizer. *to make my name good: A Re-examination of the Southern Kwakiutl Potlach.* Berkeley: University of California Press, 1967.

Filwod, Alan. "Averting the Colonizing Gaze: Notes on Watching Native Theatre." In *Aboriginal Voices: Amerindian, Inuit, and Sami Theatre,* edited by Per Brask and William Morgan. Baltimore: Johns Hopkins University Press, 1992.

Frisbie, Charlotte J., ed. *Southwestern Indian Ritual.* Albuquerque: University of New Mexico Press, 1980.

Gill, Sam D. *Sacred Words: A Study of Navajo Religion and Prayer.* Westport: Greenwood Press, 1981.

Glancy, Diane. *Claiming Breath.* Lincoln: University of Nebraska Press, 1991.

Green, Rayna. "The Pocahontas Perplex: The Image of Indian Women in American Culture." *The Massachusettes Review* (Autumn 1975).

Grose, Burl Donald. "Here Come the Indians: An Historical Study of the Representations of the Native American upon the North American Stage, 1808–1969." (Ph.D. diss., University of Missouri–Columbia, 1981.)

Hitakonau'laxk. *The Grandfathers Speak: Native American Folk Tales of the Lenapé People.* New York: Interlink Books, 1994.

Hobsbawm, Eric, and Terence Ranger, eds. *The Invention of Tradition.* Cambridge and New York: Cambridge University Press, 1983.

Jahoda, Gloria. *The Trail of Tears: The Story of the American Indian Removals, 1813–1855.* New York: Wings Books, 1995.

Jenkins, Linda Walsh. "The Performances of the Native Americans as American Theatre: Reconnaissance and Recommendations." (Ph.D. diss., University of Minnesota, 1975.)

Jorgensen, Joseph G. *The Sundance Religion: Power for the Powerless.* Chicago: University of Chicago Press, 1972.

Le Pore, Jill. *The Names of War.* New York: Random House, 1997.

Luckert, Karl W. *Coyoteway: A Navajo Holyway Healing Ceremonial.* Tucson and Flagstaff: University of Arizona Press and Museum of Northern Arizona Press, 1979.

Matthiessen, Peter. *In the Spirit of Crazy Horse.* New York: Viking Penguin, 1991.

Momaday, N. Scott. *The Way to Rainy Mountain.* Albuquerque: University of New Mexico Press, 1969.

Nabokov, Peter, ed. *Native American Testimony.* New York: Penguin, 1991.

Rathbun, Paul. "American Indian Dramaturgy: Situating Native Presence on the American Stage." (Ph.D. diss., University of Wisconsin–Madison, 1996.)

Rathbun, Paul, ed. *Native Playwrights' Newsletter* (Vol. 1 Spring 1993–Vol. 12 Fall 1996).

Riddington, Robin. *Trail to Heaven: Knowledge and Narrative in a Northern Native Community.* Iowa City: University of Iowa Press, 1988.

Roach, Joseph. "Mardi Gras Indians and Others: The Cultural Politics of American Performance." *Theatre Journal* 44 (December 1992): 461–481.

Schechner, Richard. *Between Theatre and Anthropology.* Philadelphia: University of Pennsylvania Press, 1985.

Schechner, Richard, and Willa Appel, eds. *By Means of Performance: Intercultural Studies of Theatre and Ritual.* Cambridge and New York: Cambridge University Press, 1990.

Sellers, Maxine, ed. *Ethnic Theatre in the U.S.* Westport, CT: Greenwood Press, 1983.

Silko, Leslie Marmon. *Ceremony.* New York: Viking Press, 1977.

Swann, Brian, and Arthur Krupat. *Recovering the Word: Essays on Native American Literature.* Berkeley: University of California Press, 1989.

Tedlock, Dennis and Barbara. *Teachings from the American Earth: Indian Religion and Philosophy.* New York: Liveright, 1975.

Tooker, Elisabeth. *The Iroquois Ceremonial of Midwinter.* Syracuse: Syracuse University Press, 1970.

Turner, Frederick W., III, ed. *The Portable American Indian Reader.* New York: Viking Press, 1974.

Weeks, Philip. *The American Indian Experience: A Profile.* Arlington Heights, IL: Forum Press, 1988.

Wiget, Andrew. "His Life in His Tail: The Native American Trickster and the Literature of Possibility." In *Redefining American Literary History*, edited by Brown Ruoff and Jerry W. Ward. New York: MLA, 1990.

————. "Telling the Tale: A Performance Analysis of a Hopi Coyote Story." In *Recovering the Word: Essays on Native American Literature*, edited by Brian Swann and Arnold Krupat. Berkeley: University of California Press, 1987.

Wyman, Leland C. *Blessingway*. Tucson: University of Arizona Press, 1970.

Wyman, Leland C., ed. *Beautyway: A Navajo Ceremonial.* New York: Pantheon, 1957.

Web Sites

Algonkuin Players Theatre Company
http://members.aol.com/algonkuin/index.html

The Centre for Indigenous Theatre
http://www.interlog.com/~cit/cit.html

Native American Authors
http://www.ipl.org/ref/native/

Native American Women Playwrights Archive
http://www.lib.muohio.edu/~wortmawa/nawpa

Spiderwoman Theater
http://www.lib.muohio.edu/nawpa/Spiderwoman.html

Representative Cultural Institutions
That Produce Native Theatre

American Indian Community House
708 Broadway, 8th Floor
New York, NY 10003
(212) 598 - 0100
(212) 598 - 4909 (Fax)
Web: http://www.abest.com/~aichnyc/

The Group Theatre
Box 45430
Seattle, WA 98145-0430
(206) 441 - 9480
(206) 441 - 9839 (Fax)
Web: http://www.speakeasy.org/concierge/group/index.html

The Joseph Papp Public Theater/
New York Shakespeare Festival
425 Lafayette Street
New York, NY 10003
(212) 539 - 8500
(212) 539 - 8505 (Fax)
Web: http://www.publictheater.org

La MaMa Experimental Theater Club
74A East 4th Street
New York, NY 10003
(212) 254 - 6468
(212) 254 - 7597 (Fax)
Web: http://www.nytheatre~wire.com

Mark Taper Forum
135 North Grand Avenue
Los Angeles, CA 90012
(213) 972 - 7353
(213) 972 - 8051 (Fax)
Web: http://www.taper-ahmanson.com/ctg

Mashantucket Pequot Museum and Research Center
110 Pequot Trail
Box 3180
Mashantucket, CT 06339-3180
(860) 396-6800
(860) 396-6867 (Fax)
Web: http://www.mashantucket.com

National Museum of the American Indian
1 Bowling Green
New York, NY 10004
(212) 514 - 3700
(212) 514 - 3800 (Fax)
Web: http://echonyc.com:70/0/cul/nma/

Theater for the New City
155 1st Avenue
New York, NY 10003
(212) 254 - 1109
(212) 979 - 6570 (Fax)
Web: http://members.aol.com/tnctheater

Dr. Mimi Gisolfi D'Aponte is Professor of Theatre at the Graduate Center of the City University of New York (CUNY) and at Baruch College, where she chairs the Department of Fine and Performing Arts. Her ongoing scholarship concerns Italian theatre, particularly during the twentieth century, and with special emphasis on the work of Eduardo De Filippo. Her articles and chapters have appeared in *Black American Literature Forum, Bryn Mawr Alumnae Bulletin, Centerpoint, Commonweal, Communication Education, Encyclopedia of New York City, Educational Theatre Journal, Italica, Modern Drama, Other Stages, Performing Arts Journal, Theatrical Directors: An International Dictionary, The Bronx County Historical Society Journal, The Companion to Pirandellian Studies, The Drama Review, The Journal of Dramatic Theory and Criticism, The Italian Quarterly, Themes in Drama* and *Western European Stages.* She and Nello D'Aponte, her husband, translated Andrea Perrucci's *La Cantata dei pastori* as *Shepherd's Song* (Studia Humanitatis, 1982). Her work on Italian ritual theatre was published in *Italian: Teatro religioso e rituale della Penisola Sorrentina e la Costiera Amalfitana* (Studia Humanitatis, 1984). She and Jane House translated Federico Tozzi's *L'Incalco* as *The Casting,* anthologized in *Twentieth-Century Italian Drama* (Columbia University Press, 1995). Her sampling of New York City festivals, *Celebration City!,* written with Laura Hansen, was published by City Lore in 1997.